MW00445264

THEY KILLED FREDDIE GRAY

THEY KILLED FREDDIE GRAY

THE ANATOMY OF A POLICE BRUTALITY COVER-UP

JUSTINE BARRON

FOREWORD BY RABIA CHAUDRY

Arcade Publishing • New York

CONTENTS

IV SYSTEMS OF ACCOUNTABILITY

FOREWORD

BY RABIA CHAUDRY

IN APRIL 2015, THE ATTENTION of the nation turned to Baltimore city, where the death of a young black man named Freddie Gray took place in police custody. My attention was already on Baltimore, as it had been for almost two decades. Since 1999, I had been pursuing the exoneration of a young Baltimore man by the name of Adnan Syed who was wrongfully convicted of murder.

That pursuit unfolded in front of the world with the explosion of the hit podcast *Serial*, which brought hundreds of millions of eyes to the case. What *Serial* did not bring was a critical gaze, much less an interrogation, toward a criminal justice system, and the actors in it, that would lead to an innocent person being convicted of crime he did not commit. The complete failure of that wildly phenomenal show to investigate and report on the endemic corruption and history of misconduct inside the Baltimore Police Department led to the launch of my own podcast, *Undisclosed*. I teamed up with two other attorneys to reinvestigate and report on not only Adnan Syed's case but on dozens of other innocence cases from around the country over the course of the following years.

One of those cases, which was never publicly examined as an innocence case, was that of Freddie Gray. In 2017 our team produced a series on the killing of Freddie Gray investigated by Justine Barron and Amelia McDonald-Perry. By this time, I had already learned my lesson the hard way on the dereliction of duty the media practiced in reporting on criminal matters, on the insidious way state agencies circled wagons to protect their own, and on the lies and disinformation spread by law enforcement agencies to deflect from their own culpability. Together, Justine and Amelia reported one of the most impactful and deeply investigative series we ever ran.

Since then, so much more has been revealed about the killing of Freddie Gray and the cover-up that began in real time as he struggled to survive in the back of a Baltimore city paddy wagon. Justine Barron has gathered that information and woven it into this compelling, highly detailed narrative documenting the many injustices in this case.

The story of what was done to Freddie Gray, both in his life and afterward, is a master class in how authorities are able to manipulate and misdirect the attention of the public away from the facts and real issues at play, and how the media is complicit in the propaganda—or, as some pointedly call it, copaganda.

While right-wing media focused on Gray's "rap sheet," spread lies about alleged gang ties, and bolstered the Baltimore Police Department's narrative about the legality of his detainment, arrest, injury, and ultimate death, mainstream media did no better. If anything, they caused even greater damage than conservative media by willingly entertaining and keeping the public engrossed in a twenty-four-hour news cycle of red herrings.

Why did Gray run from the police? Did Gray have a knife? Was it an illegal switchblade? Was he properly restrained in the van? Was he subjected to a "rough ride"? Will the mystery of his death ever be solved? Was his life just one big tragedy after another, from poverty to lead paint poisoning to drug dealing to an unforeseeable, unfortunate injury that caused his death?

This last pontification, about the "tragedy" of Freddie Gray's life, was pervasive in the reporting on the case, and perhaps the greatest journalistic malfeasance of the many that occurred in this story. The widespread use of the passive, non-accusatory word "tragedy" might have made Freddie Gray a sympathetic character, but it did so at the cost of the truth of the matter. This media portrayal of the circumstances of Gray's life and death made it seem as if all were the result of a calamitous series of events that no one had control over. The truth is much harder to swallow—that every difficulty and challenge that Gray faced in both his childhood and adulthood was the result of a deliberately designed, long-standing, deeply entrenched, and very American system of racial inequity and oppression.

If this angle was unconscionable, the idea spreading through the media that Freddie Gray injured himself by banging around the back of the van was beyond irresponsible. It was reprehensible.

The media just as uncritically turned an enamored eye to State's Attorney Marilyn Mosby, who emerged as a hero on the national stage, having pressed charges against six officers in the death of Gray. For at least the previous decade, the country had been witnessing the killings of unarmed black boys and men at the hands of law enforcement and also witnessing the lack of accountability for involved officers. More often than not, charges were never brought. If charges were brought, indictments failed. In 2014, before Gray's death, the brutal killings of Eric Garner, Michael Brown, and Tamir Rice were all caught on camera, and each sent the nation into a tailspin of rage and mourning, but no officers involved were ever prosecuted, much less served a day in prison.

In the wake of dismal outcomes in such high-profile cases, Mosby's actions did indeed ring heroic. Here was a young, Black, female prosecutor who understood the BPD's history of brutality against Black men and was going to hold this group accountable. What the media failed to take notice of was that these superficially valiant prosecutions were based on the same false narrative the Baltimore City Police Department itself was hoping everyone would buy into. And they did—hook, line, and sinker.

That it was a "rough ride" that killed Freddie Gray became the prevailing truth across every media platform and also inside the courtrooms, where not a single officer was convicted. There might have been convictions in the case had the State's Attorney based their theory of the killing on the statements of the many witnesses who stood watching, some recording on their cell phones, how Gray was handled by officers on the morning of April 12, 2015. But most of these witnesses—witnesses who could have demonstrated that Gray was killed not by a "rough ride" but most likely by police actions at one of the van's notorious stops—were not called to testify.

Just as egregious was the investigation itself, in which the collection of vital evidence didn't take place for days and sometimes even weeks.

Mosby's failure to secure a single conviction was yet one more avoidable injustice in Freddie Gray's story, followed by another—the refusal of the Department of Justice to bring any charges.

Had any of the investigating or prosecutorial entities done a fraction of the work put in by Justine Barron and Amelia McDonald-Perry, the work of interviewing witnesses, examining cell phone videos, obsessively reviewing CCTV footage, diligently unpacking BPD records and statements, there may have been some semblance of justice for Freddie Gray. As the official record stands, there is near to none.

Barron's years-long dedication to excavating every detail of Gray's story, to separating fact from fiction, to calling out all those complicit in covering up the truth, is nothing short of remarkable. Her ongoing work on the case, and this book, is evidence that the hearts of the people who bore witness to the killing of Gray and the aftermath of lies and deflection will not be satisfied until the truth is widely known. At the heart of that truth is likely this: in my estimation, like my many other *Undisclosed* cases, Gray's case too was one of innocence. And if there is to be a seminal text investigating the truth about the killing of Gray and the ensuing cover-up, this book will be it.

INTRODUCTION

TRUE CRIME

IN THE SUMMER OF 2016, a message appeared painted on a billboard over the corner of North Avenue and North Charles Street, at the center of Baltimore City: WHOEVER DIED FROM A ROUGH RIDE, it said in stark black all-capital letters over a peeling gray-white backdrop. THE WHOLE DAMN SYSTEM . . . , it responded in smaller print. Two Baltimore artists, usually known for colorful public murals, collaborated anonymously on the political message.

The rough ride message was a reference to the explanation given by some Baltimore leaders for how Freddie Carlos Gray Jr. was fatally injured in police custody the year before. On April 12, 2015, Gray, a twenty-five-year-old Black man, was chased by police from the corner of West North Avenue and North Mount Street in West Baltimore, nearly two miles west of the billboard. He was stopped, arrested, and loaded into a police transport van in the Gilmor Homes housing project. About fifty-five minutes later, he was found by medics to be in a coma at the Western District police station, only five blocks away.[1]

For three weeks after Gray's arrest, tensions escalated in Baltimore. A cell phone video shot by Gilmor Homes resident Kevin Moore went viral. It shows a heavyset officer restraining Gray on his belly and bending his legs all the way back while Gray screams. Two officers then carry Gray to the police van, his legs dragging, while he continues screaming. Gray died in the hospital on April 19, after one week in a coma. Protesters gathered at the Western District police station, accusing the department of withholding information. "Forty-two unaccountable minutes," one protester shouted, repeating the timeline provided by the Baltimore Police Department (BPD). "What did they do to him in that forty-two minutes? They killed him. That's what they did."[2]

Gray was the eighth person to die from injuries sustained during a police encounter in Baltimore City that year and the first to get national media attention.[3] News outlets sent their reporters from DC to Baltimore, only an hour east but rarely on their radars, to capture sound bites from eyewitnesses and officials. BPD offered a slow drip of information over three weeks that didn't sate the public's thirst for an explanation. The media capitalized on the mystery, reporting headlines like "The 45-Minute Mystery of Freddie Gray's Death" in the *Baltimore Sun*.[4]

On the streets of Baltimore, demonstrations grew in size as organizers and supporters showed up from across the country. On April 27, after Gray's funeral, riots broke out across West Baltimore. To the eyes of the world, as filtered through news reports, Baltimore spontaneously combusted. In reality, police and city leaders took provocative steps toward a violent response, including occupying parts of West Baltimore and restricting civilian movement. The Gray case and the subsequent public protests, known as the "Baltimore Uprising," became one of the most reported stories in the country in 2015.

The attention wasn't entirely welcome. "Stop reporting that we're thugs," activist Kwame Rose told Fox News's Geraldo Rivera during a protest, in a moment that went viral.[5] "I want you and Fox News to get out of Baltimore City, because you are not here reporting about the boarded-up homes. . . . You're here for the Black riots that happen." It wasn't just Fox News. Liberal news outlets were also reporting on the "Black riots" and statements from officials. Sometimes they ran a piece or two on the boarded-up homes, but there was almost no reporting on endemic police violence in Baltimore. "We're the ones that need protection," Rose told Rivera.

The intensity heightened on the streets and in the media during the last week of April. After April 27, the city established a curfew, and Governor Larry Hogan sent in the National Guard. Meanwhile, news outlets offered a rapid succession of stories that promised different explanations for the cause for Gray's death, which was still a mystery. A mass protest was planned for the first weekend in May.

The tension built to a crescendo. And then, suddenly, there was quiet. On the morning of Friday, May 1, newly elected State's Attorney Marilyn Mosby announced charges against six officers in Gray's death, including a second-degree murder charge for the van driver. She outlined a six-stop van ride. After the van left its second stop, she said, "Mr. Gray suffered a severe and critical neck injury as a result of being handcuffed, shackled by his feet, and unrestrained inside of the BPD wagon."[6] A year later in court, her prosecutors referred to the van driver giving Gray a "rough ride," a practice known to have injured prisoners in the past.

In her speech, Mosby issued a call for peace. "To the people of Baltimore and the demonstrators across America. I heard your call for 'No justice, no peace,'" she said. "Your peace is sincerely needed as I work to deliver justice on behalf of this young man." It worked. The planned demonstration for that weekend became a "victory rally" of about two thousand people.

After the press conference, Mosby was celebrated in the streets of Baltimore and by the national media. Yet over the next year and four trials, she was unable to win a conviction against any of the officers or offer compelling evidence that Gray was killed because he wasn't seat-belted. "Baltimore Trial Leaves Unanswered Question," a *New York Times* headline noted in December 2015: "What Happened to Freddie Gray?"[7]

The "rough ride" billboard popped up during the summer of 2016, just after prosecutors lost their third of four trials against the officers, this one against the van driver. By then, many of the activists who originally supported Mosby came to feel that what she had achieved on May 1, 2015, was not so much accountability as the manufacturing of consent and silencing of dissent.

For many in Baltimore and around the world, there had to be more to the story of what happened to Gray than the official explanations, especially given the disturbing video of his arrest. The "rough ride" billboard seemed to voice this discontent, though, like a poem, its meaning was ambiguous. "Whoever died from a rough ride" wasn't necessarily a question; it had no question mark. "The whole damned system" wasn't a direct answer. The billboard evoked the bitterness and skepticism of a city still unsettled by Gray's death and its aftermath. It hung in judgment over a criminal justice system that was (and is still today) policed by the same officers involved in Gray's death and led by some of the same officials who helped to cover it up.

* * *

It was also the summer of 2016 when journalist Amelia McDonell-Parry and I were asked to look into the Freddie Gray case by producers associated with the *Undisclosed* podcast. True-crime podcasts were extremely popular at that time, following the success of *Serial*. The countless miscarriages of justice that news outlets had either overlooked or sold to the public from the police's point of view were suddenly available fodder for investigators, both professional and amateur.

The true-crime boom of the mid-2010s created an appetite among mainstream audiences for stories that flipped the usual crime genre conventions, often by portraying "criminals" as victims who were wrongfully convicted and police and prosecutors as corrupt or incompetent. However, popular true-crime media after *Serial* did not make room for the stories of people killed while in police custody, a major conversation in the news at the time. The raw material for a compelling true-crime mystery was available in the deaths of Freddie Gray, Michael Brown, Sandra Bland, Alton Sterling, and other less well-known cases in which the police accounts were not easily reconciled with known evidence or common sense. Yet most true-crime content at the time showed police at worst bumbling through investigations and covering up their mistakes, not murdering people in the line of duty.

During the mid-2010s, there wasn't much room generally for Black stories in popular true-crime media. A *Vulture* list from 2018, "52 Great True-Crime Podcasts," included only a few podcasts about Black victims or with Black hosts.[8] Amelia and I, two white women, benefited from a new media genre that easily absorbed white creators from various fields. In some ways, we were naive about the ramifications of telling a death-in-custody story as a true-crime mystery with a focus on evidence and cover-ups. Our podcast, which aired in 2017, was improved by another host, Georgetown University historian Marcia Chatelain, who provided historical context for race and policing in Baltimore.

I realized early on that Amelia's mind could manage a lot of information at once and followed its own hunches rapidly from one topic to another, like one of those social media memes of a person solving a conspiracy. She dove into the second-by-second details of what happened on the morning of Gray's arrest, contrasting public statements with hard evidence and eyewitness reports. Her investigation led us to a new theory of how Gray ended up with a broken neck resulting from police actions that weren't largely known or discussed. Meanwhile, I sought to sort out incompetence from corruption in the police investigation and prosecution. The Gray case, we learned, was marked by a series of messy, overlapping cover-ups from parties with various interests, aided by a largely gullible media that helped smooth out the bumps.

Our podcast pressed some buttons locally. Before the first episode aired, the Baltimore chapter of the Fraternal Order of Police sent *Undisclosed* producers a cease-and-desist letter threatening a lawsuit based on the podcast's subtitle alone, "The Killing of Freddie Gray." Amelia and I could have anticipated the pushback from police and their sympathizers, including online harassment. What we didn't anticipate was that local Baltimore reporters who had just spent the last two years covering the Gray story weren't interested in learning about newly obtained evidence.

Almost three years after the podcast, the entire discovery file in the criminal case and the internal affairs investigation file landed in my lap, prompting a renewed investigation. The two files included dozens of critically important and unreleased interviews, videos, photographs, and documents, the main source material for this book. The new evidence exposes how many powerful people in Baltimore knew—and knew early on—what happened to Gray and covered it up, making his death, in many ways, a mystery by design.

Gray's death activated a bureaucratic machine across multiple city and state agencies—from internal affairs to crime scene units, from medical examiners to prosecutors—that effectively shield police when they cause harm. These agencies often produce highly technical documents and evidence that are taken at face value, without critical examination, by other agencies and the media. Frequently, police cite the technical aspects of policing to insist that their work is necessarily inscrutable to the public and therefore cannot be overseen by civilians. In fact, it does require some technical knowledge as well as critical scrutiny to understand how this bureaucracy functions to protect police after a death in custody, from how force is investigated to how autopsy opinions are determined.

In the Gray case, a multiagency bureaucracy erased from history the original trauma of his fatal injury as well as the accounts of those who witnessed it. As a global media circus swirled around this case—as Gilmor Homes became a literal tourist destination—the residents who saw and heard what happened to Gray were gaslighted out of their own experience.

THEY KILLED
FREDDIE
GRAY

CHAPTER 1

THE TIMELINE

It took the Baltimore Police Department (BPD) several weeks of press conferences and media statements to unfold the story of what happened during Freddie Gray's arrest. According to the police account, Gray was arrested and placed in a transport van on the early morning of April 12, 2015. The van subsequently went on an approximately three-mile journey in a loop, stopping a total of six times, before he was found unconscious. Each stop involved different officers interacting with him. The official story of Gray's arrest was complicated.

The six-stop narrative was repeated by a mostly uncritical media and became canon. It was used by the medical examiner to determine Gray's cause and manner of death. It was also used by the state's attorney's office (SAO) to determine how to charge and prosecute the officers who interacted with Gray at the various stops. It had enormous power, influencing the systems that are supposed to hold police accountable, yet the official narrative isn't the full story of what happened during the morning of Gray's arrest, nor is it entirely supported by evidence.

* * *

According to BPD, Gray was chased by three officers on bicycles from West North Avenue down North Mount Street at about 8:38 a.m. on April 12, 2015. Two of the officers, Garrett Miller and Edward Nero, apprehended him on the 1700 block of Presbury Street in front of Gilmor Homes. They searched his pockets and reportedly found a switchblade knife, which is illegal under Baltimore City code. The third officer on a bike was Lieutenant Brian Rice, who was the shift supervisor that morning. The officers called for a transport van, which was driven that morning by Officer Caesar Goodson. The back of the white van was divided down the middle by a metal partition to form two separate compartments for prisoners. Gray was loaded into the right side.[1]

This was the official story of Gray's arrest at what became known as Stop 1. (After May 1, the media settled on a uniform number system to describe the six stops.) Police described Stop 1 as uneventful, aside from a crowd of bystanders. Gray gave up "without the use of force," a BPD official told the public.[2] Stop 1 was well known to the public from cell phone videos that showed Gray screaming while restrained and carried by police, his legs dragging.

The van's second stop was around the corner. Officer Goodson left Stop 1 at 8:46 a.m. and headed south on Mount Street. He stopped at the next intersection, Baker Street, still inside of Gilmor Homes. This was known as Stop 2. According to police, two things happened at Mount and Baker. First, the bike officers took Gray out of the van to put shackles around his ankles because he was combative. Second, the officers completed the arrest paperwork so they could send Gray straight to Central Booking, Baltimore's pretrial detention facility. The media accepted the police's Stop 2 story, so it never became as controversial as Stop 1. Police and prosecutors effectively minimized and/or buried evidence of what really happened at both of the first two stops.

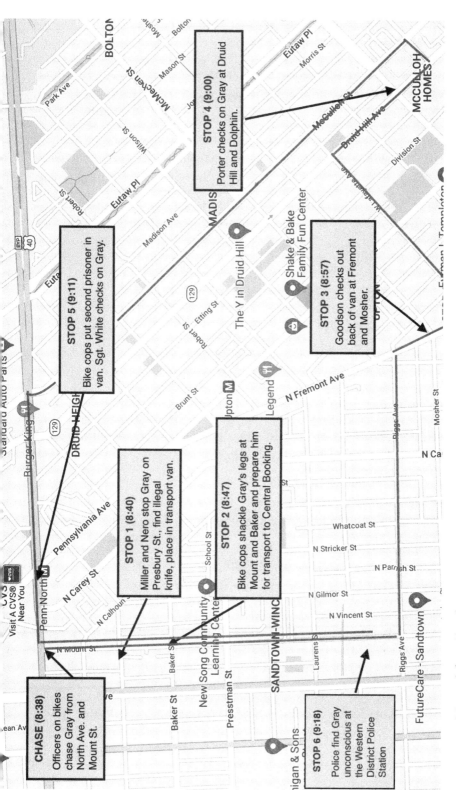

Map of the official van route according to Baltimore Police Department, with annotations by the author.

STOP 4 (9:00)
Porter checks on Gray at Druid Hill and Dolphin.

STOP 5 (9:11)
Bike cops put second prisoner in van. Sgt. White checks on Gray.

STOP 3 (8:57)
Goodson checks out back of van at Fremont and Mosher.

STOP 1 (8:40)
Miller and Nero stop Gray on Presbury St., find illegal knife, place in transport van.

STOP 2 (8:47)
Bike cops shackle Gray's legs at Mount and Baker and prepare him for transport to Central Booking.

CHASE (8:38)
Officers on bikes chase Gray from North Ave. and Mount St.

STOP 6 (9:18)
Police find Gray unconscious at the Western District Police Station

According to BPD, Goodson left Stop 2 at 8:54 a.m., heading toward Central Booking, which was about three miles east, near downtown. While on this journey, he reportedly stopped the van twice to check on Gray. First, at 8:57 a.m., officials said he pulled over at North Fremont Avenue and Mosher Street, about a mile southeast of Stop 2, and briefly checked on Gray. This was known as Stop 3.

Next, just after 9:00 a.m., Goodson reportedly stopped the van at Druid Hill Avenue and Dolphin Street, farther east in the Central District, where he met up with Officer William Porter, who checked on Gray. This was known as Stop 4. Gray's condition at this stop was debated during the trials, with both prosecution and defense drawing from Porter's descriptions.

After meeting up with Porter, Goodson reportedly circled back from Stop 4 to the Western District with Gray still in the van. He was summoned by the bike cops, who had arrested another person, Donta Allen. Goodson parked on West North Avenue near Pennsylvania Avenue, just over a block east from where Gray took off running that morning. This was known as Stop 5. The bike officers loaded Allen into the van's left compartment, on the other side of the metal partition from Gray. Sergeant Alicia White, the second-in-command working the district that morning, also showed up at Stop 5, where she briefly checked on Gray.

From Stop 5, Goodson drove Gray and Allen down Mount Street to the Western District police station, known as Stop 6. There, according to BPD, several officers discovered Gray unconscious and called for a medic at 9:24 a.m. Medics transported Gray to the University of Maryland Medical System R. Cowley Shock Trauma Center by 10:00 a.m. As with most of the morning's events, unreleased evidence complicates the official story of Stop 6.

In statements to detectives and court testimony, officers spoke about Gray's arrest as a routine day of policing, with the shocking and inexplicable discovery of a prisoner in a coma. Officials released to the public videos from the van's journey to help support its official narrative. What was missing from the public release of videos reveals much more about Gray's arrest than what was included.

* * *

Gray's fatal injury in police custody was investigated by six different legal bodies, each promising independence. BPD's Force Investigation Team initiated the original police investigation on April 12, while Gray was in a coma in the hospital. After Gray died, on April 19, BPD established a task force to take over the criminal investigation, involving investigators from different departments. The task force collected evidence during the last two weeks of April, as the street protests and riots in Baltimore became a national news story.

The medical examiner's office initiated its investigation after Gray died, completing the autopsy report on April 30. Gray's death was determined to be a homicide caused by "acts of omission"—namely the officers' failure to seat-belt him or call for timely medical attention. The report describes Gray being killed by a single "high energy injury," causing a break in his cervical spine.[3]

The office of State's Attorney Marilyn Mosby also conducted its own "independent investigation," she said, culminating in criminal charges against six officers, which she announced on May 1, 2015.[4] Goodson, the driver, faced the most serious charge of second-degree "depraved heart" murder—or killing "with malice aforethought," according to the statement of charges. Prosecutors offered other options for convicting Goodson, including manslaughter, or killing "without malice aforethought"; grossly negligent manslaughter by vehicle; criminally negligent manslaughter by vehicle; and second-degree assault. He faced up to sixty years in prison on these charges.

Mosby charged Lieutenant Rice, Officer Porter, and Sergeant White with manslaughter and second-degree assault. Officers Miller and Nero, who played a prominent role in the viral video of Stop 1 shot by Gilmor Homes resident Kevin Moore, were charged with second-degree assault but not manslaughter. While the charges sounded violent, in her May 1 speech, Mosby didn't claim that any of the officers used excessive force directly on Gray. Rather, she described them as behaving negligently.

Mosby also charged the three bike cops—Rice, Miller, and Nero—with false imprisonment over what she described as an unlawful arrest for a legal knife. Finally, she charged all six officers with "misconduct in office," which required proof that they knowingly operated in a corrupt manner. The grand jury later added a "reckless endangerment" charge for all the officers, a misdemeanor that offered an easy option for holding the officers accountable.

Mosby's prosecution was controversial. She was cheered on by some for challenging the routine business of police misconduct, including improper arrests and negligent treatment of prisoners. She was criticized by others for seeming to stretch the legal definition of charges like assault and murder to passive behaviors.

Trials of four of the officers took place from December 2015 to July 2016. Prosecutors argued that Gray was fatally injured between Stops 2 and 4 from Goodson driving recklessly while Gray was unrestrained. Defense attorneys argued that Gray was injured during the last leg of the six-stop journey, either from an accident or from Gray harming himself.

Despite so many options for holding the officers accountable in Gray's death, Mosby's office was unable to win any convictions. Porter's trial, the first scheduled, ended with a hung jury. After that, the rest of the officers selected bench trials, giving Judge Barry Williams the power to decide the verdicts on his own. Williams had a background prosecuting police misconduct for the Department of

Justice, giving hope to some of those who sought accountability. He found Nero, Goodson, and Rice not guilty on all charges, citing the state's failure to offer conclusive proof of what happened to Gray. On July 27, 2016, Mosby dropped the remaining charges against the officers. "I must consider the dismal likelihood of conviction at this point," she announced.[5]

While Maryland law did not allow the trials to be broadcast publicly, reporters put in the work of informing the public about each day's proceedings. There were important revelations in court that escaped media attention, however. For one, during the course of the trials, prosecutors radically shifted their theory about a key part of their story, which, by implication, should have called their entire theory of Gray's death into question.

Two more investigations were launched into Gray's death by outside entities. The Department of Justice opened a civil rights investigation, and two outside counties in Maryland were contracted by BPD to conduct the internal affairs investigation. Both of those investigations concluded by the end of 2017, with none of the officers determined to be at fault. The failure of any of these investigations to result in accountability in Gray's death contributed to the perception that the officers weren't responsible. Yet none of the investigations were as independent or thorough as promised.

The story outlined in this chapter has been told many times over the years. It is the well-known story of Gray's death, beginning with the official six-stop timeline and ending with the state's failure to hold any officers accountable. What follows is another story of what happened to Gray, illuminated by evidence that was unreleased and/or underexamined.

I

THE ARREST

CHAPTER 2

FOOT CHASE

"WHY DID POLICE APPROACH HIM on April 12, why did he run, and why did they chase him?" an April 24, 2015, *Baltimore Sun* editorial asked.[1] It was a set of questions people began asking right after Freddie Gray's arrest.

One of the only morsels of information BPD would provide early on was that Gray was chased by officers on bikes. "A number of officers made an arrest of a man who fled from them near the area of Gilmor Homes," Deputy Commissioner Gerimino ("Jerry") Rodriguez told the public the day after Gray's arrest. "Officers ... observed him committing what they believed warranted a contact."[2]

Rodriguez provided what would become the official response on April 20, the day after Gray died: "A lieutenant begins pursuing Mr. Gray after making eye contact with two individuals, one of which is Mr. Gray. Both males take off running southbound from that direction." The officers were "deployed in an area that is called a hot spot because of the high crime area," he said.[3]

Gray was chased because he ran, police said. In an essay in the *New Republic* titled "Looking While Black," Stacia L. Brown writes about the "tense" calculation Black people face regarding whether to look an officer in the eye. "Averting eye contact when confronted with whites was one of the unwritten rules of Jim Crow," she explains.

"No black man is eager to initiate a staring contest with the cops, especially not a man with prior arrests."[4]

The minimal explanation given by Rodriguez for how and why Gray was chased left room for the media and public to speculate. BPD never filled in the known details of what Gray was doing before he was chased. Rodriguez spoke about the incident in a serious and concerned tone, with caring eyes, while he subtly created suspicion and an atmosphere of guilt around Gray.

* * *

On Sunday, April 12, 2015, Gray started the morning in bed with his longtime girlfriend, Jamia Speller, both twenty-five. They were in her West Baltimore apartment, where she lived with her seven-year-old daughter, whom Gray often escorted to school during the week. Speller left early that morning for work as a nursing assistant. Just before 8:30 a.m., Gray met up with two of his closest friends, Brandon Ross and Davonte Roary, around Gilmor Homes. His morning started with three of the people who knew him best, who would describe him as hilarious, loyal, and full of life.

Gray and his friends took off walking around the neighborhood known as Sandtown-Winchester, or Sandtown, in West Baltimore. Spring had finally arrived that weekend, with temperatures near 70°F in the afternoon, but it was still cool that morning. Gray wore a light gray hoodie, zipped up, and sweatpants under his jeans. The three friends walked up Mount Street, passing two quiet blocks of row houses, and turned right on North Avenue, a heavily trafficked street at the north end of Sandtown. They walked two blocks into the commercial area around the Penn North transit station.[5] According to Ross, they were going to a breakfast spot south on Pennsylvania Avenue, but it was closed early Sunday morning, so they retraced their route back toward Gilmor Homes.[6]

Gray and his friends were probably not thinking about the network of closed-circuit television (CCTV) and security cameras that were filming them along their entire walk, catching Ross bending over to tie his shoe at one point. They weren't doing anything illegal.

As Gray and his friends arrived back at North and Mount, they stopped to talk to a few other men, including Shawn Washington. About thirty seconds after arriving on the corner, Ross spotted an officer on a bike riding toward them. It was Lieutenant Rice. Officers Miller and Nero followed behind by about a block. "Time out!" Ross called out, warning everyone about the police.[7] Gray and Roary took off running. They immediately turned left into a cut off Mount Street and then down an alley behind the row houses. Rice followed close behind them on his bike.[8]

The alley ended after a block, putting Gray and Roary back onto the street, with Rice still close behind. The young men both ran toward Gilmor Homes. "A lot of them that's in trouble, that's their comfort zone. It's the projects where he grew up," says Jernita Stackhouse, a neighbor. "He just ran for dear life because he had to get back to his neighborhood so somebody can see him, not knowing this was gonna be his last day on this earth."[9]

Washington also noted a practical advantage to crossing into the projects when he spoke to detectives in 2015: "Once you come into the parking area, unless you can take the bicycle and jump over the steps, the basketball court sits low.... If he beat them, he gone." Washington described Gray as a fast runner who would've gotten away if the officers were on foot instead of bikes.

Roary ran straight ahead down Mount for another block and eventually made it into Gilmor Homes ahead of police, escaping into a building on the far end of the complex. Gray took a different route. He ran into a narrow cut between two buildings on the other side of Mount Street and down an unkempt path with tall grass between the row houses. Rice followed him into the cut but couldn't ride his bike easily on the grass. Gray could have gotten away, except that Miller and Nero had split up on either side of the path behind the houses. They were "going to head him off," Washington said. "Next thing you know, he come out the cut, and they met, in perfect harmony." Washington and Ross ran down to watch what happened next.

Gray ran across Presbury Street toward Gilmor Homes, with Miller right behind him and Nero ahead of him. He was finally cut off by both officers on a wheelchair-accessible ramp at the entrance to Bruce Court, one of the Gilmor Homes courtyards. Then, according to police and civilians alike, Gray surrendered. "He surrendered right here on the rack," Roary told an investigator. He "put his face on the ground, put his hands on the ground, and got down."[10]

* * *

BPD's explanation for how and why Gray was chased—eye contact and running—didn't entirely satisfy the public, but it did serve other goals. Rodriguez's repeated references to crime in the neighborhood revealed an early and deliberate effort to prepare the officers' legal defense.

While police must have probable cause of a crime to arrest or search someone, they may pursue, detain, and briefly pat down a suspect with only "reasonable articulable suspicion" that a crime might be taking place. This legal pat-down is known as a "Terry stop," from the Supreme Court decision in *Terry v. Ohio* (1968), or more commonly as a "stop-and-frisk." After Gray died, on April 19, BPD told the public that the chase and pat-down resulted in the discovery of an illegal knife. But the question was whether the officers had the right to chase and detain Gray in the first place.

Terry v. Ohio was followed by a series of Supreme Court decisions that further defined reasonable suspicion, mostly by chewing holes in the Fourth Amendment. In *Wardlow v. Illinois* (2000), the Supreme

Court gave police reasonable suspicion to chase, stop, and frisk some-one who runs from them in a "high crime area." Rodriguez made it repeatedly clear that Gray ran from police in a "hot spot," or an "area with a history of drug dealing and violence."[11]

"'High crime area' has no precise legal meaning," according to Seth Stoughton, University of South Carolina law professor, criminal justice professor, and former police officer. Prosecutors often estab-lish it in court by having officers "testify about the number and types of crimes in that area," he explains.[12]

The attorney for Officer Nero, one of the bike cops, emphasized his client's *Wardlow* defense in court. He asked Ross if drugs are typ-ically sold around Gilmor Homes. "Where drugs not being sold at in Baltimore City?" Ross responded, providing a trenchant critique of *Wardlow*.[13]

BPD's vague explanation of the chase served another purpose beyond legal justification: It left room for the department to insin-uate that Gray was actually dealing drugs before he was chased. Putting out two parallel stories about what happened—an official story in statements to the press, which could be presented in court, and an unofficial story through leaks and insinuations—was a com-mon tactic for the police. BPD made sure the public never saw the video evidence of Gray's long morning walk or how he wasn't on the corner long enough to set up shop before he was chased. BPD also never told the public that there were a handful of people who witnessed the chase and ran down to watch what happened next.

Deputy Commissioner Rodriguez implied more than once that Gray was dealing drugs. On April 20, he said the officers "believed that Mr. Gray had either just committed or was committing a crime and that's why he ran." Rodriguez said he wasn't "validating" the officers' beliefs: "I'm merely stating the facts of what they gave us."[14] Yet none of the officers made that assertion in statements they gave on the afternoon of Gray's arrest. Lieutenant Rice said only that

Gray made eye contact and ran. The other two bike cops said they followed their boss.

Fox News was a strong advocate for the theory that Gray was arrested for drug dealing. On May 1, Sean Hannity hosted an anonymous BPD officer who insisted that Gray was "observed in a hand-to-hand transaction, small items in exchange for currency."[15] Fox successfully shielded the guest's appearance but did a poor job of disguising his thick Baltimore accent, as it sounded like a robot's voice on top of his regular voice. Hannity's guest said dealers either toss drugs when chased or swallow them. "Nine times out of ten, they'll stick the drugs right in their mouth, chop them up, hit the bottle water, swallow them, and then they'll never recover." He said Gray would have suffered "adverse effects," from swallowing a pile of drugs, to "his respiration, his heart rate, his thinking, and his actions." The officer also noted that Gray's "preliminary toxicology report" turned up "positive for heroin and marijuana."

"Woah, woah, woah, so this hasn't been made public before," Hannity said. Gray's toxicology results wouldn't be made public until the autopsy report was leaked to the media two months later. Hospital records do show that Gray tested positive for cannabinoid and opiate antibodies upon admission, but, as the officer noted, he was given a preliminary test known as an antibody-based immunoassay. His medical records indicate "confirmation not performed." The hospital never performed the more accurate follow-up test, using gas chromatography and mass spectroscopy, which would have determined the specific opiate.[16]

Regardless, Gray might not have had any opiates in his bloodstream. His lactate levels were described as "elevated upon admission" and remained concerning through his stay. Studies show high lactate levels can cause false positives in preliminary antibody-based opiate testing.[17] Nothing in Gray's medical records indicates any evidence of an overdose.

In his 2015 statement to investigators, Washington denied Gray was dealing drugs on April 12, but he did say drugs came up in the conversation. He said Ross asked who had "weed for cheap" because they had run out. He also said Gray ran because "they was gonna beat his ass either way." He described policing as a game of "hot potato": "It lands on you, tag you it. You're going to jail. And that's the process on the streets."

Stackhouse says it was a "known fact" that Gray sold drugs, but she doesn't believe he was selling drugs that morning. "He went to the corner to get his breakfast. Everybody go up there on North and Pennsy and get their breakfast in the morning."

* * *

The popular belief that Gray was arrested on April 12 for dealing drugs was supported by his widely circulated arrest history. CNN noted a list of "more than twenty arrests" from public records.[18] CNN never looked into how many records were repeated from the same case transitioning from district to circuit court or were dropped by prosecutors. Of his sixteen separate arrests, prosecutors dropped six cases and "stetted" one, giving it an indefinite postponement for up to three years. Gray was also found not guilty in one case for possession of less than ten grams of marijuana, which has since been decriminalized, and he could have expunged that record after three years. Of Gray's remaining eight arrests, three were still open at the time of his death.[19]

The actual story of Gray's arrest history says as much about policing in West Baltimore as it does about his life. About half of Gray's arrests occurred in 2017, when he was eighteen years old. He was arrested three times just after turning eighteen. That date is meaningful, according to Jenny Lyn Egan, a Baltimore City juvenile public defender. Officers often "taunt" kids with their upcoming eighteenth birthdays, given that the adult criminal system is harsher than the juvenile system. "It's a form of psychological warfare and torture," she explains.[20] In 2009, Gray spent two years in prison for possession with intent to distribute narcotics, a felony. He stayed out of police custody for about a year after that, but with a record and no high school diploma, he struggled to find employment.[21]

Gray seemed to have been a police target again for the last two years of his life. He was arrested six times, usually for minor offenses that were dropped. In 2014, he was arrested for playing dice for money and "trespassing," meaning that he was outside in a Gilmor Homes courtyard. In Baltimore, it is illegal for anyone not named on a lease to be on Housing Authority property, even though the projects provide some of the only community spaces in neighborhoods like Sandtown. Gray was arrested again five months later for burglary and trespassing. In fact, police chased someone else into a Gilmor Homes apartment and found Gray outside of the apartment on the stoop. All of the charges in both cases were dropped. (When Officer Miller spoke to internal affairs investigators in 2017, he said that he regretted not adding trespassing to the April 12 charges against Gray, even though Miller had chased Gray into Gilmor Homes.)

In two of Gray's last arrests, the probable cause statements describe him operating as a lookout. The charges in both of those cases were also dropped. Only once in the four years before his death did police ever describe Gray in the act of exchanging drugs for money. That case was still open when he died.

Gray's behavior on the morning of April 12 did not fit the pattern of any of the drug dealing described in prior arrests. There were no stash, customers, lookouts, or alleys. He was walking for more than ten minutes with two of his closest friends into a busy commercial area. Gray also had never been arrested with Roary or Ross before.

Gray's legal history offers a case study in the way the war on drugs puts young Black men into what Michelle Alexander, in *The*

New Jim Crow: Mass Incarceration in the Age of Colorblindness, calls an "undercaste, permanently locked up and locked out of mainstream society."[22] Alexander traces how this undercaste is built, from "the absence of significant legal constraints on the exercise of police discretion"—including constraints around who police choose to stop and arrest—to the imposition of second-class citizenship that "begins the moment you are branded a felon."[23]

One reason Gray may have been considered a high-priority target during the last two years of his life was his placement in a state program called the Violence Prevention Initiative (VPI). VPI's objective was "to identify that relatively small core group of offenders who are most likely to engage in violent crime" and to subject them to "enhanced supervision" and "containment."[24] Gray was put on this list without ever having been arrested for a violent crime, only nonviolent drug offenses. In all of his sixteen arrests, he was never even found holding a gun. With VPI, the state of Maryland seemed to stretch the definition of violence beyond violence—beyond even gun possession—to dealing drugs or standing near people dealing drugs. Gray appeared to have landed on the VPI list following a 2013 arrest with a dealer named Johnson, who did have a violent record. The charges against Gray were "stetted," or effectively dropped, in that case.

In *The End of Policing*, Alex Vitale describes how lists like VPI and gang databases affect young people: "Wherever they go they are hounded by government officials, who treat them as always-already criminals. The effect is what sociologist Victor Rios calls the 'youth control complex,' which undermines their life chances by driving them into economic and social failure and long-term criminality and incarceration."[25]

Gray did face one complaint for a violent act, two months before he died but years after he was placed on the VPI list. An older friend accused Gray of breaking his car window with his foot and hitting him in the face when they argued. Nearby officers approached the scene and declined to charge Gray. They recommended the friend fill out his own complaint at the courthouse, which he did. The complainant told *Undisclosed* that he had never had trouble with Gray before and was caught off guard by his behavior that day. Gray died before that case could be investigated. The story of Gray kicking in a window became lore around the Western District police station and was repeated to investigators, with various details added to the story. In many renditions, Gray was kicking out the window of a police SUV.

Gray's long list of arrests was used to portray his death as a result of his own poor choices and character, a portrayal that flooded conservative media. "I mean, this rap sheet. It's amazing for somebody twenty-four years of age," Rush Limbaugh said. "Look at how many times the police did not kill Freddie Gray."[26]

"There is no point in confusing Freddie Gray with a singer in the church choir, the way some in the media did," former Maryland governor Larry Hogan wrote in his 2020 memoir. His book describes Gray as a "Crips gang–connected, street-level drug dealer with a long criminal rap sheet, well known to the Baltimore City police."[27] No evidence ever tied Gray to any gangs.

The campaign to characterize Gray as a menace started on the day of his arrest. In their statements to detectives, officers described Gray as acting crazed and dangerous. Officer Porter testified in court that Gray would "usually act out and yell and feign some type of injury" when arrested. In sixteen probable cause statements, Gray was never described as resisting arrest, acting violent, or claiming to be injured. In fact, during the 2013 arrest that put Gray on the VPI list, Johnson escaped from his cuffs, kicked open the van door, and tried to flee. Gray did not follow him.

Governor Hogan went along with the police's characterization of Gray as a threat to the officers, writing, "Officers would say later that they kept the handcuffs on because Gray had been so unruly while they were attempting to place him in the van, the cuffs couldn't be safely removed." It was another Hogan invention. Police officers don't remove prisoners' handcuffs when they put them in a transport van. Hogan might have been thinking about the officers' decision not to seat-belt Gray. Nevertheless, video evidence shows Gray in compliance with the police at all points. His only documented acts of resistance were his loud, persistent screams.

* * *

It is typical for police to characterize the people who die in custody as dangerous, requiring excessive force. Yet police violence is disproportionately used on the most vulnerable. In 2016, the Ruderman Foundation found that a third to one-half of people killed by police are disabled.[28] About 55 percent of Black disabled men are likely to be arrested by age twenty-eight.[29]

Police are more likely to harm people who appear easier to abuse, can't hear or understand commands, have physical difficulty complying, respond sensitively to restraint, and/or have a non-neurotypical response to authority. Sandra Bland told the officer that pulled her over in July 2015 that she had epilepsy, and he replied "good."[30] Laquan McDonald reportedly had learning disabilities and complex post-traumatic stress disorder. Eric Garner had asthma.

Gray was disabled by early exposure to lead paint, as many news outlets reported. The levels of lead in his blood were so high from early childhood that he and his two sisters—Fredericka, his twin, and Carolina, their older sister—won a 2009 lawsuit against a landlord. All three siblings were diagnosed with attention deficit hyperactivity disorder (ADHD). In a deposition, Gray said he was placed in special education classrooms. According to Carol Ott, a local housing advocate and expert, lead paint is known to cause difficulties with self-regulation. "The fact that he ran, that does not surprise me at all," she says.[31]

Gray's death brought a wave of media attention to the mass disabling of families from lead paint in Baltimore. While the level of lead in Gray's blood was documented, the media made a number of assumptions about the nature of his disability. He was often portrayed as more physically and cognitively limited than his friends and neighbors report. Gray may have had a few or many disabling conditions as a result of lead paint exposure. Still, his ADHD was documented in the civil case. His friends have described him as "hyper." The media missed an opportunity to represent Gray as a young man with ADHD, discuss how police engage with people with ADHD, and/or analyze how ADHD affects success and placement in school, especially for Black children. Instead, Gray became a poster child for lead paint poisoning, vaguely understood and recklessly applied by the media.

The media's framing of Gray's lead paint poisoning was especially problematic in stories that discussed the high correlation between lead paint poisoning and criminality or aggression. "It's not just about learning disorders," a *Daily Beast* article claimed. "More recently, research has gone beyond that realm and has been starting to make more direct links between childhood lead poisoning and social dysfunction of the sort Gray exhibited, and even a tendency toward violence and crime."[32] Yet Gray didn't have a documented history of violence, aside from the one incident written up by his friend. In a deposition, Gray described his twin sister as "the aggressive one." Witnesses recalled the officers, not Gray, acting with aggression during his arrest. The media never explored the medical causes of the officers' aggression.

The Ruderman Foundation report outlined some common issues with media coverage of disabled victims of police violence, including: not mentioning the disability, blaming the disability for the police violence, mentioning disability as an "attribute without context," and using an impairment "to evoke pity or sympathy for the victim." The coverage of Gray's lead paint poisoning suffered from all of these issues. Many news stories blamed his death on his disability, directly or indirectly. The *Daily Beast* headline, "Why Freddie Gray Never Had a Chance," was referring to lead paint poisoning, not police violence. It was a prevalent framing that not only let police off the hook but portrayed disability by itself as a death sentence.

As much as Gray's disability story was about lead paint poisoning, it was also about how police respond to someone they disable in custody. Unreleased evidence, including witness and officer statements, showed that Gray's complaints of pain provoked police to respond with further aggression at both of the first two stops of his arrest.

Gray was also relatively small at the time of his arrest—a physical vulnerability if not a disability. He was five feet nine inches but weighed only 132 pounds when he arrived at the hospital. His older neighbors use language like "skinny little boy" to describe him. Officer Miller, who weighed 240 pounds, compressed Gray on the ground to the point where it is hard to see his body at all from one angle on Moore's cell video.[33] Moore's video begins with Gray screaming, mid-outcry, ". . . breathe!" followed by, "I need attention." Several witnesses and even some officers said he complained about not being able to breathe during his arrest. The police were unwilling to acknowledge Gray's physical vulnerability until he died. Then, it became useful to them. Some cops leaked an unverified story that he had a prior back injury.

Gray became an avatar for whatever political meaning people ascribed to him. Stories about his life usually centered around poverty, disability, and criminality. Maryland governor Wes Moore offered a rebuttal to Hogan's characterization of Gray as a reprobate. In a 2020 Instagram video, Moore said, "This is a person who was born underweight, premature, addicted to heroin, and poisoned by lead. And by this point in his life, he's two years old."[34] Appearing on ABC's *The View*, Moore said, "It wasn't just about the horror of his death. ... It was the horror of his life that he was forced to live."[35]

Headlines and articles referred to Gray's life as "sad," "hard," and "doomed." He certainly faced challenges, as his family revealed during the lead paint case. His mother, Gloria Darden, had an admitted drug dependency and lived on small disability payments. When he was a child, his family was so poor they sometimes had no food or electricity. They accepted a cash payout in the lead paint case by selling the settlement to a predatory company, losing hundreds of thousands of dollars in the deal.[36]

While Gray had his share of obstacles, the sympathetic portraits often reduced him to another collection of socioeconomic tropes—a mythology of sadness instead of danger. They didn't always sound sympathetic. CNN referred to Gray as the "son of an illiterate heroin addict."[37] A *Washington Post* article on Gray's lead paint exposure described Gray's life as "defined by failures" and his teenage aspiration of getting into brick masonry a "stretch to some."[38]

Ott discusses how kids with lead poisoning are often "written off" by mainstream society due to "disruptive behavior." The irony is that some of the reporters and politicians drawing attention to lead poisoning seemed to be doing the same.

* * *

Gray's personality was often left out of media stories on his life, especially early on. This left room for his life to be defined by court records and the psychologists who spoke to him once for the lead paint lawsuit. To the people who knew Gray, he wasn't a scoundrel or a lost cause. He was known to his friends and neighbors as "Pepper," "Pep," or "Lil Pep" and was commonly described as generous, fun-loving, hyperactive, charismatic, popular, fashionable, loyal, flirtatious, and quick-witted—so funny he could have been on *Saturday Night Live*, according to author D. Watkins.[39]

"He was a good guy," Gray's friend Jamel Baker remembers. "He was hilarious, always cracking jokes . . . always full of life." He describes the neighborhood as "pissed off" when Gray died. "He was so close with everybody. We really felt it, especially in the projects."[40]

Sierria Warren hung out with Gray and Ross a few years before his death. "Oh my goodness, he was too funny," she remembers. "If you're sad, you will not be sad no more." Warren says Gray had troubles, but he didn't show them outside his tight circle. "He was a good person to be around. He looked out for people. If you knew him, you loved him." Like others, she remembers Gray often hanging out with his two sisters and being an uncle figure to kids in the neighborhood.[41]

"He used to buy us ice cream, used to take us out to eat. I miss him so much," a girl named Briana told a reporter during a protest. "He was like a brother."[42]

Washington told detectives the story of meeting Gray for the first time, six months before his death: "When I first met him, I was homeless, and he was selling weed." He said Gray gave him a sandwich, some cash, and a job finding customers.

The longtime older residents of the Sandtown-Winchester community—most of whom have no love for the violence brought on by the drug trade—all remember Gray fondly in the same specific ways. Most of them watched him grow up. "He was a nice young fellow," Alethea Booze says. "He used to come past and called me, 'Ma, do you want a soda?' Ask if I need help with anything."[43]

Stackhouse remembers Gray as "joyful," generous, and a jokester. "There wasn't a day that you didn't see Freddie Gray. Too much, you know?" she says, laughing. He would ask if she needed food or anything else and hire her boyfriend to do small jobs, like fixing his bike.[44]

Jaselle Coates and Harold Perry lived in a row house on the corner of Mount and Presbury, across from where Gray was arrested. They allowed an artist to paint a large mural in honor of Gray covering one side of their house, one of three public art pieces honoring him at that intersection. The mural shows Gray's face behind bars, surrounded by various figures from civil rights history, including Martin Luther King Jr.

Peter Moskos, a professor at John Jay College of Criminal Justice, calls the mural a "disgrace" in an article on his website titled, "He Shouldn't Be Up There with Martin Luther King." Moskos was a BPD officer for about a year and used the experience to write a book, *Cop in the Hood: My Year Policing Baltimore's Eastern District.*[45] Since then, he has been a go-to media expert on Baltimore crime. In a *Baltimore Sun* op-ed, he describes Gray as "an occasional drug dealer who dropped out of school and never held a steady job." He writes, "Nobody cared about Freddie Gray until police placed him into custody."[46]

But Coates cared. "This young man came past me and spoke every day," she says. "I like to keep that young man's spirit alive, and that's why I was all for the mural wall."[47]

Gray's friends and neighbors acknowledge that Gray had faults, including his participation in the drug trade. "He was a nice boy, but he got involved with the wrong crowd," Booze says.

"Nobody is perfect," Warren says. "It wasn't like he was going around murdering people or killing people like that. He sold a little drugs. That's how he fed his family. Where we come from, that's the first job as a male that you get in the projects." Warren remembers the police having a "grudge" against Gray during the last few years of his life that seemed outsized compared to his crimes. She wondered if it was because he was particularly dark-skinned, though she admits he talked back. "Police do not like people that are not yes-men," she says.

In his 2015 statement to detectives, Washington summed up the Gray he knew: "Freddie had a lot of mouth, but he didn't back down. But he wasn't violent. Everyone will say the same. He was a smart mouth, but he would give you the shirt off his back."

CHAPTER 3

THE LIEUTENANT

LIEUTENANT BRIAN RICE, FORTY-ONE, STARTED the morning of Sunday, April 12, leading roll call at 7:00 a.m. for the Baker patrol shift at the Western District station. Roll call ended by 7:30 a.m. with these words: "Back each other up."[1] Rice was the shift commander, the "09" on the radio, overseeing the entire squad that morning and working without supervision.

Rice could have taken it easy on Sunday morning, which is usually quieter on the streets, with about a 30 percent drop in the number of drug arrests.[2] Normally, the 09 would stay back to complete inspections and paperwork. That wasn't Rice's style. It was the first warm weekend of spring, and he decided to go on bike patrol for the first time that year, leaving Sergeant Alicia White behind to handle shift-wide duties. He was joined by Officers Garrett Miller and Edward Nero, who had completed BPD's bike training program. The three officers had made plans the day before and arrived in special uniforms, with yellow shirts, a black helmet for Rice, and white helmets for the other two officers.

The bike cops left the station and headed up to North Avenue around 8:30 a.m. Rice was about a block or two ahead of his officers when he initiated the chase of Freddie Gray and Davonte Roary into an alley off Mount Street, yelling "foot pursuit" or "foot chase."

At 8:39 a.m., he told dispatch there were "two on Cumberland," which he then revised to "South on Calhoun, south on Calhoun!" Cumberland was a mistake. "I can't ride a bike and talk at the same time, hang on," he told the dispatcher.[3] He followed Gray into a narrow cut between two buildings on Mount, with a grassy path, but lost him. About a minute later, Miller got on the radio and announced that he and Nero had one of the men in custody on Presbury Street at the entrance to Gilmor Homes.[4]

* * *

BPD tried and failed to establish regular bike squads more than once in its history, but there weren't enough volunteers willing to ride for ten to twenty miles a day and get teased by fellow officers. The department reintroduced bike patrol in 1993 with a media campaign, promising that officers on bikes were a part of community policing.[5] Baltimore residents haven't always experienced them that way. "The yellow bikers, you know, they think they can do whatever they want to do to people," an unidentified witness to Gray's arrest told an investigator.[6]

Lieutenant Rice went on bike patrol with some frequency, weather permitting. It was a unique choice in a busy and violent district like the Western. Lisa Robinson, a retired BPD captain, says it "made absolutely no sense" for Rice to be out. "You're the shift commander, the only command that is ranking. You're supposed to run the shift. You shouldn't be out."[7]

"Why the fuck is the 09 shift commander on a bike?" another retired commander asks. "You're responsible for the whole district. What if someone gets shot? To me, it sounds like he was fucking up."[8]

Carrie Everett, a retired BPD patrol lieutenant, offers a different perspective. She and Rice were in the same class in Police Corps, a federal training program for college graduates piloted in 1998 to elevate police standards and training. "We rode bikes. We got to do special ops. We didn't do regular policing," she says. "It would not shock me that he was on a bike," Everett says, though she acknowledges that not every one of her classmates took the community model to heart. "Half of my Corps class probably shouldn't even be police," she says.[9]

* * *

At about 1:30 p.m. on April 12, 2015, Lieutenant Rice went downtown to give a videotaped statement to the BPD Force Investigation Team (FIT) about the events of Gray's arrest. Like most of his colleagues, he waived his Fifth Amendment rights and gave a voluntary statement. With nearly twenty years on the job, he looked like a lot of middle-aged white BPD officers—blond hair, balding, fair skin, blue eyes, and a square-shaped jaw. Rice provided FIT detectives with a confident, nonchalant run-through of the various stops and then answered some questions. He spoke as if he assumed he was believed and trusted. At the same time, he made bold claims that didn't match video evidence and left out a lot of information.[10]

Rice provided a brief and simple description of Gray's arrest on Presbury Street, or Stop 1: "They had him handcuffed and called for a wagon," he said. "The wagon got there pretty quickly." That was also how officials described it to the public: a quick arrest with a quick arrival of the wagon. In reality, Stop 1 was a complex incident with multiple events and five additional cops providing backup.

As Miller and Nero apprehended Gray at 8:40 a.m., Rice biked down to check on them before heading back behind the row houses across the street. He told detectives he was looking for "the second guy." For about the next four minutes—as Miller and Nero restrained Gray, Gray screamed, and a crowd formed—Rice stayed behind the houses, out of view of CCTV cameras.

There aren't many places for a suspect to hide behind those houses. The walkable path is no more than 150 feet, and most of the back-yards are surrounded by tall fences. There are a few vacant houses with unfenced yards. Rice told detectives he looked "under a couple porches and in the back alley" before giving up. After about a minute out of view, Rice radioed dispatch to send a unit "to the rear of 1707 Mount," saying, "There is one back here hiding." That address was actually on the other side of Mount Street, around the corner from where Gray was being held. Less than a minute later, three vehicles pulled up and stopped in front of 1707 Mount.

What makes the story of Rice's roughly four-minute manhunt suspicious is the behavior of the officers who responded to the backup call. Unreleased CCTV video shows them walking slowly through a vacant lot as they head behind the houses on Mount. The officers are staring at the ground, as if they are looking for land mines.[11] Video from another camera shows three officers about a minute later, pacing in the middle of a lot behind Mount Street, still staring at the ground.[12]

The officers told investigators they were helping Rice find the other suspect, but suspects don't hide on the ground in the middle of a lot that is visible to the street. That might be a place to look for contra-band. The alleys, cuts, and vacant lots behind Mount Street are where Western District cops describe local dealers keeping their stashes. Gray could have tossed something during the chase, but he didn't run through that lot, and Rice told detectives he didn't see Gray throw anything. Whatever instructions Rice gave these officers weren't trans-mitted on the police radio, at least not on the dispatch audio played during the trials. The officers all got the idea to search the ground from somewhere. According to dispatch reports, Rice also used "CADAPP," a cell phone application, to communicate at this time.

The behavior of the police during Stop 1 was further suspicious because the transport van was one of the vehicles that pulled up to

1707 Mount, speeding right past where Miller and Nero were hold-ing Gray with lights and siren on. The van stayed at 1707 Mount for more than a minute as the crowd observing Gray's arrest around the corner grew from a few onlookers to more than a dozen. The driver, Officer Caesar Goodson, told internal affairs investigators in 2017 that he was one of the officers searching the lot.

Why would Rice wait more than a minute to call for a van to pick up Gray and then, once the van arrived, hold it up the street from a screaming suspect and growing crowd? One explanation is that he was still looking for a reason to arrest Gray before putting him in the van. In their statements to FIT detectives, Miller and Nero only ever said they found an illegal pocketknife on Gray, a minor offense and a rare charge by itself. Rice never even men-tioned the knife in his statement, nor did he mention any reason why Gray was in custody.

Officer Nero gave the only statement suggesting Rice was look-ing for something besides another suspect. Speaking to internal affairs investigators in 2017, he said, "I remember him saying something to the effect of, like, he was looking for something or maybe it was the other suspect, but he was looking for something—whether they had discarded something or—I don't know." Later, he said Rice didn't find anything, so they charged Gray for a knife.

As the van driver and backup officers arrived in front of 1707 Mount, a fourth officer, William Porter, showed up to assist Rice behind the houses on Presbury Street. Altogether, five officers arrived to help Rice with his search, leaving only a sergeant and two patrol officers to cover the rest of the district.

BPD made sure the public never learned about Rice's entire Stop 1 production. Officials buried the video evidence showing the van parked up the street. Ironically, Rice's extended search was one rea-son the public became aware of Gray's arrest. Kevin Moore didn't run outside and start filming until just after the van passed by.

Eventually, Miller requested over the police radio that the van come quickly. "Get us a wagon quick," he said. "Gilmor Homes is starting to empty out." Goodson pulled the van around, and the officers who were searching the ground ran diagonally across the intersection to assist Miller and Nero. Rice finally biked back after two officers loaded Gray into the van; he was the last of the eight officers at Stop 1 to return to the scene of the arrest.

The last minute or so of Moore's full cell video shows Lieutenant Rice riding his bike through the crowd, threatening bystanders: "All right, you're gonna leave the area immediately or you're going to be arrested!" he yells. "Off the streets or you're going in the car! One more warning and you're coming with us!"

"We live right here!" Brandon Ross yells back. CCTV video shows Rice continuing to follow Ross even after the van drives away.

* * *

Lieutenant Rice joined the force in 1997 and came up during the era of Baltimore policing known as "zero tolerance." Mayor Martin O'Malley sought to replicate what the Rudy Giuliani administration achieved in New York City during the 1990s with "broken windows," a mass incarceration program marketed as community policing. O'Malley brought New York Police Department leaders to BPD to implement his vision.

Carrie Everett says the Police Corps program offered training in broken windows as it is purely designed but rarely practiced. "I loved it because you could talk to people when it wasn't bad, when they didn't need you, and they didn't have to call 911," she says. "You came to have a rapport with the community."[13] She was trained to attend community meetings, visit recreation centers, and even help with trash. She describes O'Malley's brand of zero tolerance policing as inhospitable to what she learned. She remembers her bosses trying to force her to arrest people for how they rode their bikes in violation of an obscure city code. Everett, who is Black, recalls asking if they were "doing that out in Roland Park," a mostly white neighborhood.

Mass incarceration was a national trend in the 1990s, a product of a drug war that gave the United States "the highest rate of incarceration in the world," according to Michelle Alexander in *The New Jim Crow*. The war on drugs targets Black communities despite "remarkably similar rates" of using and selling illegal drugs across races. "No other country in the world imprisons so many of its racial or ethnic minorities," Alexander writes. "The United States imprisons a larger percentage of its black population than South Africa did at the height of apartheid."[14]

Baltimore went famously far with mass incarceration. In 2003, BPD made more than 110,000 arrests in a city of about 650,000. The criminal justice system couldn't contain that many arrests. Tens of thousands of Black residents annually would spend a night or two in jail without a charge. Ray Kelly, a longtime West Baltimore resident and executive director of the Citizens Policing Project, says, "Even those of us that weren't really engaged in the trade, you couldn't stop and speak to your neighbor because you had to assess the whole situation. If it was too many people, then the police may jump in and grab everybody, and everybody would miss a day of work."[15]

The pilot episode of HBO's *The Wire* (2002) comments on the ineffectiveness of zero tolerance policing under O'Malley. Homicide Detective Jimmy McNulty tells a judge why key high-level drug dealers are being left alone to control the Westside.

"Who's working them?" the judge asks.

"Nobody really. We're a little busy making street rips, you know? Community policing and all that," McNulty responds sarcastically.

In 2005, *Time* magazine named O'Malley one of America's top five best mayors for improving the quality of life and reducing crime in Baltimore. About 100,000 arrests corresponded to about thirty-five fewer homicides annually. A year later, Baltimore was sued by the American Civil Liberties Union (ACLU) and the National Association for the Advancement of Colored People (NAACP) for a pattern of unconstitutional and inhumane arrests. The lawsuit offered evidence that BPD was rewarding officers for maximizing arrests.[16]

O'Malley left office in 2007. In 2010, the ACLU and NAACP won their lawsuit. The victory came with a settlement package and a demand for change. BPD issued a memo titled "No Zero Tolerance Policing," which ordered the end of arrests for quality-of-life crimes, including disorderly conduct, failure to obey an order, littering, and trespassing. Those crimes constituted about 16 percent of Lieutenant Rice's arrests by 2010.[17] After the new policy, BPD cut arrests nearly in half while the homicide rate also decreased about 27 percent. The era after zero tolerance offered evidence against its theory of change.[18]

In March 2014, three years after zero tolerance ended on paper, Rice arrested a man for littering. Porter wrote up the arrest but described himself in the probable cause statement as following Rice's orders. The man threw a lit cigarette on the ground and didn't want to pick it up and put it in the trash. He also talked back to Rice. He was further charged with failure to obey an order. Rice imprisoned a dozen people in 2014 for similar crimes, exploiting loopholes in the "No Zero Tolerance Policing" policy.

* * *

At some point toward the end of Gray's arrest on Presbury Street, Lieutenant Rice hatched a plan to finish the arrest on the street and send Gray straight to Central Booking: "To deescalate the entire situation, I had my officers leave, I had the wagon leave, and I said, 'We'll take the guy down Mount Street a couple of blocks and we'll pull him back out of the wagon where it's a little more relaxed," he told detectives that afternoon. The van parked at Mount and Baker Streets, which became known as Stop 2.

Rice said the officers took Gray out of the van briefly to put leg shackles on his ankles because Gray had run from them, presumably referring to the initial chase, but he was hazy on some other details. He wasn't sure if Gray was sitting or standing when they took him out, and he wasn't sure at first how they put him back in the van.

Rice was far clearer on two other points. First, he remembered that Gray was so combative inside of the van that he was causing the vehicle, which weighed more than 9,500 pounds, to shake.[19] He saw Gray "shaking the wagon violently" as he biked over to Stop 2, and he saw it shaking again after they put Gray back inside of it. "As I got the door closed, he was up and banging and the wagon was just violently shaking." One of the detectives asked if he was sure Gray was back up on his feet. Rice responded that Gray must have gotten up to have the "leverage" to do "that much banging and that much rocking back and forth of the wagon," though he acknowledged that it was "just an assumption."

Rice made an additional assumption about Gray's behavior at Stop 2: "He looked like he was hitting his head in the back of the wagon," he said. He mimed banging his own head backward. "When he got back into the wagon, the wagon began shaking violently, and he was hitting his head, and kicking the door, and just making a lot of noise," he said. Detectives didn't ask Rice how he knew Gray was hitting his head behind closed doors.

Two CCTV videos show the van at Stop 2 from the front and above. The cameras are preprogrammed to constantly rotate, so they don't capture everything. Neither of them shows the van visibly shaking at any point.

The CCTV videos don't capture what was happening in the back of the van, where the action took place, but Ross caught some of it on a cell phone. His video is jumpy because he was arguing with the officers while filming. A few seconds of the video show Gray's body facedown on the floor of the van and his lower half hanging out of the back. His knees and shins are on the ground. For the first time on video, Gray is not screaming, talking, or moving. The bike cops are huddled around the back of the van. BPD never shared Ross's Stop 2 video with the public, but Deputy Commissioner Rodriguez described it—or, more precisely, misrepresented it. He said it showed Gray "conscious," "speaking," and "able to move."[20]

In a couple of blink-and-you-miss-them moments, Rice climbs all the way into the van as Nero lifts Gray's legs. Rice then climbs back out, as Gray's body is all the way inside the van.

Gray was laid down on the floor of a space measuring only about four feet high and one and a half feet across, next to an enclosed bench.[21] It would not have been easy for Rice to get in and out of the van if Gray were violent and kicking. Rice neglected to tell the FIT detectives that he climbed into the van, but he admitted to leaving Gray on the van's floor.

Ross's video recorded a conversation he had with Officer Porter, who pulled up in his car as Rice was climbing into the van. "Hey, Porter, can we get a supervisor in here please?" Ross calls out. "Okay, can we get somebody else up here please?" Ross asks. "There's gotta be someone else out here that can come out here and calm this down. That's not cool. That's not cool."

Porter responds, "Brandon, you know where [unclear] goes at. Go to the news."

Ross's video cuts to black after this conversation, but it still plays sound. A high-pitched voice in the distance, sounding like Rice, yells, "Jail, jail, jail." Ross told reporters that Rice threatened him with a Taser.[22] CCTV video does show Rice at that time leaning on his bike, facing the witnesses, and seeming to raise his Taser-side arm toward them.[23]

Stop 2 was the last time Rice interacted with Gray. He made it clear to detectives that Gray was not only conscious and healthy at

Stop 2 but behaving in an aggressive and self-destructive manner. So whatever happened to put Gray into a coma, Rice implied, had nothing to do with him.

* * *

On April 20, 2015, BPD put Lieutenant Rice and five other officers involved in Gray's arrest on administrative suspension, or desk duty, while it completed its investigation. The next day, the *Guardian* published the first of a series of articles exposing Rice's history of allegedly harassing and threatening his ex-girlfriend, Karen Crisafulli, and her then-husband, Andrew McAleer.[24] Crisafulli is the mother of Rice's child and also a BPD officer. The Associated Press (AP) contributed to the evolving story. Rice's unreleased disciplinary records from BPD's Internal Affairs Division (IAD) complete and update these stories. Disciplinary records were not available to reporters in Maryland in 2015.

The news stories and IAD files outline several major incidents, all after Rice was promoted to lieutenant in 2011. Some are backed up by police reports. In April 2012, Crisafulli reportedly asked local sheriffs to check on Rice following an alleged suicidal outcry. Carroll County law enforcement confiscated six personal firearms, including an "AK-47–style rifle." Rice was given an emergency petition and hospitalized. The AP reported that Major James Handley asked deputies not to fax over the police report from the incident to BPD. Instead, he would have it picked up.[25] (Handley, who is white, later sued BPD for racial discrimination.)

Two months later, McAleer informed IAD that Rice was using his departmental cell phone to send videos and photographs of "lewd acts'" to Crisafulli, including "almost daily" pictures of himself masturbating. "Rice has been harassing and abusing for some time," the disciplinary record states. Crisafulli "fears that his powers will affect her job." After a year-long case, Rice received a "severe letter" and was suspended for thirty-five days.

A week after filing that complaint, on June 22, 2012, McAleer called police to his home at 2:15 a.m. Rice was reportedly arguing outside with Crisafulli, who was holding their infant son. The family had returned from a vacation to find Rice in their driveway. Westminster Police Department (WPD) officers wrote reports describing Rice as refusing to give his name and intimidating Crisafulli into not speaking with them. McAleer later wrote up a version of this incident in which he claimed that a drunken Rice removed a semiautomatic gun from his trunk. According to police reports, Rice left the scene on foot, and the WPD officers spent the rest of a long night trying to locate him and convince him to pick up his car.[26]

There is a very brief record of this incident in Rice's IAD file for "tracking only." It is labeled as a "domestic incident" and states that "Rice failed to identify himself" to local law enforcement.

After that incident, the conflict escalated between Rice and McAleer, with McAleer ultimately filing a criminal complaint against him on January 19, 2013 and having him arrested.[27] Two days later, McAleer filed a peace order, or a "plea for protection" against Rice. Over ten pages, he outlined a years-long campaign of "harassment, stalking, trespassing and serious threat of bodily harm," including the incidents above and a few others. He wrote that Rice and Crisafulli were required by the courts to meet at a local police station to exchange their child.

McAleer's complaint finally got BPD to pay more serious attention. Rice's IAD record shows that he was suspended by Western District's new captain, Erik Pecha, who took away his gun and badge. Crisafulli gave a statement saying that she was "in fear of" Rice. She later accused him of obtaining a confidential email she had sent to IAD. Rice seemed to be off the streets for most of 2013 and parts of 2014.[28]

Crisafulli and McAleer separated and were divorced by 2015, but the issues continued between the two men. On March 29, 2015, Rice was at the Westminster police station at around three in the morning, demanding McAleer be arrested, flaunting his status as a BPD lieutenant, and refusing to provide an accurate phone number or identification, according to a police report.[29] IAD opened an investigation into this complaint too. Two weeks later, Rice was leading his squad into a chase and arrest that would end a human life and foment an uprising.

* * *

Rice's history with Crisafulli and McAleer was only a part of his complete disciplinary history. If made public, his "rap sheet" of complaints would have outrivaled Gray's arrest history in volume alone. Over seventeen years, Rice faced thirty-two IAD complaints. In 2006, Rice was accused of striking a twenty-one-year-old man until he was unconscious and breaking his arm. The complainant was the young man's mother, Pamela Foote. She still recalls the incident, but she says the IAD record got it wrong: her son's arm was already broken and in a cast. He had just come out of physical therapy when Rice assaulted him and "snatched him" by his broken arm, she says. Her son went to the hospital after Rice's assault.

Foote was demoralized by the IAD process. "They tried to look at my son's background, prior things that happened," she says. "That's not an excuse for why an officer had a right to assault nobody." An attorney advised her to stop cooperating with the investigation. "My son is not the only person Officer Rice hurt around there. He hurt other people."[30]

In 2008, a woman filed a complaint claiming Rice pulled her out of a car during a traffic stop, slammed her to the ground, "pushed her shoulder to the ground," and yelled, "Shut the fuck up." IAD investigated this case thoroughly for about a year and then closed it without explanation. The finding was "not sustained," which means not enough evidence to determine guilt or innocence.

An IAD record states that, in January 2013, Rice pulled a gun on an unarmed man who was having a mental health episode and broke the back door of his house. The man's mother agreed to drop the complaint but requested "Lieutenant Rice to stay away from her home."

Rice's disciplinary records include several complaints about him following, stopping, searching, and harassing people without cause. In 2008, a man complained after Rice reportedly arrested him twice in one week for loitering and trespassing. He said Rice harassed him and constantly compared him to his father, "who had trouble with the law." In 2009, an elderly woman called Rice, then a sergeant, to complain about his officers harassing her and using homophobic language with her son. According to the woman, Rice "berated" and hung up on her.

After Rice became a lieutenant in 2011, he faced fewer allegations from the streets and more from his commanders. He faced back-to-back complaints in January 2015 over failing to comply with direct orders in how he supervised, including allowing two officers to share a car. It does seem that eyes were on Rice in 2015. Yet by then, he was serving under his fourth major in three years.

Most of Rice's IAD complaints were closed without a clear explanation. Only one was determined to be entirely "unfounded," meaning he was determined to be not guilty. IAD detectives have tools for closing cases without a resolution, including "not sustained" or "administratively closed." An ACLU study found that only 8 percent of external complaints against BPD officers from 2015 to 2019 were sustained.[31] Not all issues make it into personnel files. In August 2014, Rice made a U-turn in the middle of the street, ramming his police car into the front of another car, according to the police report of the incident. The driver and passenger sued. That incident was never investigated by IAD.[32]

A summary of Rice's IAD file was sent to the commissioner on the day after Gray's arrest. It lists only two sustained cases: a 1998 incident involving drug evidence left in his car, for which he received counseling, and the sexual images he sent to Crisafulli. It also notes the January 2015 incidents concerning his supervision. The list sent to the commissioner was the tiny tip of a very deep iceberg, whereas the entire world learned about every time police arrested Freddie Gray, even when charges were dropped.

* * *

Rice's actions on April 12, 2015, reflect someone with nearly twenty years of experience in quickly responding to an incident by seeming to protecting himself. On the streets and in his statements, he was deft at crossing back and forth between performing as a supervisor and performing as just another officer on a bike, with limited involvement.

After medics took Gray to the hospital, Rice went more clearly into supervisorial mode—or, arguably, cover-up mode. At 10:13 a.m., he got on the radio and asked the dispatcher, "Did the crime lab respond to the station in reference to an arrest on Mount and Presbury?"

Then he said, "I'm gonna call you," and dialed a direct number to reach the dispatcher from his phone.

The dispatcher picked up the phone line and let him know, "This line is recording." Rice told the dispatcher the situation was a "potential death." Seth Stoughton identifies two reasons for an officer to call dispatchers on a landline instead of communicating via radio: "To avoid sharing information with anyone listening on that radio channel" and/or "to avoid the information being recorded."[33]

What Rice said next isn't entirely clear on the dispatch audio played in court, but it sounds like he asked for CSU to wait for an hour. Notably, one hour later, according to BPD timelines and dispatch reports, someone from FIT checked with the dispatcher to see if CSU was requested and was told Rice had requested it. It did, in fact, arrive about an hour after Rice's request. "If you need CSU, you want CSU there promptly," Stoughton says. "I've never heard of delaying CSU an hour." Before CSU arrived, Officer Goodson took the van, a major piece of evidence in the potential death of a prisoner, away from the station, supposedly for gas. "That makes no sense to me," Stoughton says.

At 10:45 a.m., FIT detectives arrived to take over the investigation. Rice became officially an "involved officer," which is a police euphemism for a suspect. He went downtown to give a statement. For much of the interview, he spoke more like a colleague of the investigators than their subject. "From my standpoint or a supervisor's standpoint," he said, there was "no use of force."

Toward the end of his statement, Rice began shifting the detectives' attention to two of his officers. Sergeant Alicia White checked on Gray at Stop 5 and would have the most information about his last known condition, he said, spelling out her first name. Rice also pointed the detectives toward Goodson, the van driver, who became the source of most of his observations. "Officer Goodson said that he felt concerned that the guy was lethargic, didn't look good. He had run from us, that kind of stuff, and he was hitting his head against the wagon." Goodson was the only officer who declined to give a statement. On the way out, Rice asked where the cameras in the interview room were located.

* * *

Lieutenant Rice benefited from ineffective accountability systems and a handful of supporters in high places. The local Fraternal Order of Police (FOP) president, Gene Ryan, who used to work with Rice, told the *Baltimore Sun*, "I would be very surprised if he did something like that," referring to McAleer's ten-page complaint.[34]

Rice was also supported by the FOP's attorney, Michael Davey, another former cop, whose firm has an exclusive contract with the FOP for internal disciplinary cases. The firm subcontracts to other law firms when there are multiple parties involved or criminal cases. Rice called Davey's firm on the afternoon of Gray's arrest and put Davey as his contact when he was booked on May 1. The other officers listed family members as their contacts.

Davey spoke out shortly after Gray's arrest. He said he spoke for all six suspended officers; however, at the same time, he identified himself specifically as Rice's attorney.[35] In doing so, Davey explicitly tied the fates of the other five officers to Rice's interests. They would have to go along with the FOP's agenda, which was likely Rice's agenda, to get their legal needs met. As for McAleer's complaint, Davey said, "People file peace orders all the time. The only thing I'd comment on is, any issues similar to this had nothing to do with his ability to perform his duties as a Baltimore police officer."

A former BPD major discusses the way in which Rice was protected, even as some of his commanders were suspending and writing him up. "I'm not sure if he was guarded by a larger internal force. There is a likeness to protect some based on who they are aligned with and also to avoid the exposure of others involved." This commander, who requested anonymity, described BPD as "all about sex, lies, and cash."[36]

Carrie Everett likewise describes a system of advancement and protection within BPD based on "manipulation," "team players," and even "blackmail," with sex and cash at play. Everett was in her thirties and with a military background when she joined the force, so she wasn't easily manipulated. "I'm not scared of policing, and the criminals weren't my problem," she says. It was BPD leadership. "They don't honor people who work hard."[37]

CHAPTER 4

FREDDIE'S CREW

Freddie Gray's arrest in Gilmor Homes was witnessed by nearly twenty bystanders who shared their stories with investigators and reporters. Some of the witnesses were also Gray's close friends who had started the morning with him or showed up in response to his screams. They subsequently dealt with the double trauma of losing a close friend and witnessing police abuse. Some of them faced further trauma as a result of coming forward in a city where being a young Black man and a witness are both high risk factors.

Brandon Ross, one of Gray's two longtime friends with whom he took a walk that morning, was thirty years old in 2015. Also known as B-Low, he was tall and built, with a smooth manner and movie-star looks. He walked out into the chilly April morning in a long-sleeved ribbed white shirt over another shirt, while everyone else was in jackets. Ross described Gray as his "godbrother" in statements. They had been friends for about ten years.

Davonte Roary, then twenty, was known as Little Daddy or Daddy Daddy. He got that nickname because he was the youngest of the group of friends but acted like everyone's father. He spoke in an intense and instructive manner, using his voice to punctuate the importance of his points. Roary had known Gray since childhood.

Gray and Roary took off running from Lieutenant Rice. Roary ran ahead into a building in Gilmor Homes, looking back just before entering. Ross ran down to Presbury Street after them. Both Ross and Roary saw Gray being apprehended by police on a wheelchair-accessible ramp.

Duane Day was walking east on Presbury Street when he saw his friend from childhood being arrested. Day was lanky and an animated talker, his arms and body in constant motion when he spoke. He wore an extra–wide-brimmed baseball hat, angled to the side. During Gray's arrest, he borrowed someone's bike and rode it around the scene.[1]

As Day approached the scene, Kevin Moore heard a person screaming about the officers tasing someone, so he ran out of his Bruce Court apartment. He quickly pulled out his phone to record the last two minutes of Gray's arrest. Over six feet tall, Moore was wearing head-to-toe black clothes, with long dreadlocks pulled back into a ponytail. A husband and father, with another child on the way, he worked at a nearby corner store. Moore offered Gray an assuring presence. "Don't worry, Shorty. We recording this shit," he said. He moved closer to the officers to get a better angle. By that time, the officers had moved Gray about seventy feet east, from the ramp in Bruce Court to a short stone wall in Bakbury Court, where the transport van could park.

Gray's friends observed the rest of his arrest until he was loaded into the van. As the van pulled off, they assumed it was taking him to the nearby police station and they would catch up with him later. Several other witnesses stayed outside, talking. Ross walked into Bakbury Court and borrowed a neighbor's phone to call 911 and report "an altercation between a police officer and a citizen" at Gilmor Homes. "They are being rowdy," he told the dispatcher, referring to the police.[2]

Two minutes after the van left Stop 1, the remaining bystanders shifted their attention in the direction of Mount and Baker Streets around the corner. They could hear Gray's screams all over again.

CCTV video shows them running down the street or through the courtyard to see what was happening. Ross interrupted his story to the dispatcher, saying, "Matter of fact, they fighting on someone else over here!" and hanging up.

A smaller crowd started forming around the van at Mount and Baker Streets, or Stop 2. Ross started filming what he saw on the phone he borrowed to call 911. "After they had him in the fucking— After they had him in there! They got in the car at Mount and Presbury!" he yells in his video. Like everyone else, he didn't understand what Gray was doing out of the van again.

"Don't worry about it," Moore shouts. "We got him on camera." Ross then shouts about hearing Gray being tased "again."

In his apartment in Bakbury Court, Jamel Baker was woken up by Gray's screams. His second-floor window looked right out on top of the van. Known as Snap—but sometimes known as Fool for his propensity to use the word to describe others—Baker had become close friends with Gray over the previous four years. "We'd just hang out, kick it, talk trash, you know, crack jokes and stuff like that," he recalls. "We wasn't hurting nobody."[3] Baker is young-looking, with a soft-spoken manner that belies his wry sense of humor. He was working as a janitor at a hospital in 2015. He is also a single father and refers to his daughter as his "best friend."

Gray's friends—Ross, Roary, Day, Moore, and Baker—gave taped statements to investigators in the hours and days after the arrest and made multiple efforts to get the truth out, often at personal risk. The stories they told investigators were largely consistent and important in reconstructing what really happened to Gray. They provided a level of detail that was missing from news reports and during the trials. The public never heard their original statements. Both police and prosecutors buried the recordings.

* * *

Kevin Moore was the first of Gray's friends to speak to FIT detectives at police headquarters on the afternoon of the arrest. He gave a videotaped statement at 1:50 p.m. to detectives Michael Boyd and Joseph Poremski. Boyd led the questioning, as he did for most of the interviews that day. Moore was friendly and cooperative. He had no idea that Gray was in a coma, and the detectives gave him many reasons to trust them. Boyd shook Moore's hand, cracked jokes, and called him "brother." (Boyd is white.) They chatted about the best places to get tattoos.[4] Moore gave the detectives his phone and password so they could download the cell video of Gray's arrest.

"Apparently, you have some video. You video-recorded some of this incident on your cell phone, yes?" Boyd asked.

"Well, a small portion of it," Moore answered. "I didn't really catch any of the illegal stuff," he said. "All I caught was—"

Boyd interrupted. "Lemme backtrack a little bit for what we do," he said. He explained that the subject of their investigation was the police, not Gray. "So we're not necessarily investigating what he did to be arrested. We're investigating the officers' actions."

Boyd had misunderstood Moore. "Well, that's what I'm talking about," Moore explained. "The officers that arrested him, I didn't really get anything illegal, all you see was them arresting him." He witnessed a lot more than he taped, he explained, including actions he later described as illegal.

Moore played the video of Stop 1 for detectives and signed a paper giving them unrestricted access to his phone. He then provided a run-through of the events of the morning: "I was in my house, me and my wife were talking. You know, husband-and-wife things. And I hear screaming. And one of my friends, which I really prefer not to name, yells out the window, 'They're tasing him, they're tasing him.' So I run out. I'm down the steps." On his own cell video, Moore can be heard shouting, "Shorty, that was after they tased the fuck out of him like that! You wonder why he can't use his legs."

Moore described police restraining Gray "like a crab" with his arms and legs pulled back.

Moore became well known for his video and eyewitness account of Stop 1. But most of his first-day statement to FIT detectives was about what he saw around the corner. "But the second time, when they stopped down on Baker Street … and when I tell you, dude, I wish I could've recorded it," he said. "They pulled him out the paddy wagon, tased him again, and then threw him back in."

"And you physically saw that yourself?" Boyd asked.

"I saw that myself, but I didn't have a chance to record it," he said. He described the prongs that shoot out of the Taser. "They're on him. You know?"

"You can physically see the prongs?" Boyd asked.

"I can physically see the prongs in this guy's leg!" Moore responded, touching his right knee. He also described the wires connecting the Taser to the prongs.

"See, that's why we're doing the talk," Boyd said. "You got more information than you thought!" Right before this interview, Boyd had interviewed Lieutenant Rice, who assured him that Gray wasn't tased at any point.

"And what did it sound like?" he asked.

"It sounded like electricity, dude, like voltage," Moore responded. Boyd asked him to demonstrate the sound. "*Zzh zzh zzh*," Moore responded.

"What color was the Taser? Did you see the Taser?" Boyd asked.

"The Taser was black, and it was gold," Moore responded. The officers' Tasers were black and yellow.

Moore filled in some of the other details Rice had left vague about Stop 2. He said the officers "drug him out" of the van "by his feet," before tasing him, then "threw him back in." He said the officers went into cover-up mode when the witnesses approached, responding hastily. "They lift him up, wet noodle, throw him in the back of the paddy wagon," Moore said, miming someone being picked up and casually thrown.

"Feet first or headfirst?" Boyd asked.

"Headfirst," Moore responded. "We're flipping. I mean, like, we're zagging out." Moore also described one of the bike officers harassing the witnesses. He quoted the officer saying, "You'd better get the F away from here," and then pointing at the witnesses, saying, "One, two, three. Jail, jail, jail." Moore's sincerity and guilelessness in his statement to FIT detectives—together with the fact that he didn't yet know the outcome of the arrest—lend extra weight to his recollections. He spoke to detectives only hours later and remembered details that were corroborated by other evidence, like Rice's triple jail threat, which can be heard at the end of Ross's Stop 2 video.

* * *

As Moore was being interviewed downtown, Jamel Baker, the single father who witnessed Stop 2, was interviewed outside of his apartment. He spoke to FIT Detectives Charles Anderson and Syreeta Teel at 1:42 p.m. on the afternoon of Gray's arrest. The interview was audio-recorded. Baker too was unaware of the outcome of the arrest. From the interview, it also sounded like he didn't realize that the person in custody was his very good friend.[5]

Teel asked Baker to recount the morning's events. "Early this morning, I was in bed sleep—well, trying to sleep," he said, "and I heard something that sound like somebody was being killed, I mean, like really screaming. So looked out the window." He said the prisoner was "on the ground, behind the wagon" and lying on his stomach. The man was yelling before he got to the window, "aaah, aaah, aaah, real loud," he said.

Baker had trouble seeing the full action, so he took the screen out of his window. He said three officers grabbed Gray by his feet and handcuffs, two on one side and one on the other. "As I'm getting the screen out the window," he said, "they're like picking him up off the ground and throwing him in—like, putting him in the wagon." Did Baker see the officers "put" or "throw" Gray into the wagon? "When I got to the window," he said later, "they was just flipping him in the wagon." At another point, he said they were "lifting him into the wagon."

Detective Anderson, whose interview style was to dig into specific details, sought clarity on this question. "Did they shove him in there, slide him in there?" he asked.

"Yeah, kind of like sliding him in there," Baker answered, tentatively.

"Was it a forceful slide or did they just slide him in?"

Baker wasn't sure. Later, he said, "Well, it wasn't—I don't know. It wasn't really *forceful* forceful, but they . . ." and then he trailed off. Anderson asked if the officers were doing anything else, like hitting or kicking Gray. "No, I didn't see them do anything like that, but someone was doing something, because that man sounded like he was dying," Baker responded.

Baker was very clear on the rest of what he saw, most of which was confirmed by Ross's video of Stop 2. He recognized five officers on the scene, three on bikes in yellow shirts who were "Caucasian" and two Black officers "on foot." He recognized the van driver as a Black man. He remembered the second Black officer staying back by his car, talking to one of the witnesses. (This was Officer Porter talking to Ross.)

Baker also identified which officers he saw pick Gray up from the ground and put, throw, flip, lift, or slide Gray into the van: namely, the van driver and two of the bike cops. One of those bike cops, he said, was the supervisor. He knew this based on the conversation he heard between Ross and Porter. "Someone was like, 'Can I speak to your supervisor?' or something. The other guy was like, 'That's the supervisor there,'" pointing to one of the bike cops that handled Gray.

According to Baker, the man in custody was no longer screaming like he was dying at the end of the stop. "He wasn't moving when I looked out there. He wasn't doing nothing." Detective Anderson asked Baker to come downtown to provide a videotaped statement, but Baker didn't have anyone to watch his then-eight-year-old daughter. Anderson took his phone number. BPD never called Baker to give a full statement on video. He was interviewed for only eight minutes on the street, surrounded by people and noise.

* * *

The next day, April 13, FIT Detectives Teel and Poremski interviewed Brandon Ross downtown at headquarters on video at 3:16 p.m. He was the only civilian to capture any of Stop 2 on camera. It was on his neighbor's phone, but he wouldn't share her name. Detectives obtained a copy of the video later the same day from someone in the neighborhood who received it via email.[6]

Ross's video of Stop 2 had been circulating over the prior twenty-four hours among Gray's friends. BPD was fully aware it was out there. That day, an investigator printed out Facebook posts from a woman named Kiona Craddock, who shared a still image of Gray's legs hanging out of the van at Stop 2. She wrote that "Pepper" was tased and beaten and had lost his pulse at one point.[7]

Ross provided detectives with a detailed run-through of what he witnessed during Gray's arrest.[8] He saw a lot, more than any other witness. He was cooperative, but he wasn't upbeat. He knew that his godbrother was in a coma. Detective Teel was also a frustrating interviewer, lacking patience with his answers and not always following which part of the story he was sharing. By the end of the interview, Ross had his head in his hands.

"I don't want to get you all frustrated," Poremski said when Teel stepped out of the room for a moment.

Ross's story started with Gray running from the corner of Mount and North "before the officers even came." Teel seemed incredulous of this. "That's Freddie. Freddie's hyper," he explained. "It's a nice day out there. We walking, enjoying ourselves." He described the bike officer that chased Gray as older-looking with blond hair "cut low."

Ross then ran down to Gilmor Homes, where he saw Gray surrender "flat on the ground" on the ramp in front of Bruce Court, something only a few people witnessed. Ross demonstrated an officer putting his knee into Gray's back while handcuffing him: "He was handcuffed immediately, simultaneously with knee, boom, hand behind his back, handcuffed." He then described the same officer dragging Gray to the wall in Bakbury Court by his wrists and his shirt. There, Ross said, the officer tased him.

"What color was the Taser?" Teel asked.

"Yellow," Ross answered.

"Describe the sound of the Taser to me," Teel demanded. Ross imitated a rapid clicking sound.

"Lemme make sure I have this straight," Teel asked later. "You see your godbrother Freddie get tased by an officer?"

"Right," Ross responded. He was not positive if the officer used the Taser in direct contact mode, against the skin, or by shooting out prongs. Detectives didn't ask Ross exactly where he was standing.

Ross's story included a lot of specific details that didn't become public until the trials. He knew one officer biked down Bruce Street, which is parallel to Mount, and cut Gray off on the ramp. He remembered the other officer jumped off his bike to catch Gray and then yelled, "Yo, grab my bike," to his partner, which both officers confirmed in their own statements.

Detective Teel asked Ross how Gray entered the van at Stop 1. He took a few beats to think about it and then said, "If I can recall,

I'm saying, he even like ducked his head down. I'm trying—I'm trying to remember. He got down, he bent his head down." It was an accurate response. On Moore's video, Gray lowers his head to enter the van. Despite Gray's legs dragging as officers carried him to the van, his ability to move his neck, speak, and bear his own weight while entering the van at Stop 1 was used by police and prosecutors to deny that he had suffered his fatal injury by that point. Even Ross didn't think Gray was seriously hurt during Stop 1. "He was completely healthy, fine being carted off, aside from his leg," he told a reporter the next day. "It's nowhere near how he's sitting in the ICU right now."[9]

Ross told detectives that while he was in the courtyard speaking to the 911 dispatcher, he heard Gray screaming again. Unreleased CCTV video shows Ross suddenly running from a stoop inside Bakbury Court and through a cut between two buildings that exits onto Mount Street at 8:48 a.m.[10] "When I hear him screaming, I hear a Taser," he told detectives. He said the Taser noise stopped when he was still in the "split" between the buildings.

Ross raced out onto Mount Street and found himself facing the rear doors of the van, where a lot was going on. "I seen the wagon, about three or four officers surrounding the back of the wagon, with Freddie, like laying in the gutter," he said. "And they pick him up again and threw him headfirst, threw in the wagon." Ross ran closer to the van to get a better view and began filming. "When they threw him in the wagon headfirst," he said, "you can hear him kicking and yelling."

After leaving Stop 2, Ross and two others walked down to the Western District station to complain. The door was locked, and nobody answered when they knocked. He looked around the back of the police station, where he recalled seeing the transport van. He borrowed the phone of a "white lady" he knew in a house nearby to call 911 again.

"I witnessed an assault," he told the dispatcher. "I seen the officers assault this guy, and I have it on a camera, and I want to file a complaint." Ross gave the name "Rodney Clark."[11] In court, Ross explained why he gave a fake name: "Because I knew what was going to come of this, and I knew I was going to be harassed by the police officers," he said.[12] Ross was a frequent police target, with a deeper record of arrests than Gray and a couple of extended prison stays.

* * *

The statements provided by Moore, Baker, and Ross in the immediate aftermath of Gray's arrest are detailed and credibly supported by other information. Their statements are also nuanced, especially on the issue of Gray being tased. Moore told detectives he heard from someone yelling outside *about* Gray being tased at Stop 1, but he actually saw and heard tasing at Stop 2, including prongs in Gray's leg. Later, Moore told reporters that he did hear (but did not see) Gray being tased as he ran out to film Stop 1, though it was common for the witnesses' memories to shift a bit over time. Meanwhile, Ross told detectives he saw *and* heard Gray being tased at Stop 1, but he only heard the sound as he was running toward Stop 2. The sound stopped before he got out onto Mount Street. Later, he saw Rice point a Taser at the witnesses in a threatening manner. If Gray's friends were going to lie about him being tased, they would have benefited from a simpler story. The media conversation around Gray's arrest never made room for this level of nuance. Detectives Boyd and Teel barely had patience for it.

Police denied the existence of these witness statements. On April 20, BPD Deputy Commissioner Rodriguez announced, "We have no evidence—physical, video, or statements—of any use of force."[13] Rodriguez's magic trick was to promise transparency while making one provocative statement after another that gaslighted the witnesses and public.

Anyone watching Moore's video might reasonably feel that police were holding Gray in a position that was excessive and forceful. Gray's legs were pulled behind his back in a hold called a "leg lace," making it impossible for him to move. According to Seth Stoughton, who cowrote a book titled *Evaluating Uses of Police Force*, "The leg lace is supposed to be quickly used and then transitioned away from as soon as possible. You don't keep someone on their chest. To avoid positional asphyxia, police training is you get them into that position, you get them out of that position as quickly as possible by rolling them onto their side and hopefully have them sit up or stand up soon."[14] Miller held Gray in that position for around a minute and a half.

* * *

BPD became focused on managing and containing the witnesses after Gray's death. Detectives talked to Gray's longtime friend Duane Day on April 21, after he appeared on CNN and claimed an officer walked up to Gray and "straight hit him in his mouth, slammed him, put the cuffs on him, tased him."[15] Day also told a local TV station that Gray had coffee in his hand when he was stopped and dropped it. That part of his story was not supported by any evidence.[16]

In a videotaped statement, Day told detectives the same story he told reporters but without the coffee detail.[17] He also said he biked over to Stop 2, where he saw Gray tased again: "I saw the prongs shoot out. It's like—he was out. He wasn't moving, and he wasn't responding. It's like he was gone right then and there. I'm like, oh my God."

Day told detectives that after Stop 2, he walked with Ross to the police station, confirming that nobody answered. "Someone punched their time card that morning. They did not come to the door. They did not want to tell us what was going on with our family or our friend," he said.

* * *

Davonte Roary—or "Daddy Daddy," the precocious professor of the group—was the last of Gray's close friends to talk to authorities. He never spoke to police, only the state's attorney's office (SAO). Roary and a few other young men took an SAO investigator, Wayne Williams, on a walk along the path Gray took when he was chased, zigzagging through the cuts and alleys behind Mount Street.[18] In the video of their walk, Roary remembers being baffled by Rice's aggressive chase, calling it "harassment." He says he even tried to turn around and talk to Rice at one point.

At the end of the first alley, Roary says, "I ran straight. I wish Gray would've ran the same way." The young men then bring Williams along the route Gray took instead, through the grassy path on the other side of Mount and down to the ramp in Bruce Court. Roary demonstrates Gray surrendering on his belly. One of the other young men says the police went the "extra mile" by putting a knee in his back and pulling on his arm.

The video of Roary's interview is useful but frustrating as evidence. It has no date on it. The young men aren't identified, though they seem to know a lot about what happened. Williams, in an expensive-looking suit, doesn't ask any questions.

* * *

After Gray died, on April 19, Kevin Moore was getting frustrated with BPD's secrecy and lies. He felt an obligation to speak out, so he began talking to reporters. His friends and neighbors "designated me to do that shit," he says, because he was the only one brave enough to speak out. Moore wasn't close with Gray, but they were friendly in the neighborhood. He wanted Gray to have a voice.[19]

Within weeks, Moore became a major media figure, identified with the case and the protest movement. He told reporters the officers kept Gray "folded like a crab or a piece of origami," and he described Gray's screams as "straight out of a horror movie." He delivered sincere and media-savvy sound bites that challenged the dominance of the police's story.

The *Baltimore Sun* did a headline story on Moore on April 23.[20] "He didn't put himself in a coma. He didn't fracture or crack three of his own vertebrae," he told the reporter, Catherine Rentz. The story amplified Moore's cutting insights about the case in general, but it didn't corroborate his specific witness testimony. "Moore thought he heard a Taser go off," Rentz wrote, "but Rodriguez said that while one officer drew his Taser, it was not used on Gray." Intentionally or not, journalists began correcting witnesses with the police version of events.

As for Stop 2, "Moore said he heard Gray screaming again at that time and raced down the block to get more footage," Rentz reported, "but by that time, a crowd of police had surrounded the van." Moore told Rentz he saw Gray's body at Stop 2, "but he wasn't moving."

Most of Moore's media appearances around that time focused on the details of Stop 1, without reference to everything he told detectives about Stop 2. But he remembers telling reporters much more. "I definitely remember stressing to everyone that listened how bad it was when they got around that corner," he says. "It was awful just to, like, see how they ragdolled him and threw him, like a sack of damn potatoes." He blames the police for "controlling the narrative" by keeping violence at Stop 2 mostly out of the media. At the same time, Moore acknowledges that, in 2015, he believed Gray was "strangled or some shit" at Stop 1 and so may have highlighted that stop in his interviews. He now believes Gray's death was caused by a "pile-up" of abuse from both of the first two stops and an unrestrained ride around town.

Moore's April 23 headline story in the *Baltimore Sun* seemed to catch the police department's attention. One day later, BPD announced at a press conference that police were looking for witnesses to Gray's arrest. "We're gonna share with you today some more witnesses that we have caught on cameras," Commissioner Anthony Batts said. "We would like them to come forth and share information."[21] The media then circulated a shadowy image from a CCTV video of someone filming Gray's arrest at Stop 1, asking for help identifying him.

It was obviously a picture of Moore. He took it as a threat. "What is so important that you have to plaster my picture over the Internet? I've already spoken," he told Rentz.[22] If witnesses were afraid to talk to the police for fear of retaliation, that ominous photo probably didn't help.

* * *

Between 911 calls, cell videos, knocking on doors, and statements to investigators and reporters, Gray's friends tried to help. Some of them may have paid a price for it. Three days after Gray's arrest, Roary was dragged out of bed on a warrant filed that day for an incident in March. He got out on bail and then, five days later, was picked up on disorderly conduct and resisting arrest. All of these charges were dropped in June. It was the beginning of a tough period for Roary, who'd had a light arrest record before. He became a target, with officers using cell phone tracking technology on his phone in one case.[23] While all of this was happening, case files show that investigators were trying to speak to him as a witness to Gray's arrest.

After speaking to the press, Moore became a target of ongoing police harassment. He describes BPD officers driving past him with their cell phone cameras up and watching him take his kids to school. He was arrested on April 30 after leaving a protest on North Avenue with two members of CopWatch from Ferguson, Missouri. A police SUV and two helicopters followed their car back to Bruce Court, where police in military gear arrested them. They hadn't violated curfew, he says. Moore was never charged with anything. "So basically, you're kidnapping me now?" he says. He recalls police pointing a rifle at his pregnant wife. "I'd rather be around the Bloods and Crips. The police don't give a fuck. They will shoot your ass in broad daylight," he says.[24]

Moore breaks down in tears over the guilt he feels for not intervening to help Gray, even knowing he could have gotten killed. "I felt like just standing by recording this shit, it just wasn't enough, you know?" He also feels guilty for his role in any damage caused during the riots. He wishes he could have "thought about shit" before acting back then. "My life is still fucked up behind that shit. I still can't sleep," he says.

* * *

Most of Gray's friends stepped back from speaking about the case after the disappointing results of the trials. For several years, Jamel Baker was Gray's only close friend willing to keep speaking on the record about what he had witnessed. His auditory memory has remained stronger and clearer than his visual memory. "I heard one scream and it was just, it just sounded horrible," he says. "I live in the projects. There's always noise. But it just was like a scream like I never heard before." Like Moore, Baker has described the screams as if someone was stabbed in a horror movie. Baker then heard a pause followed by more screams, so he went to the window. "By the time I looked out the window, he wasn't making any noise. I heard them screams, and then I ain't hear nothing, you feel me?"[25]

Gray was Baker's first friend to die, and the loss was deeply felt. "It felt like, in that short amount of time that we started hanging together, like, it seemed like we've been friends our whole life, you know?" he says. Gray's absence affected the group, which stopped hanging out as much. "It just seemed like a piece was missing. You got a puzzle and you put the whole thing together, and then just that one piece that's just gone and it's not complete. Like, he held us together."

CHAPTER 5

NEIGHBORS

Alethea Booze woke up around six in the morning on Sunday, April 12, to start cooking dinner. By 8:30 a.m., she had prepared turkey wings, which she planned to bake and serve alongside mashed potatoes and greens. Booze cooks enough for twelve or more neighbors every Sunday, putting food in containers for them to take home. "Everybody comes past," she says. "'Oh, you fixing it today,' they say."[1]

She was in the kitchen in the back of her row house on Mount Street when she saw a young man running past her window, chased by a police officer on a bike. "I knew within myself that it had something to do with drugs, because of the drugs within the neighborhood," Booze says.

Then, she heard her younger brother, Tobias Sellers, shouting, "Come on Alethea, come down here!" He lived in the row house next door. They walked around the corner to Presbury Street together. Booze and Sellers were just two of many older neighbors who rose with the sun—or with Gray's screams—and witnessed his arrest.

Harold Perry was lying in bed next to Jaselle Coates, flipping the TV channels. They lived in the row house Coates owns on the corner of Presbury and Mount. Usually, Coates was the one finding the

Sunday morning local preacher show, but she had been up late the night before. Perry was on his own.

Perry needed help with the channels because he is visually impaired. He began losing his vision in 1997 due to glaucoma, but treatment from the Veteran's Hospital helped him maintain some of his vision for many years. In 2015, he was still able to make out shapes and colors. "So I was just scanning the channels, and I'm lying there, and I hear someone holler, 'Let me go. I haven't done anything. Why are you grabbing me?'" Perry looked out the window, where a young man was being arrested in a rough manner.[2]

"Harold woke me up," Coates remembers. "I said, 'Who in the world is that hollering and screaming like that first thing in the morning?'"[3] Perry wouldn't let her rest. By the time Coates looked out the window, she saw the scene captured on Kevin Moore's phone for the world. She missed most of Gray's initial arrest, but Perry didn't. He was one of a few people to witness what happened when Gray was first detained.

Across Mount Street, Jernita Stackhouse was also compelled out of bed by the screams. "The cry I heard was—I'm a mom, so it was like a child pleading he was hurt." She stepped outside. "I didn't know it was gonna be Freddie Gray out there, lying on the ground."[4]

CCTV video shows a small handful of people observing the first two minutes of Gray's arrest. Then, at 8:43 a.m., people start pouring out, presumably because of the sound of Gray's screams. Booze and Sellers are recognizable among them.

What happened during the first two minutes of Gray's arrest, before Moore started filming, was a source of some public speculation given how distressed he seemed. Gray's friends saw him surrender on the ramp, aside from Duane Day, who described an officer walking over to him and knocking him down. Danielle Holloway likewise told CNN she saw Gray stop running and walk toward the officers. "As he was walking towards them, they proceed to just throw him on the ground."[5]

Shawn Washington told detectives that an officer "picked Gray up and slammed him" with his "feet vertical to the sky."

"Did you see him when he hit the ground?" a detective asked.

"No, but I heard him scream," Washington said. His boss had already called him back to the corner, he said. "I never heard a man scream like that. And God willing, I never heard that again." He described the screams as what would happen if nails were hammered into a penis.[6]

Yolanda White described a particularly violent arrest to homicide detectives in a long April 24 audiotaped interview. She recalled an officer repeatedly kicking, tasing, and "stomping on" Gray while he was on his side. This was after Gray was handcuffed and "brought out of the court." Her recollections carry weight. She correctly recalled parts of the incident that weren't yet known to the public, including that three cops on bikes chased two men, one into an alley, and that Miller dragged Gray to the wall in Bakbury Court. She also recalled three police cars in a row pulling up to the scene at the wall, which is confirmed by CCTV video. White knew Gray to be a nice, non-violent young man who previously sold her James Brown, a kind of heroin.[7]

The variations in the accounts of Gray's initial arrest made it easier for investigators and even reporters to dismiss the witnesses en masse. Yet most of the witnesses were only interviewed for a few minutes and never asked when they came outside or where they were standing. Officer Miller admitted he restrained Gray on his belly at least three different times during Stop 1, once at the ramp and twice at the wall. The witnesses could have been describing any part of that.

Over time, some of the witness recollections may have been shaped by their beliefs about how Gray was killed. "He was hurt right there at that wall," Booze says. "They put their knee in his back or neck. That there was the cause of his death." Booze expresses a popular belief, even outside of Baltimore, that Gray was killed in the same manner as Minneapolis's George Floyd. On Moore's video, Miller appears to restrain Gray lower down his body, but Moore only filmed the end of Gray's arrest.

* * *

From his window right across the street from Bakbury Court, Perry witnessed more of Gray's initial arrest than most of his neighbors. News stories and notes from detectives highlighted Perry's blindness, often dismissively, yet his impairment did not get in the way of—and might have heightened—his other observational skills. At the time of Gray's arrest, he could see enough to walk every day to the store around the corner and purchase food and cigarettes.

Perry has reported the same specific details in interviews since 2015. "They drug him out of the street right down there at the end of that building, where that railing begins, and they pulled him right over to that side and threw him down," he says.[8] He was one of few witnesses to see Gray moved from the ramp to the wall. He describes a large officer "slinging" Gray around, "like a morsel in his hand." Perry then heard "some sort of scuffle," with Gray crying out, "Let me go, you're hurting my neck, get off my back. . . . I can't breathe."

Perry next recalls two police cars pulling up to the scene right after officers moved Gray to the wall, as confirmed by CCTV video. (A third police car was behind them.) Perry remembers a "white shirt," meaning a high-ranking officer, run over to the scene from the first car, yelling, "Put him on the ground. He's not shackled right to be transported." Perry recalls the officer's keys jangling as he ran. According to Perry, the white shirt then jumped on Gray's back, as Gray pleaded, "Get off my back! You're hurting my back!" The officer yelled back, "Shut the F up!" The CCTV video rotates away from the scene after the cars pull up, so it's unclear if anyone got out, though the video also shows the three police cars driving away from arrest scene seconds later.

While Perry's exact memory of the white shirt isn't shared by the other witnesses, there are overlaps. Brandon Ross and Yolanda White had clear memories of Gray being abused after he was moved from the ramp to the wall. Washington told detectives he saw a third bike officer on the scene, who yelled, "Shut the fuck up," the same words Perry heard. Lieutenant Rice was with the other bike officers briefly when they first detained Gray at the ramp, but CCTV video shows him biking away from the scene before the three cars pulled up.[9]

Years after Gray's death, Perry most vividly recalls Gray's helplessness. "That boy seemed like he was just looking at me laying there with his head up, like this," he says, cocking his neck. "And he was saying, 'Somebody help me.' And I felt that, and I still feel it today." He talks about the "inconsistent rest" he has experienced as a blind man and how he still hears Gray's voice in his waking sleep.

Many of the older Stop 1 witnesses also lucidly remember Officer Porter refusing to help. "We said to him, 'Do something! Do something!'" Booze says. "He totally ignored us and kept walking to his car." She had to stop her brother from going after him.

They didn't know Porter by name, but they recognized him as one of the only Black officers on the scene. "How can you stand there and watch this happen to someone of your race, same color as you?" Perry asks. Not only was Porter Black, but he grew up in their neighborhood.

* * *

Gray's death followed decades of racial and economic policies that have impacted life for the Sandtown-Winchester neighborhood, where about 95 percent of residents were Black in 2015.[10] Sandtown was a commercially and culturally lively area during the first half of the twentieth century, like Harlem's cousin in Baltimore. Nearby factories and businesses along Pennsylvania Avenue sustained Black families. Testifying in his own trial, Officer Porter emphasized that the area around "Pennsy and North" was once a popular jazz area— "Cab Calloway would go there, and Lena Horne would go there"— before it became the "heroin capital of the East Coast," he said.[11]

According to Ray Kelly, a community organizer who has lived in Sandtown since 1978, "When I came home from prison and rehab, I kind of had a realization that people return to Sandtown because they can count on the activity." He describes Sandtown as if it were Wall Street of the drug trade. "Sadly, my community is that environment. This is the place where drugs are prevalent."[12]

After Gray died, news outlets spotlighted Sandtown's distressing indicators. In 2015, more than 50 percent of residents lived below the federal poverty line. The median income was around $24,000. Unemployment was at least 20 percent.[13]

Sandtown's fall from its cultural heights is not unique among Black neighborhoods in US cities over the last sixty years, but it is an extreme example of the trend. And it has seen no recovery. The history of Sandtown's decline is often told through major social events—the construction of two highways through West Baltimore, the 1968 riots, the crack cocaine epidemic—but it can also be told through the sustained disinvestment by civic leaders in all aspects of public life, apart from policing. By 2015, Gilmor Homes was under constant surveillance by police cars and cameras, but there were no grocery stores within easy walking distance and very little recreational programming for children.

Most of the older witnesses to Gray's arrest know this history firsthand. They grew up in Gilmor Homes or the row houses surrounding the projects. "That whole area used to be so beautiful," Coates remembers. "We had beautiful yards, chained fences, beautiful

flowers. We had a clean block. We had guidance and mannerism [*sic*]."
She moved into Bakbury Court in Gilmor Homes in 1957 and raised
her children in the same projects before, in the late nineties, buying
the large row house on the corner of Mount and Presbury on which
is painted the mural of Gray.

Booze grew up in Gilmor Homes with seven siblings. Her father
bought four row houses in the surrounding neighborhood. "We had
a real good life," she says. "The police used to come around when we
were young, and they would buy us ice cream and stuff. We went to
church, and we were taught to respect elderly and the police." She
raised two boys in one of her family's houses while working as a
project coordinator for defense contractors for forty years.

Gilmor Homes was built in 1942 in the center of Sandtown as
a solution to overcrowding and substandard living conditions in
Baltimore's poor neighborhoods with the mass migration of Black
Americans from the South.[14] Originally, the development had playgrounds, recreation centers, and social services. "The thing that most
people don't know is that there was never any money allocated for
long-term maintenance," Baltimore housing specialist Carol Ott
says.[15] The city was forced to cover upkeep with minimal revenue.
Conditions became substandard, and the budget for services and
amenities was cut. In 2015, a group of women filed a lawsuit against
the Housing Authority, claiming Gilmor Homes maintenance staff
were requiring sex in exchange for repairs.[16]

The "Black Butterfly" is a phrase defined by Dr. Lawrence Brown,
professor of Community Health and Policy at Morgan State University.
His book of the same title describes the systematic and historical
neglect and abuse faced by East and West Baltimore, which form butterfly wings on a map of the city. Brown contrasts the conditions in
Black neighborhoods with the resources and tax incentives poured
into the "White L," or the neighborhoods that extend north from the
Inner Harbor and east to Fells Point and Canton. In the Black Butterfly,

public schools have gone without functional air-conditioning or heat for years. Former governor Larry Hogan canceled a budgeted transit line that would have connected Sandtown to jobs and services, while free tourist-friendly buses are available to the residents of the White L.[17]

The city government's relative priorities become evident if one takes a walk from Sandtown to Bolton Hill, a predominantly white neighborhood a mile east in the same zip code. It looks like a different planet. Bolton Hill has green walking spaces and parks with landscaping, benches, and playgrounds. Its sidewalks are lined with trees; its curbs are clean.

Civic neglect has caused Sandtown's population to collapse by about 40 percent in forty years.[18] Booze and Coates say most of their elderly friends and relatives have fled the neighborhood and live in senior homes. The two women refuse to budge. "My father worked too hard for their houses," Booze says. The walls of her home are covered with pictures of her brother and husband, who both died in recent years, and dozens of siblings, children, and other relatives who left the city.

Sandtown's drastic population decline has left about 33 percent of its homes vacant, their facades marred by boarded-up windows and untended yards, some with trees growing in the middle of them. Ott maintains a website called Slumlord Watch that documents and calls out neglectful owners of vacant properties that contribute to crime, environmental issues, and fires. She guesses about 50 to 70 percent have out-of-town owners.

In 2019, Stackhouse lived in one of the neighborhood's abandoned row houses, which she called a "free mansion," with her boyfriend and cats. Though her ceiling was rotted out in parts, she decorated the house with brightly colored print fabrics, similar to the printed dresses and headscarves she wore outside. Her boyfriend worked in a nearby convenience store and helped keep the block clean.

Sandtown's residents have been left to help themselves and each other. One of Moore's favorite memories of living in Bruce Court was when he and others fixed a basketball court. The city wouldn't help. "You close down all the swimming pools, the basketball court's falling apart," he says, "so we took it upon ourselves, money out our pocket, to go buy paint and paint brushes."[19] A local group built a community garden in the vacant lot across from Booze's house. The garden is designed to help address Sandtown's food desert, though Booze complains about the rats it attracts.

Baltimore leaders abandoned the Sandtown neighborhood to the drug trade, its only viable industry, and then aggressively punished the neighborhood by policing that trade. One by one, Sandtown's older residents describe police acting like an organized gang, pulling people from cars without cause; beating, tasing, framing, and stealing from them; and threatening stores with code violations for not cooperating with investigations. "They don't try to have any rapport with the people," Perry says.

Even Booze, who would like to see more policing of drugs and guns, acknowledges local police cannot be trusted. "A lot of them are just as crooked as the people out there," she says. "It would have to take a whole lot of changes for them to get the respect that they used to have." By 2015, the city put a more than $450-million valuation on BPD out of a nearly $3 billion total city budget, while Sandtown was further stripped of its resources.[20] The city tipped the already unbalanced scales all the way against its Black residents. And this played out in who got to tell the story of what happened to Freddie Gray.

* * *

While Moore's Stop 1 video drew national attention to Gray's story, it also helped officials divert attention from what happened around the corner at Stop 2. A few minutes after Gray was loaded into the van on Presbury Street, another set of neighbors was disturbed by screams, this time on Mount and Baker Streets. Like Jamel Baker, some residents were woken up by his screams, unaware of what had happened up the street. Others had just returned home from watching Gray's arrest and heard screams all over again.

Sellers and Stackhouse were still outside on the corner of Presbury and Mount, assuming the arrest drama was over. They watched the van drive south on Mount Street, headed toward the police station. They were surprised to see it suddenly stop at the next corner. Before they knew it, they were watching another scene of police abusing Gray, seemingly for no reason.

Most of the Stop 2 witnesses who came forward told the same story as Gray's friends, with minor variations: Gray was pulled out of the van, thrown flat on the ground on his belly, shackled at the legs, and thrown back into the van—"like he was a dang rag doll," according to Sellers.[21] A few witnesses also described tasing and additional beating at Stop 2.

"They did what we call 'hogtied' him and threw him back in the truck," Stackhouse says. "They tossed him in the back. They didn't escort him or help him in there." The witness accounts of Stop 2 are more consistent than the accounts of Stop 1, a reflection of how many people were watching at the same time from within a more narrow radius. The narrative of Stop 2 also remained uncorrupted by media conversation.

* * *

Sierria Warren was woken up by screams so loud they reached her bedroom on the other side of her apartment. She looked out of the first-floor window of her thirteen-year-old daughter's bedroom, and she saw the police van and several officers on Mount Street directly in front of her. "They had somebody on the ground, I didn't know who it was," she told detectives that afternoon.[22] She found out later it was her friend. Gray and Ross used to come by her apartment, where she sold clothes and did hair.

Warren was interviewed after Gray's arrest by "everyone," she says. Investigators were "flooding the projects."[23] At about 3:00 p.m. on the afternoon of the arrest, FIT Detectives Teel and Anderson interviewed Warren outside of her apartment. The interview was audio-recorded. She told detectives she saw bike officers cuff Gray's ankles while he lay on his belly on the ground. "I heard everyone yelling, 'Why you tasing him? Why you tasing him? You got him in cuffs.'"

Then, she told detectives, "They just threw him in back of the paddy wagon, like really *threw* him in the back of the paddy wagon." Asked to clarify, she said, "They picked him up, like how he was laying, facedown, and threw him in the wagon." She described the police as "aggressive" with Gray. Asked to explain what she meant by "aggressive," she said, "Just like how they threw him in the paddy wagon—like *threw* him in the paddy wagon." Warren also told detectives she heard an officer threaten to tase one of the bystanders.

Detective Anderson didn't press Warren on the "throwing" part of her story like he had with Baker an hour before. Instead, he questioned her about how Gray was behaving on the ground while his ankles were cuffed. "Was he kicking?" Anderson asked.

"Not really kicking but he was squirming," Warren answered.

"So he was pretty much resisting?" he asked. She wouldn't concede to resisting, only squirming.

"Let's break down squirming," Anderson said. "Was it his upper torso moving or was his lower legs moving?" This went on, while Warren kept insisting that Gray wasn't resisting, just squirming a little. Warren ended her interview by repeating again that the officers "threw" Gray into the van.

Warren was reluctant to speak about the case for a while. Like others, she felt disappointed by what came from trying to help in 2015. "I could feel some kind of way about all of you in my house recording me saying shit, and y'all ain't even use it," she says. "Where did that information go? Where are those recordings?" She was confused after Ross was called to testify at the first trial. "Why the fuck they ain't calling me? If you're ready to go to court, I should be going to court too," she says. "We seen the same shit."

At the time of Gray's death, Warren didn't consider the significance of what she saw. She assumed Gray was fatally injured from being knocked around in the wagon. She feels differently now. "Mount and Baker, that's when it got real. I think the bike cops and the paddy wagon driver that actually put him in the back—*threw* him in the back—and that's where I think they broke his neck." She believes the absence of official evidence of what she saw at Stop 2 is incriminatory. "That's why I know that's what killed him, because they never showed that footage. They never used my statement," she says. "They didn't use any of the shit that was true. They just used the shit that would possibly help them out."

Warren grew up fast in West Baltimore and spent seven years in Mountmor Court in Gilmor Homes. She describes the projects as "the hood within the hood," in terms of its intensity and risk. She remembers moving around the corner one year, out of the projects, and experiencing the neighborhood in an entirely different way. "There's a lot of gang shit going on," she says about Gilmor Homes. "But Baltimore police is the biggest gang."

Warren spent her childhood surrounded by drug culture and "traumatized" by too many funerals. She lost her mother at a young age. She lost a child, who died as an infant. She also lost a good friend to murder right outside of her house. As a teenager, she raised her nephew and her own daughter on her own. Despite the obstacles, Warren pulled through. By 2015, she was working full-time as a phlebotomist. Her background, steady job, and clarity about what she saw could have played well in court. "I'm a very convincing person," she says. "People believe me because I'm telling the truth. I have no reason to lie about any of this."

* * *

Kiona Craddock, like Warren, was a young mother in 2015. She filmed the end of Stop 1 from behind the van and posted her video on YouTube two days later. It showed the officers dragging Gray to the van. "His leg look broke! Look at his fucking leg!" she cries out in the video. On April 14, as her video started going viral, Craddock gave an audiotaped statement at SAO headquarters to investigator Wayne Williams. Williams was a brusque interrogator with a tone that sounded accusatory. Craddock, in a soft, high-pitched tone, sounded apologetic in response at first, but she stayed resolute. She described Gray's legs as "twisted up" while he complained that he couldn't breathe at Stop 1.[24]

Craddock's story about Stop 2 seemed at first incidental. She returned home from Stop 1 to her apartment and heard screaming again. "I'm thinking they got somebody else now, like everybody else was rounded up." She looked out of the window in her daughter's bedroom and saw Gray lying flat on the ground. "Then I just seen they picked him up, but they threw him in the back of the paddy wagon, but facedown," she said.

"And what happened after that?" Williams asked.

"And after they threw him back in the paddy wagon, they just drove off. And everybody just—was just mad," she said. At the end of the interview, Williams asked how Gray last appeared to Craddock. She replied: "The last physical condition what I saw with my own two eyes was, when they threw him in the paddy wagon, he just looked limp. He just looked lifeless. I dunno, they just threw him in there. He wasn't screaming no more either." Craddock's interview makes it clear that not just BPD but also SAO learned about violence at Stop 2 very shortly after Gray's arrest.

* * *

A few houses down from Warren, Jacqueline Jackson, a grandmother, was in her kitchen, cooking and cleaning. "And I just hear some noise, and I hear a lot of commotion going on," she told *Undisclosed*. She looked outside and saw the same scene as Warren—officers "yanking" on a young man on the ground.[25]

Of all the known eyewitnesses, Jackson was the first to express the certainty that she saw Gray killed at Stop 2. "When I looked out my window, the police had Mr. Gray and threw him up in the paddy wagon headfirst," she said. "They didn't put him up there. They *threw* him up there. That's how he got all the injuries." She heard a noise, like a loud thump, followed by Gray making moaning sounds. She said the police "looked scared" after it happened. "I just got angry right then and there, because why would you all throw him in headfirst?" She asked them, "'What is you all doing to that man?' And they told me I need to mind my M-Fing business. And I told them it is my M-Fing business."

It is not known how far Gray was thrown or at what angle. The passenger space of that side of the van was only about one and a half feet wide on the floor because of the metal partition dividing the back of the van into two compartments. Most of the space was taken up by a bench that had an enclosed bottom.[26] If Gray had been carelessly thrown headfirst into the van, there would have been a lot of hard surfaces in his path.

On the early morning of April 23, at around 3:00 a.m., CNN broadcast an interview with Jackson. "He wasn't responding. His head was down," she said, demonstrating her head bent to her chin.

"And they picked him up and threw him up in the paddy wagon."[27] According to the autopsy report, Gray's fatal injury happened when his neck was "hyperflexed," or bent forward.[28] In the same story, CNN broadcast footage from Ross's Stop 2 video, the first time it aired publicly, showing Gray not moving or speaking. CNN's story did not gain traction, even within the network.

The *Baltimore Sun* also posted a video interview with Jackson to its website on April 24. The same video features several other eyewitnesses, including Earl Williams, who lives in the neighborhood and was a father figure to Warren growing up. "They picked him up and literally threw him back in the wagon," he said. "You know, that's crazy."

Jackson's eyewitness account didn't make the evening news or become a headline story. A sound bite of her saying Gray was thrown into the van continued to appear in the occasional CNN or *Baltimore Sun* report, but out of context from the rest of her statement and without corroboration. Hers was just another anecdote in the cacophony of abuse stories that officials insisted didn't happen.

Jackson remembered an SAO investigator visiting her house after she appeared on CNN. "They came and told me I didn't see what I seen. They said, 'How could you see that, when it didn't occur?' I told them it *did* occur." SAO never recorded the interview or invited her to give a longer statement on the record.

Like many other witnesses, Jackson remained haunted for years by the trauma of Gray's death. "I haven't been sleeping since all this happened. It's a nightmare," she told *Undisclosed* in 2017. "And me being a mother. You know, that's somebody's child. And, you know, to witness that, you know, it was bad."

Jackson passed away in 2019. Her death left an emotional hole in Mountmor Court, which Warren said had a more familial vibe than Bakbury or Bruce Courts. Warren knew Jackson as "Momma Jackie" or "Aunt Jackie." On a typical day, there could be a stream of her grandchildren and their friends in and out of her apartment.

* * *

Finally, Michelle Gross, another mother figure to the neighborhood, witnessed the last part of Stop 2. She had lent Ross her phone to call 911, and he ended up using it to film part of the stop. Unreleased CCTV video shows Gross leaving her porch and running behind Ross as he charged through the "split" onto Mount Street. "Is he all right?" she calls out on Ross's video.[29]

"No, he ain't all right," Ross responds.

After Lieutenant Rice threatens them, Gross says, "Let me get the fuck out of here," and convinces Ross to leave the scene. "Brandon, go ahead please. Walk. Just walk." While she and Ross walk away, she says she could hear Gray "kicking the cruiser."

On April 28, 2015, Gross gave independent journalist Robert Brune a walk-through of that morning. Brune asked her to point out when Gray stopped screaming. Gross broke down crying just as she approached the split. She was so emotional, they had to take a break from filming. When they resumed, Brune asked what she heard when she got onto Mount Street.

"I didn't hear nothing," Gross said. "He was just laying there."

"Not making a sound?" Brune asked. And she shook her head. "From that corner to this corner," he said, pointing the camera from Stop 1 to Stop 2.

She repeated, "From that corner to this corner," gesturing from Stop 1 to Stop 2. Gray was screaming, and then suddenly he wasn't making a sound.[30]

With Stop 2 getting almost no media attention, Gross gave a copy of Ross's video to the *Baltimore Sun*, which published a story about it on May 20. The reporter, Catherine Rentz, provoked mystery around the stop, pointing out how Gray appeared silent and motionless on Ross's video and how police removed CCTV video from Stop 2 from its YouTube page. Her story did not, however, incorporate anything that Jackson, Williams, or other witnesses said happened at Mount and Baker Streets. Gray was "placed," not thrown, into the van at Stop 2, Rentz reported, "head first and on his stomach."[31] Mosby had filed charges earlier that month based on the idea that the officers might have handled Gray negligently at Stop 2—placing him in an unsafe position in the van—but not that they were violent with him. Asked about the absence of witness statements from that story, Rentz says, "The article was focused on the *new* video and was not an all-encompassing 'what happened at the second stop.'" She also says she originally wrote a "longer version" that was "edited" to fit "time and space constraints."

* * *

Altogether, there were eleven known witnesses to Stop 2. Nine of them described police throwing Gray headfirst and/or facedown into the wagon. For the most part, the public never learned about this part of the story. Most of the Stop 2 witnesses also described Gray no longer screaming or moving, which is how he appears on Ross's video.

Witness accounts, especially those of women and elderly witnesses, were generally erased, minimized, or ignored by officials and the media. BPD never asked any women or elderly witnesses to give longer videotaped statements downtown, only three younger men. Prosecutors never invited any women or elderly witnesses to testify in court, only two younger men. Media outlets continued interviewing Moore, not Jackson.

When BPD officially closed the Gray case in 2017, it released several binders of documents to media outlets. The binders include official transcripts from the statements given by officers and medics but not civilian witnesses. The witnesses are reduced in the binders to mug shots, criminal histories, and brief notes by investigators.

CHAPTER 6

LIEUTENANT RICE'S CREW

"I didn't see any malice in the heart of those police officers. I don't think those officers involved are those you would put in the class of bad or malicious or evil police officers." —Commissioner Anthony Batts, July 27, 2016

STATE'S ATTORNEY MARILYN MOSBY WAS accused of a "malicious prosecution" in lawsuits from the officers who were charged in Freddie Gray's death and in articles by their supporters. To this day, she is criticized for going after "good apples," unlike the drug-dealing and gun-planting criminals on the force who were later indicted as part of the Gun Trace Task Force scandal. Even Lieutenant Rice was perceived as more troubled than corrupt or criminal. As for the rest of the "Baltimore 6," as they were called, many were still young and well regarded.

Garrett Miller, twenty-six, and Edward Nero, twenty-nine, joined the force only two months apart in 2012 and were both assigned to the Western District after six months in the police academy. "Since being out on the street in the Western, we did everything together," Miller said in court, testifying in Nero's trial.[1] BPD doesn't have traditional partners like on television cop shows. In fact, two patrol officers weren't allowed to share a car in 2015, something Rice got in trouble for allowing. Yet unofficial partnerships were common, and Miller and Nero often functioned as one such pair.

The officers could have been cast as a duo in a movie. Nero was tall and thin with long, angular features, dark hair, and a nervous manner. He came from suburban southern New Jersey, where he had been an emergency medicine technician (EMT) before joining BPD, so he was a few years older than his colleagues. Miller was heavyset, with receding blond hair and a round, wide face. Like Lieutenant Rice, Miller came across as confident and blunt. He even looked like a younger Rice, and a few witnesses mixed them up on the street.

Also like Rice, Miller was an aggressive street-level enforcer, making a lot of arrests, mostly for low-level offenses. During 2014 to 2015, about 70 percent of Miller's arrests were for simple drug possession or zero tolerance offenses like disorderly conduct. Half of Miller's drug possession arrests were for less than ten grams of marijuana. Nero's arrest patterns were similar, though he was the arresting officer in about half as many cases as Miller. When Miller and Nero made arrests together, Nero tended to follow Miller's lead.[2]

There are only a few ways for BPD officers to advance either in rank or out of patrol into specialized detective squads. Aside from passing tests and following orders, they are evaluated based on the number of arrests they make, regardless of quality. According to a 2016 Department of Justice investigation into BPD, "Many officers believe that the path to promotions and favorable treatment, as well as the best way to avoid discipline, is to increase their number of stops and make arrests for those offenses . . . with or without requisite reasonable suspicion."[3] Prosecutors declined to charge in about half of Miller's and Nero's arrests during 2014 and 2015.

"We look at the arrest rate, but we never look at the conviction rate compared to the arrest rate," retired BPD Captain Lisa Robinson says. "It's just really all a smokescreen if you didn't have a legitimate arrest."[4]

Miller not only made more arrests than his colleagues but also racked up more IAD complaints. In October 2013, he was charged with breaking a young man's arm after allegedly smelling marijuana on him. As the IAD report states,

> *P/O Miller grabbed Thomas by the arm and forced him forward. At that time, believing Thomas was resisting arrest, P/O Miller took him to the ground. Thomas heard his arm pop then he blacked out. When he came to, his face was bloody, he was handcuffed, and P/O Miller told him, "You're [sic] arm ain't fucking broke."*

Thomas was taken to the hospital "where he was diagnosed with a broken arm," the case record states. A witness saw another officer kicking Thomas in the head. Miller was found guilty of excessive force, yet he never faced any discipline or criminal charges.

In December 2014, Miller stopped a man in his car and threatened him with arrest unless he signed a repair order for a broken headlight. The man signed it but then went straight to the police station to show the officers on duty that his light was working fine. The complaint was "administratively closed." Nero faced half as many complaints as Miller, none involving excessive force or abusive language. His more serious complaints happened when he was with Miller.

Text messages among the officers after Gray's arrest reveal more of their personalities and history. Miller and Nero participated in an ongoing text conversation with some of their colleagues, in which Nero mentioned that they should be careful in what they say about the case.

Miller was especially vocal and opinionated in the conversations, with a bent for dark humor. He often invited the officers over to his house for food and drinks. "Everyone is more than welcome to come up to the house anytime. Esp if news starts showing up unannounced," he texted. "Doors are unlocked but the owner is armed."[5]

At some point before Gray's arrest, Miller got in trouble for buying
and wearing his own body camera. He received only a warning. One
officer texted about wanting to leak the story to the *Baltimore Sun*.

Miller complained in his texts about protesters, the media, and
the city's handling of the case. "Good luck with that word-twisting
political agenda," he warned a fellow officer headed in for a Force
Investigation Team (FIT) interview.[6] He had many positive things to
say about then-sheriff David Clarke of Milwaukee County, who went
on Fox News and blamed Gray's death on liberal politics. "David Clark
[*sic*] for President!" he texted. "He's the man! I follow him on Twitter."

Like nearly 80 percent of the force in 2015, all three bike officers
lived in politically conservative counties outside the city. Miller lived
in Freeland, Maryland, a rural area almost an hour north of Baltimore
near the Pennsylvania state line. Nero lived in Bel Air, a suburb about
an hour northeast in Harford County. On workdays, the officers left
their large homes in areas composed of at least 90 percent white
residents to patrol a predominantly poor Black area with one or two
murders per week. "I wonder if this is our ticket out of the Western,"
Miller texted his fellow officers the day after Gray's arrest. A few
weeks later, he said he missed the district.

Nero wasn't as involved in the dialogue on the text chain. On
April 30, the day before charges against the officers were announced,
he opened up about how the case was affecting him emotionally.
"I'm not healthy mentally or physically with all this going on," he
said. He described suffering "extreme anxiety" and said he might
need medication to relax. "I don't even want to wake up in the
morning to see what more hatred against us has brewed overnight."

"I'm gonna puke if I'm in this ride anymore," Miller shared during
that conversation. "That probably explains why I have the shits for
no reason."

* * *

Six hours after arresting Gray on April 12, Officers Miller and Nero gave videotaped statements to FIT Detectives Boyd and Poremski. Boyd seemed mostly concerned with making sure the officers never saw any signs of Gray in medical distress. Both officers denied they had, although Nero did say that Gray asked for an inhaler after he was arrested.

"Is it looking like he's having an asthma attack?" Boyd asked.

"No, he was, like I said, he was talking. He's more like screaming than anything," Nero said. "He wasn't screaming in pain. He was just making, like he was trying to attract people to come out. He wasn't saying, 'I can't breathe.'"[7] Whether or not Gray was screaming to attract people, numerous people present at Stop 1, including Officer Miller, heard Gray say he couldn't breathe during Stop 1. Kevin Moore's video begins with Gray screaming, ". . . breathe!" and then saying, "I need attention."

Nero appeared to struggle and overthink his responses. Describing Gray in the wagon at Stop 1, he said, "And at this point, 'cause also, I'm sorry, in the wagon, he's just literally banging everything. I don't know if he's kicking into his head. I don't know what he's doing." Nero would often make exaggerated, vague claims about Gray being combative, like "kicking into his head," when he seemed unsure how to respond.

By contrast, Miller gave short, straightforward responses. While he seemed a little nervous, he also came across as unbothered by the implications of what he said. More than once, he admitted that he acted with some force. "We had put him back down on the ground. He didn't want to go on the ground. So we put him back on the ground," he said. Miller had admitted that Gray complained "he was having trouble breathing" the first time Miller put him on his belly at the wall in Bakbury Court, but then he admitted to forcing Gray on his belly again. At Stop 2, Miller admitted, he and Rice pulled Gray out of the van by "his leg" and put him "on the ground, on his belly" to shackle his ankles.[8]

Despite being together for hours during and after the arrest on April 12, the bike cops didn't always have their stories together. They were the most inconsistent around how they got Gray back into the van at Stop 2—notable, given the clarity and consistency of the witnesses. Nero said, "It takes all of us to put him, like, back into the wagon.... We actually had to—had to—had to like push him into the wagon." Later, he said, "We had to slide him on to the floor."

Miller had a different story. "I think LT [Lieutenant Rice] did.... I think they had to drag him in. I think, if I remember correctly, I think LT was actually in the wagon with him." Miller insisted Nero had no contact with Gray at Stop 2 and that he himself was "standing off to the side." Unreleased CCTV video does show an unidentifiable bike cop in a yellow shirt standing away from the wagon for a lot of Stop 2.[9]

Meanwhile, Rice told detectives, "I think we just slid him back up onto the floor." He also said they "lifted him up" into the wagon "because he was shackled arms and legs." Gray's leg shackles had a sixteen-inch-long chain between the two cuffs.[10] He could have walked into the wagon if he were willing and able. A homicide detective even made a demonstration video showing someone in the same type of shackles doing just that.[11]

From their statements, it seemed the officers were figuring out how to describe two things that happened: First, as numerous eyewitnesses reported, a few officers picked Gray straight up off the ground, where he was lying on his belly, and threw him in the van, headfirst and facedown. Ross started filming just after witnessing Gray being thrown into the wagon. His video shows the second event: Rice pulled Gray's limp body into the van, while Nero assisted by lifting Gray's legs. Miller was standing right next to Nero for that part.

After the van doors closed at Stop 2, Miller said, Gray kept kicking the door and "shaking the wagon." Nero said he saw Gray "flail around again and bang around." On two CCTV videos of Stop 2, the van appears to be still.

* * *

A major focus of Miller's and Nero's statements was to deny that anyone used a Taser on Gray. Miller told investigators that he did yell, "Taser, Taser, Taser! Get on the ground!" as he was pursuing Gray but claimed he never deployed it. "I think that's where the whole crowd was saying, 'Oh, they tased him,' but it was just a scare tactic," he said. According to BPD policy G-19, officers are supposed to "loudly announce that the ESD Electronic Shock Device is going to be discharged" before use. There are numerous Taser demonstrations on YouTube where someone yells, "Taser, Taser, Taser," before firing. Invariably, the victims scream out in serious pain after being shot, even when they knew it was coming. Miller's statement about tasing became the official BPD story: "There was an officer that was attempting to stop Officer [sic] Gray that took his Taser out, preparatory to using it, but never deployed the Taser," Deputy Commissioner Rodriguez said on April 20.[12]

Prosecutors accepted BPD's claim about Taser usage based on the downloaded reports and the autopsy examination. Rice, Miller, and Goodson all had their Taser information downloaded two days after Gray's arrest. According to BPD, they were the only officers wearing Tasers that day. (In Moore's video, Nero doesn't appear to be wearing a Taser.) Taser usage is downloaded into a system known as Evidence.com, which allows one to filter date ranges and types of events before printing them onto simple word-processing tables. The printouts show Taser device numbers on them, but the officers' names are handwritten on top.

BPD included Taser reports in the binders released publicly in 2017, after the Gray case was finally closed. The reports show that, at the beginning of each shift, the officers tested their Tasers by operating them briefly in three settings—armed (with the safety switch off), trigger (when the Taser is deployed), and safe (with the safety switch on).

The available downloaded records for all three officers are atypical in different ways. Miller's records show his Taser in armed mode on April 12 at 8:37 a.m., then in safe mode. This supports the story that he prepared to deploy his Taser but didn't. Yet at 8:37, Miller was supposedly on his bike, not even beginning to chase anyone. The company that manufactures Tasers discusses a phenomenon called "clock drift," which can happen if the device isn't connected to the online system for a while. The phenomenon has been used in court cases by both sides to explain when records don't match stories.[13] Miller's Taser was last connected to the system two months before, according to police records.

Goodson's records for April 12 are missing any activity, even testing. He was reportedly working overtime, but he didn't test his Taser the day before, either. Each day that Goodson worked during the week before, he tested his Taser.[14] From the records, it looked as though he wasn't wearing a Taser on April 12, although he was photographed wearing one later that day at police headquarters.

For Rice's Taser, the publicly released records end at October 31, 2013, with no records at all for the day in question. Years later, BPD provided records from April 12, 2015, in response to a request, and they show normal testing and no other usage, but their absence in the original files is glaring. Together, these printed-out tables with handwritten names, missing entries, and clock drift were used to dismiss nuanced same-day and next-day accounts of tasing from eyewitnesses whose statements were otherwise corroborated by evidence.

A Crime Scene Unit (CSU) technician went to the hospital on April 12 to take pictures of Gray's body as he lay in a coma. In one picture, there are two small circular marks about an inch apart just under Gray's right kneecap. They could be from a Taser, which shoots out side-by-side prongs. Moore told detectives, hours after Gray's arrest, "I can physically see the prongs in the guy's leg" at Stop 2. As he said this, he put his hands over his right kneecap, exactly where the two circular marks appear. On the day of his arrest, Gray wore two sets of pants, which could have made Taser marks fainter and harder to read. His body wasn't examined by the medical examiner until one week after his arrest, and the autopsy did not mention Taser marks.

The CSU technician also took photos of the officers and their Tasers on the afternoon of Gray's arrest. In their pictures, Miller and Goodson were wearing their Tasers, but Rice's Taser holster was curiously empty. As with the other two officers, his Taser wasn't hooked up to the Evidence.com system until two days later.

In close-up pictures, both of Miller's hands look bruised or otherwise inflamed on each of the knuckles and joints on all the fingers. There could have been many explanations for the marks. BPD investigators never asked Miller about his hands or even made note of them.

* * *

A still image from Moore's Stop 1 video circulated online with the names of the officers labeled on the image. Miller, Nero, Rice, and Goodson were identified in the picture, though Rice was mislabeled. The thin, dark-haired man in a blue uniform helping to carry Gray to the van was Officer Zachary Novak, twenty-five. Novak was at three of the six stops on the official BPD timeline that morning. He handled Gray's body twice, and he had a major role behind the scenes in this case. Yet he was never suspended or indicted.

Novak was close friends and colleagues with Miller and Nero; he went to the police academy with Nero and lived near him in

Bel Air. Some of the other Western District officers confused him with Nero because of their similar appearances and because both last names began with "N." Tall and slender, with close-cropped brown hair, Novak pursued public service after finishing college. When he graduated from the academy, he was given an award as the recruit demonstrating the best commitment to public service. After only a few years on the force, Novak already had a brand: he made himself appear helpful. He was the Eddie Haskell of the Gray case.

Novak participated in the text chain with Miller and Nero. The texts came from his personal cell phone, which he turned over as part of an agreement with prosecutors in exchange for immunity. After the riots, he texted, "I was with a hump officer all day who didn't want to get into anything or back anyone up. The four of us would've had a fucking blast. Sadly, I did not get to kick anyone's ass—but the funs only just begun."[15]

After the charges, on May 5, Nero and Novak had a private text conversation about the loss they felt since Gray's death. "Wanted to let u know i miss working with u and the others a lot," Nero texted. "We had so much fun at what we did and we were very good at it. . . . We were like rising stars in the dept."

Novak responded: "The biggest crime is that we are split up and can't work together as the perfect team we built."

The day before Gray's arrest, Miller and Novak got into some trouble and were written up by IAD. According to the IAD record, their sergeant reported them for leaving the Western District without notifying anyone or responding to the radio at all. Novak finally told the dispatcher he was "in covert" with Miller, "watching some guys on a corner" near Bon Secours, a hospital two miles south of their assigned sector. They were supposed to be responding to calls in their sector and backing up other officers.[16] According to the Western District schedule, Sergeant Alicia White was the shift commander that day.

* * *

Novak gave the last videotaped statement by officers on the afternoon
of Gray's arrest, speaking to FIT Detectives Anderson and Teel. He was
more polished and verbally skillful than his colleagues. He provided
explanations not just for his actions but for the entire morning's events.
For instance, he explained why the officers stopped the van at Mount
and Baker, or Stop 2, even though he wasn't a part of that decision. He
often sounded more like the bike cops' attorney than a witness.

Novak started the morning of Sunday, April 12, on a quest for
gas that kept getting interrupted. He called the dispatcher at 8:38
a.m. to let her know he was headed to Front Street, near downtown,
where BPD officers fill their gas tanks. Instead, he heard Rice initiate
the chase of Gray and Roary on the radio, so he showed up to help.
Novak drove the first of three police cars to pull up in front of the
wall where Miller and Nero held Gray.

Novak then responded to Rice's request for help finding the
"other suspect" behind 1707 Mount Street. He was one of the three
officers searching the ground in the vacant lot. A minute later, Novak
ran from the lot to Bakbury Court to help Nero carry Gray into the
van. "He was doing like the floppy-fish routine," he told detectives
about Gray dragging his legs on the way to the van.[17]

After leaving Stop 1, Novak announced on the radio that he was
going to Front Street for gas, but Sergeant White asked him to pick
up some district paperwork first and drop it off at headquarters while
he was downtown. After that, instead of getting gas, he responded to
Miller asking for backup at Stop 2.

In speaking about Stop 2, Novak seemed to suffer the same memory fog affecting his colleagues. At first, he told detectives, "They
had sufficient units on scene. So I never even actually got out of my
car at that point." The second time he mentioned Stop 2, he said,
"I never even got out of the vehicle." And the third time, he said, "I

stayed in my car, didn't bother getting out." Yet on his fourth rec-ollection, Novak changed his mind: "I think I got out at one point because Lieutenant Rice was worried about, like, four or five people coming up." CCTV video shows his car pull up next to the van after witnesses had already dispersed.[18] (The camera rotated away before it could record whether Novak got out.)

Novak left Stop 2 at 8:52 a.m. He told detectives he finally had time to go to Front Street to get gas. Almost thirty minutes later, he found himself back at the police station, with Gray's unconscious head in his hands.

When medics arrived, they questioned the officers about what happened. According to Paramedic Angelique Herbert, Novak told her that Gray might have been "banging his head."[19] She relayed the same information to the hospital on the radio: "We're seen with a twenty-six-year-old approximate Black male who was found in police custody unresponsive, non-breathing. The police said that he could have been banging his head."[20]

Novak told FIT detectives later that day that he had no idea what happened to Gray, but they should look into one possibility:

> On the wall of the wagon, though, it wasn't like a lot of blood or any-thing like that, but it was like two smears. And I don't know if that's old or not, but I don't know if the Crime Lab got it. . . . We've had people in the past, like, when they're upset hit their head up against a wall. But I don't know if the banging was from kicking . . . or if he was just banging his head up against the wall. Couldn't tell you.

That Rice and Novak both suggested Gray was banging his head is notable. Gray did suffer a broken neck caused by a single force-ful injury to the head, but there wasn't a visible manifestation of the impact. The subdermal injury, behind his left ear, showed up in imaging scans and the autopsy. Rice and Novak had a number of choices for what they could have guessed happened to Gray. They both chose an explanation involving head trauma.

* * *

Four more officers were involved in Gray's arrest: Ricardo Alvarado-Rivera, Mark Gladhill, Matthew Wood, and Aaron Jackson. All but Jackson were given immunity by SAO in exchange for their grand jury testimony. The four backup officers barely made the news, but most of them were at multiple stops. They were interviewed toward the end of April, at which time they seemed excessively coached. "Nero and Miller are probably one [sic] of the most professional police officers that I know," Officer Wood told detectives, "and I know they would not do anything like that to those—to anybody." He then described the van at Stop 2. "I was at Mount and Baker after the fact, and I saw the wagon moving back and forth and that guy, screaming and kicking the door . . . kicking, headbanging, I don't know."[21] By this time, the "violently shaking" van had become an increasingly important talking point for the officers in this case.

The backup officers mostly refused or struggled to remember anything they saw with their own eyes besides a few seemingly scripted points. Officer Gladhill would talk only about the bikes at Stop 1, which he was asked to guard, and the crowd. "I wasn't really any part of that," he said, when asked about officers on the scene. "I was just [swings arms back and forth] crowd."[22]

Gladhill was slow paced in his responses and clearly nervous. FIT Detective Lakishna Lewis (then Degraffinried) recommended that he relax. He referred more than once to how much more comfortable he felt in his usual routine. "I'm a sector one guy," he said about his assigned area west of Gilmor Homes. He went back to his sector after dealing with the bikes and crowd at Stop 1.

"And how were things there?" Detective Lewis asked.

"It was actually really good," he said, smiling. "I was keeping things clear." He seemed genuinely wistful and calm for a change.

"Good job," Lewis responded.

Gladhill said he wasn't in his sector long before was called back to provide backup again for the bike cops. "I'm like, jeez. I keep trying to go back to my little area." All of the officers working the Western District Baker patrol shift early that morning, except one, were pulled into Gray's arrest and required to account for what happened.

CHAPTER 7

POCKETKNIFE

FREDDIE GRAY WAS IN POSSESSION of an illegal switchblade, police said. Officers Miller and Nero found it on him just after moving him from the ramp in Bruce Court, where he was apprehended, to the wall in Bakbury Court. That gave them cause to call for a transport van and have him arrested. At Stop 2, the officers completed the paperwork to send him straight to Central Booking from the street. This was, at least, the story that police and prosecutors told the public.

State's Attorney Mosby charged all three bike cops with one count each of false imprisonment for arresting Gray without justification. "The blade of the knife was folded into the handle," she said on May 1. "The knife was not a switchblade and is lawful under Maryland law."[1] Her claim ignited a heated public debate around whether Gray's knife was in fact legal. According to the city ordinance, it's illegal to "sell, carry, or possess any knife with an automatic spring or other device for opening and/or closing the blade, commonly known as a switchblade knife."[2]

John Jay College Professor Peter Moskos was a prominent voice in opposition to Mosby on this issue: "Gray had a knife that most likely violates Baltimore City ordinances," he wrote in an article on his website. "There's ambiguity here as to what the law means, with its reference to an 'automatic spring.' But—and get this—even if the knife were legal, it wouldn't automatically make the arrest illegal."[3]

Moskos and others discussed the legality of a knife they never saw. Neither side of the case released a picture of it to the public before or during the trials. In fact, the knife wasn't mentioned once during any of the trials, despite the controversy around it.

Then, in October 2016, months after the trials concluded, SAO finally released a photograph of the knife to a local news outlet.[4] It appeared to have a bright blue handle, with a black bottom and a hook on the end. The debate was reignited, and, like almost everything around Gray's death, media outlets were content to provoke binary controversy. "Was Freddie Gray's knife legal?" they asked, but they didn't definitively answer the question.

While reporters focused on the legality question, other important questions were ignored: Was Gray really in possession of a knife on April 12? Was Goodson really taking Gray to Central Booking on a knife charge? There are good reasons to question BPD's knife story. For one, Gray had been arrested sixteen times and never before found in possession of a knife. Also, bright blue knives are traditionally marketed to police. The knife in this case is known as a tactical or rescue knife, useful to first responders. It has a seat belt cutter, which is a hook at the bottom, and a button at the top to break glass. And then there's the fact that it took officials a full week to tell the public why Gray had been arrested. They waited until he was no longer alive to confirm or deny it.

* * *

The story of how Miller and Nero found a knife on Gray went through a few iterations, beginning with their statements to FIT detectives on the afternoon of the arrest. "He said he was having trouble breathing, so we sat him up," Miller said. "And then we started to do a precursory search where I pulled a pocketknife out of his front right pocket." It sounded like a potential Fourth Amendment violation. Officers may briefly pat down suspects with reasonable suspicion—in this case, Gray running from police in a "high crime" area—but they may not search the pockets of suspects without probable cause of a crime. Miller might have felt what he thought was a weapon during the pat-down, but he didn't make that clear.

Nero was interviewed right after Miller, and he added a detail: "The suspect said that he was—he needed his asthma inhaler. So then we lifted him back up. At that point we then see a knife that he had on." Later, Nero said, "We asked him, 'Where's your inhaler?' 'No, I don't have one.' So at that point, that's when we see the knife." Nero almost suggested that Gray gave the officers permission to search him by requesting an inhaler, but he didn't assert that explicitly. The knife seems to appear out of nowhere in his account, and the interviewing detectives didn't seek clarification.

After Miller and Nero allegedly found the knife on Gray, they didn't radio Lieutenant Rice to let him know, although this reported discovery gave them cause for the arrest. Rice, meanwhile, delayed the transport van in front of 1707 Mount Street while several backup officers searched the ground of the vacant lot behind the building for something.

Some people online thought they spotted Gray's knife in Moore's cell video. There was a small, shiny silver object on the ground near Gray. That was in fact his Motorola phone. Moore's video does catch another object that looks like the knife in question. It is about the size and shape of a pocketknife, and it appears black but also, at one angle, blue. It first shows up on the short wall behind where Miller restrained Gray on the ground. As Gray is brought to the van, Miller grabs the object. He reaches it behind him, as if to put it on the back of his own equipment belt. Instead, he picks up Gray's phone and hands both the phone and the object to Goodson.

* * *

After Gray was loaded into the van at Stop 1, Goodson was on his way to the police station. "One male from 1710 Presbury to Western District," he announced at 8:46 a.m. Gray can still be heard screaming in the background of this call. The Western District station was about a half mile down Mount Street. The bike cops could finish processing their arrest on the computers in the station.

Within seconds of pulling out of Bakbury Court, Goodson got a radio call from Miller. "Hey, meet me at the end of Gilmor Homes down there so I can toe tag this guy," he said. "We're gonna stay out." The "toe tag" was a reference to paperwork needed to send Gray straight to Central Booking instead of bringing him to the police station. The officers were going to "stay out" on the streets and keep arresting people.

Central Booking and Intake Facility opened in 1995 in the center of town to process prisoners more quickly and efficiently than at the nine district stations.[5] People who are arrested in Baltimore end up at Central Booking, but not right away. According to policy 1117, "the arrestee must immediately be transported to the district for debriefing." A "debrief" is a kind of shakedown for information. Prisoners are asked questions at the station about crime in the community that is unrelated to their arrests. This policy isn't well enforced. During 2014 and 2015, about half of arrests by the officers involved in this case skipped the debrief and sent arrestees straight to Central Booking from the street.

In order to send Gray straight to Central Booking, Miller needed to swap out his metal handcuffs for plastic flex cuffs so he could have his cuffs back for the day, which he did at Stop 2. He also needed to follow booking policies. Per policy, an officer must obtain a Central Complaint (CC) number from the dispatcher and put a wristband on the prisoner that has its own barcode number on it. The officer must write both numbers on a Charge Information Form known informally as a "toe tag"—because, to police, getting booked is metaphorically like getting tagged at the morgue. A prisoner cannot be admitted into Central Booking without the band and toe tag, which comes in duplicate. One copy of the toe tag goes to the arresting officer, and the other goes to the driver.[6]

In court, several officers testified that, after the officers shackled Gray's legs and "placed" him back into the van at Stop 2, Miller filled out booking paperwork on the side of the van while Gray was causing the van to shake. Again, in CCTV video, the van appears still at this time.

During two of the trials, the state played audio of Miller calling the dispatcher for a CC number for a "concealed deadly weapons" charge. He was referring to a state law—"concealed *dangerous* weapon"—that applies to switchblade knives as well as martial arts equipment, razors, and mace. It is more commonly used than the city's switchblade law for knives, as it comes with a higher penalty. The dispatcher gave Miller his CC number for the arrest (150404754).[7] According to BPD timelines, Miller's call occurred at 8:51 a.m., after Gray was back in the van at Stop 2, but there is no way to confirm that. Unfortunately, the dispatch audio played in court had no time stamps.

The officers gave various confusing statements about the toe tag. Miller told FIT detectives that, at the end of Stop 2, "I gave my toe tag to the wagon driver. And off he went, and then we just went right back up to North Ave. and reported to CC for the offense." From this version of events, it sounds like Miller might have called in the offense after Stop 2, meaning Goodson was headed to Central Booking without the completed paperwork to book Gray.

In May 2015, Officer Novak mentioned the toe tag when he testified before the grand jury in exchange for immunity. He said Miller was filling out the toe tag at Stop 2 with the "intended primary charge."

A juror asked, "So the primary charge is not the knife? Is that what you're saying."

Novak replied, "I believe it is . . . but I haven't seen the actual toe tag itself."

Curiously, there was never a toe tag or wristband in any of the case files or photos. Multiple sources from SAO's investigation said they tried to locate the toe tag and never found it. In response to a Maryland Public Information Act (MPIA) request, BPD officially said the toe tag didn't exist, because "Mr. Gray was not book [sic] at Central Booking and Intake Facility."[8] But he was supposedly headed there, and the toe tag was a topic during the trials. That BPD couldn't produce either copy of the toe tag, even to SAO, suggests that either it wasn't completed at Stop 2 or it was completed with different information on it from what the public was told—say, a different "intended primary charge"—and BPD didn't want the public to see it.

Lieutenant Rice discussed the toe tag with internal affairs investigators in December 2016: "I have my copy, which is probably Miller's copy," he said. The investigators didn't ask him to produce it. Rice also said he didn't know about the knife during Stops 1 and 2. "I didn't know why the arrest had been made," he said. "I didn't particularly care why the arrest had been made."[9]

There is another document that could illuminate what happened during Gray's arrest. Officers are required to write reports for each CC number they request, but BPD also couldn't locate a report for the CC number Miller received on the dispatch call. The number was "issued in error," the department officially stated.[10] Yet that CC number was part of the dispatch audio played in court, and it appears all over the case files as well. Officer Porter filed Gray's clothes and belongings into the Evidence Control Unit (ECU) under that number.

BPD seemingly could not produce paperwork to verify one of the simplest parts of its story—that Gray was arrested and sent to

Central Booking for possession of an illegal knife. Based on how several witnesses described his condition at the end of Stop 2, he was not in any shape to be booked.

* * *

At around noon on April 12, a CSU technician was called to the Western District. She was instructed to take a lot of pictures at the police station, around Gilmor Homes, at BPD headquarters, and at the hospital. She didn't photograph the knife. The knife doesn't appear in any CSU pictures or photo logs. BPD's social media accounts are filled with pictures of seized weapons, drugs, cash, and even knives and other items. From the CSU pictures, this case looked like an arrest without a crime.

The knife didn't make it to ECU until late on the night of Gray's arrest. Officer Novak submitted a "blue/black spring-assisted knife" to ECU at exactly 9:00 p.m.[11] He was accompanied by Miller. By policy, BPD officers don't have to keep track of the chain of custody for evidence before it is submitted to ECU, but this was a long delay, and Novak was not the arresting officer or directly involved in Gray's apprehension.[12] The knife's late submission raises questions about what was going on after Miller gave his statement to FIT detectives at 2:45 p.m. He stayed on the clock but didn't do anything else officially for hours besides turning in evidence to ECU, which was in the same building as the FIT offices. He first went to ECU at 6:08 p.m. to submit some drugs allegedly found on the other van passenger, Donta Allen, yet he didn't submit the knife until three hours after that.

Novak told the grand jury what happened to the knife that day: "It was given to me by Officer Miller while we were at the district. I kept it in my breast pocket throughout while I was doing the investigation."[13] Novak helped with some canvassing that afternoon and then wrote a report for FIT at the end of the day.

Over a year later, Novak had a different story for internal affairs investigators. "Did Miller mention the knife to you?" one of the investigators asked.

"The only time I remember having a discussion about the knife with Miller, when I guess he came—when I was doing the force investigation report or—and he came to submit the knife and then we had to bring a copy of the receipt of the knife."[14]

"Did you ever take a look at the knife itself?" the investigator asked.

"Yeah, I think, when he came down to headquarters, when I was typing up my report." In this version of events, the knife wasn't in Novak's breast pocket all day.

Retired BPD Lieutenant Carrie Everett says she would not have given the primary evidence in an arrest to the van driver or to a colleague if she were Miller. "You hold on to that, and I believe policy says you have to submit it to the evidence control in a 'reasonable time.'" As for why the knife wasn't filed into ECU for eleven hours in this case, Everett takes a beat to think about it. Then she says, "They were plotting."[15]

* * *

Just before submitting the knife into ECU with Novak at 9:00 p.m., Miller made a call to the dispatcher. This call wasn't played in court, and it didn't appear on any of BPD's timelines. It was disruptive to BPD's story of Gray's knife arrest, so BPD tried to bury it.

Miller's nighttime call appears on a document known as a Computer-Aided Dispatch (CAD) report, which reflects what the dispatcher entered into the CAD system in real time. Requests for CC numbers are labeled as "CASE" calls. The CAD reports can be helpful in this case because the trial dispatch was an edited production of selected calls from April 12, played back-to-back, with different calls added and subtracted for each trial and no time stamps. Officials have never made the raw dispatch audio available to the public.

When it comes to Stop 2, the CAD reports are confusing and don't match the trial audio. Miller's CAD report doesn't show a CC request during Stop 2, but one does appear on Nero's CAD report. Nero's CAD report also has the CC and CAD numbers on it that were given by the dispatcher to Miller over the radio (150404754 and 20695, respectively), so it may be that the dispatcher mistakenly assigned all of Miller's Stop 2 calls to Nero, among other possibilities.

Miller's CAD report shows something else more clearly. It registers its own CASE call at 8:42 p.m. and a different CC number, 150404962. The new number doesn't appear elsewhere in the case and is sequentially higher by several hundred than the CC numbers given that morning. What Miller's CAD report reveals is that he requested a CC number at night, while he was still downtown working on the Gray case, just eighteen minutes before he accompanied Novak to submit the knife into ECU at 9:00 p.m. According to Everett and other BPD sources, Miller didn't need to obtain a new CC number in the case if the officers simply changed their minds about, say, whether to charge for the state or city knife law.[16]

So why did Miller request a second CC number twelve hours after Gray's arrest, just before submitting the knife, and for what charge? Miller's CAD report contains another clue. The evening call includes a note from the dispatcher: "B09 advised to keep them separate and no further infor[mation]." B09 was Lieutenant Rice's unit number. Normally, if more than one CC number is requested during a complex incident, police are supposed to reconcile them in a timely manner; CC numbers are used to keep evidence and investigative materials in one place. That night, Miller was requesting a *new* CC number for Gray's arrest, more than twelve hours after the incident, and Rice wanted it kept separate from any other CC numbers. It appears the officers were holding on to different options for how to charge Gray.

Miller's 8:42 p.m. CASE call was so disruptive to the official narrative of the knife arrest that BPD tried to keep it from the public. The department didn't include his CAD report in its public release of case files with the rest of the CAD reports. When the report was finally provided in response to an MPIA request, BPD printed it out onto two pages and cut out the evening CASE call. Fortunately, another source provided the complete and intact CAD report.[17]

* * *

About two and a half hours after submitting the knife into ECU, Novak accompanied Miller to the courthouse to file a summons charge against Gray, as advised by Lieutenant Rice and the FIT investigators. The forms were signed by a court commissioner on April 12, 2015, at 11:25 p.m. They seem hastily filled out and withhold a lot of information. Miller's statement of probable cause was only six sentences, and it never mentions that Gray was going to Central Booking:

> *The above named Defendant fled unprovoked upon noticing police presence. The Defendant was apprehended in the 1700 block of Presbury St after a brief foot chase. The officer noticed a knife clipped to the inside of his front right pants pocket. The defendant was arrested without force or incident. The knife was recovered by this officer and found to be a spring-assisted, one hand operated knife. During transport to Western District via wagon transport, the defendant suffered a medical emergency and was transported to Shock Trauma via wagon.*

Most probable cause statements, even by Miller, go on for pages and include far more information, including the names of all the officers involved in the arrest, each of their roles, the time of the arrest, the submission of evidence, any notable dialogue with suspects, what suspects are wearing, and so on. They usually read like first-person, minute-by-minute novellas. Miller omitted all of that. He also left the courthouse name and address blank on his forms. These details were included in almost every one of sixty Western District charging documents reviewed from 2014 and 2015.

Miller's probable cause statement offers a new explanation for how he found a knife on Gray. He "noticed a knife clipped to the inside of his front right pants pocket." If Miller noticed a knife clip on the outside of Gray's pants, then he had probable cause to reach into Gray's pocket. He may have decided to charge Gray with the city's switchblade crime instead of the state's "concealed dangerous weapon" crime to avoid the Fourth Amendment issues around finding something concealed on a person.

When Mosby announced her own charges against the officers, she came up with a cleaned-up, composite description of Miller's and Nero's various statements: "Mr. Gray indicated he could not breathe and requested an inhaler to no avail. Officer Miller and Nero then placed Mr. Gray in a seated position and subsequently found a knife clipped to the inside of his pants pocket."[18] It didn't matter that Gray wasn't carrying an inhaler that day. He also may not have been carrying a knife.

As part of Miller's application for charges, he had to fill out a witness summons form, listing the officers who were witnesses to the arrest. He checked a box identifying himself as the "arresting officer," but he crossed out the word "arresting." During the trials, Miller was identified as the arresting officer, but on the night of Gray's arrest, he apparently hadn't settled on that role yet.

Overall, while parts of the knife arrest story remain a mystery, the documents in this case—CAD reports, an ECU report, CSU logs, a witness summons form—show BPD working out how to charge Gray and holding on to options. The quest to determine how to arrest Gray started early that morning, with the backup officers searching the ground, and lasted late into the night.

BPD still wouldn't commit to an arrest story as Gray lay in a coma during the week of April 12. The day after his arrest, on April 13, Deputy Commissioner Rodriguez said, "He has not been charged yet," and, "There are charges against him that will be filed,"[19] though Miller's statement of charges had been signed and stamped by the court commissioner the night before. The media missed the knife charge online because it was filed under "Grey," the spelling on Freddie Gray's driver's license.[20] Then, Gray died on April 19, and police immediately released to the press two pages from Miller's charging documents. Did BPD leaders have an alternative arrest story in mind in the event Gray survived?

There continued to be intrigue around the knife after Gray's death. On April 27, FIT Detective Teel, who was the lead detective on the case, checked out the knife from ECU at 11:21 a.m. An hour later, the knife was returned by Officer Novak.[21] By April 27, Novak was officially a witness in the case and shouldn't have been handling evidence. He was also under investigation himself. About ten minutes after he returned the knife to ECU, he was interviewed by Teel's colleagues in FIT.

* * *

When Mosby announced charges against the officers, she framed the terms of the conversation about the knife around its legality, igniting a media debate that ran for over a year. If the public had seen a picture of the knife sooner, there would have been no such debate, according to Xan Martin, an expert on knives and knife law. "The knife is a legal knife. There should've been no hesitation about the ruling of the knife from the get-go," he says.[22] By day, Martin sells knives in a retail store and provides expert testimony in court. By night, he maintains a collection of knives that he stores in a studio in Orange County, California. He displays knives from across the world and throughout history along the walls. He keeps smaller knives in a stack of narrow drawers. His switchblades are kept separately from the knives similar to the one in this case.

Martin is one of several knife aficionados around the country who advocate for legalizing knives generally. They are cousins to National Rifle Association (NRA) advocates. With a ponytail and colorful printed shirts, Martin doesn't seem like the type you would find at an NRA convention. Knife advocates are often more progressive than gun advocates. Most of them don't shy away from talking about racial disparities in enforcement.

Siding with Mosby, Martin offers a passionate, lengthy explanation of the mechanics of a switchblade—the "long piece of metal that is cut in the middle" and "forms a tight V shape," while a "separate spring forces a pin into a hole when activated by the push of a button, toggle, or lever." That is his short explanation. More simply, Martin compares the spring in a switchblade to a mousetrap. "It only has two positions. It compresses until it is released, at which point it opens fully, quickly."

Public paranoia around switchblades hit a peak during the 1950s, with the popularization of the stiletto, the narrow switchblade that pops open from the top. Movies like James Dean's *Rebel without a Cause* showed neatly dressed young white men circling each other with stiletto knives. But most 1950s switchblade hysteria was racist and classist. "Vicious fantasies of omnipotence, idolatry, barbaric and sadistic atrocities, and monstrous violations of accepted values spring from the cult of the weapon," Congressman Sidney R. Yates of Illinois testified in a 1958 hearing that led to the Federal Switchblade Act, banning most switchblades.[23] Baltimore's switchblade law, enacted in 1950, is a holdover from that era.

The knife in the Gray case is neither a switchblade nor an old-fashioned folding knife. It's called an "assisted opener," and it was invented in 1998, decades after Baltimore's law could have anticipated it. While switchblades *automatically* pop open upon the press of a button, assisted openers have thumbstuds and flippers, which are protruding knobs attached to the sides and back of the blade, respectively. One must *manually* press against a thumbstud or flipper to open the blade. As it extends around 40 degrees, an internal mechanism called a "torsion bar" moves along a track inside the knife and opens the knife the rest of the way. Assisted openers can be safely opened and closed with one hand, which makes them useful to electricians, farmers, rescue workers, and others.

In 2009, President Barack Obama signed into law an exemption to the Federal Switchblade Act legalizing, at the federal level, knives with a "bias toward closure," which is the resistance one faces trying to open an assisted opener.[24] Switchblades have a bias toward opening; they pop open easily.

During the Gray case, many people blamed the language in Baltimore's switchblade law for being confusing, resulting in the controversy. It didn't help that BPD officers received no training on knife law. According to the city ordinance, it's illegal to "sell, carry, or possess any knife with an automatic spring or other device for opening and/or closing the blade, commonly known as a switchblade knife."

Martin doesn't believe a torsion bar is a "device for opening and/or closing the blade" because these actions need to happen manually. Even more, assisted openers are not "commonly known as switchblades." They aren't known as switchblades by the federal government or by retailers, who categorize them with the other legal folding knives. They're only known as switchblades by police officers in order to arrest civilians for possessing them. Martin goes on to ask: "And how many retailers get arrested for selling those knives in Baltimore?" The answer is none. Police do not target Walmart, sporting goods stores, or gas stations for selling assisted openers, even though the law forbids selling switchblades.

Martin says virtually all of the knives in the cases he has studied are legal assisted openers. Peter Moskos and others excuse wrongful knife arrests based on police officers' right to be "reasonably mistaken" in their understanding of the law, as granted by the Supreme Court in *Helen v. North Carolina* (2014). That old adage about ignorance of the law not being an excuse applies only to civilians in the United States, not the professionals who enforce laws.

Nero and Miller didn't claim to be reasonably mistaken about knife law, though. "Miller, he's very good with knives. He knows, you know, the knife laws in both city and state," Nero told internal affairs investigators. "We both had a pretty good understanding of the difference between a spring-assisted, a switchblade itself, or just like a regular buck knife."[25] During 2014 and 2015, knife-related charges showed up in about 12 percent of total arrests for the officers in this case. Miller added knife charges more often than his colleagues.

In the end, Miller and Nero never had to account for their understanding of knife law in court because the prosecutors dropped the issue. They never brought up the knife once over four trials.

* * *

Mosby swung hard in her press conference announcing charges against six officers. She declared it a crime for officers to wrongly arrest someone who had a legal knife. The grand jury didn't proceed with an indictment on the charges of false imprisonment based on a wrongful arrest, but she was still prepared to argue that the arrest wasn't legal and so constituted assault. She had a knife expert ready to testify to that. Then she dropped the issue. In the end, Mosby chose not to bring before the eyes of the world proof that she was right about the knife. She couldn't; her office was complicit too.

"Mosby came out and said this knife was not a switchblade, but that message never trickled down to the line attorneys in district court," Baltimore public defender Sarah Elkins says. "While the Freddie Gray case was going on, we were defending these switchblade cases with knives that looked exactly like the knife they purported to recover from Gray."[26] Mosby's office charged someone for possessing an assisted opener just three days before she charged the officers for illegally arresting Gray for the same type of knife.

Officer Nero's lawyers filed a motion to preclude mention of the knife's legality, attaching case files from recent examples of SAO charging people who carried assisted openers, often added to other charges.[27] They also subpoenaed every assistant state's attorney in SAO's Charging Division, which approves and settles charges before prosecution. It was a kind of legal blackmail, and it seems to have worked. SAO shifted to a new theory that Miller's arrest was illegal because he had handcuffed and moved Gray before knowing why Rice initiated the chase. As Chief Deputy State's Attorney Michael Schatzow explained, "The defendants filed motions to keep out of evidence questions about whether the knife was legal or illegal, and it was our theory that the arrest was made before then, so we didn't oppose those motions."[28]

SAO stipulated away the issue around the knife's legality and never had to deal with its own history of wrongful charges around knives. Yet prosecutors took it further: They never mentioned the knife in court at all. They presented a step-by-step account of Gray's arrest without saying why he was in custody. It sounded, once again, like an arrest with no crime.

Prosecutors were unwilling to tackle the knife controversy in court, but months after the trials, SAO released pictures of the knife with an intriguing statement: "The type of knife recovered was sold to police officers by the Cop Shop, has been advertised in the Baltimore Police Department headquarters building for officers to purchase, and was in the possession of one of the defendants on the very day that Mr. Gray was arrested." The Cop Shop is a store that sells gear to first responders in Baltimore.

Schatzow explained in a press conference that one of his staffers saw a Cop Shop poster in BPD headquarters advertising a similar knife. It had "a BPD insignia on it," he said, "the very knife that Freddie Gray had in his possession."[29]

Neither statement from SAO clarified the legality issue. Baltimore City's switchblade ordinance includes an exemption for police officers on duty, and Gray's alleged knife didn't have a BPD insignia on it. SAO subpoenaed sales records from the Cop Shop, but the records didn't turn up similar knives sold to Western District cops. That "type of knife" is also available all over the internet.

However, SAO's claim about an officer having the same knife in his possession on the day of Gray's arrest did hint that maybe prosecutors thought Gray's knife was planted.[30] In 2016, an internal affairs investigator asked Lieutenant Rice about Miller "carrying the same knife as Freddie Gray." Rice wasn't sure, and investigators didn't ask Miller directly.

SAO didn't pursue any concerns with the knife arrest beyond the Cop Shop subpoena. The prosecutors' own theory of Gray's cause of death, between Stops 2 and 4, depended on nothing serious happening to him at either of the first two stops at Gilmor Homes. It was a theory that relied on Goodson heading toward Central Booking after Stop 2 with a legitimate arrest. So both BPD and SAO leaders told a story that sounded uncontroversial: Gray's knife was discovered when he asked for an inhaler at Stop 1, and police decided to send Gray straight to Central Booking on a knife charge from Stop 2. Most of the evidence that would undermine these claims was never revealed to the public.

II

THE ROUTE

CHAPTER 8

BALTIMORE IN BLACK AND BLUE

When State's Attorney Marilyn Mosby announced charges against six officers on May 1, she introduced the roles of the Black officers in this case: Officer Caesar Goodson, forty-five, who drove the van; Officer William Porter, twenty-five, who provided backup at almost all of the stops, checking on Gray twice; and Sergeant Alicia White, thirty, who checked on Gray at Stop 5 and handled some of Lieutenant Brian Rice's duties while he was on bike patrol. All three Black officers wore traditional blue uniforms that day and acted within the scope of their positions as van driver, backup officer, and sergeant, respectively.

The media circulated a grid of mug shots showing three white and three Black officers, which some used to dismiss race as a factor in the Gray case. "You can't just label this something racial," Congressman Elijah Cummings said, "when you have three African American officers involved."[1] In 2015, BPD was composed of about 48 percent Black officers, making the distribution among the six officers demographically expected.

Before the trials, some media outlets addressed the history of race in the department. Yet the question of how race played out in the Gray case never came up. Very little was known about what happened on April 12 to provide context. So, while there were stories on being a Black police officer in Baltimore historically, there were none about being a Black officer in the Western District in April 2015.

There is a reading of what happened on the morning of Gray's arrest that is reflective of the department's history of racial inequity: Three white officers, including the shift commander, chased Gray on bikes and arrested him. According to twenty or so witnesses, they handled him roughly at two stops. Three Black officers were left to manage the aftermath and clean up some of the mess. They ended up saddled with greater responsibility for what happened than the white officers. This reading of the Gray's arrest wasn't apparent in the media or in court, but it was a topic within the department.

Some nuances complicate an easy racial binary in this case. There were social alliances that crossed racial divisions, and race wasn't the only identity at play. Gender and age also factored into the roles officers were cast to play that morning. There is also Jamel Baker's clear and detailed same-day memory of which officers he saw pick Gray up off of the ground at Stop 2 and toss him into the van: Officer Goodson, Lieutenant Rice, and one other bike officer.

* * *

Officer Goodson left Stop 2 at 8:54 a.m., heading south on Mount Street. According to police, he was taking Gray to Central Booking on a charge of illegal knife possession. For the next ten or so minutes, he was alone with Gray. During that time, according to prosecutors, he committed a murder.

Goodson came up in the department with Lieutenant Rice, joining in 1999 as zero tolerance became policy. Born and raised in Baltimore, the grandson of a police officer, in 2015 he lived in Catonsville, Maryland, a middle-class, mostly white liberal suburb just west of Baltimore.

Goodson was the only officer involved in Gray's arrest to invoke his Fifth Amendment right not to self-incriminate on April 12. FIT detectives tried to interview him twice, but he asked for a lawyer both times.[2] After he was acquitted, he was required to give a statement to internal affairs investigators. His morning on April 12 began with "cleaning the garage," he told investigators. "I don't know why I was doing that, cleaning the garage," he said.[3]

Nearing retirement in 2015, Goodson had been driving the van in the Western District for more than thirteen years when Gray was injured, making only the occasional arrest. He had a nickname, "Gentle Caesar," to support his reputation for being easygoing. "He's the calmest guy that I have ever been around," Officer Wood told internal affairs investigators.[4] Others described him as always smiling and mild-mannered. He was unlikely to initiate chases, his colleagues said, but he wouldn't neglect his responsibilities.

Goodson's colleagues also described him as a wise mentor and a "seasoned veteran," according to Gladhill. "You need that experienced officer when you're the young, dumb one," Officer Novak said.[5]

The internal affairs investigators had a different take. "You never handcuff, you never search, even if a search has been done, you never put anyone in the wagon," one of them said to Goodson. "You're allowing another officer to hop in and basically do what I believe a reasonable police officer would know to be the job of the wagon man."

* * *

Mosby indicted Goodson for second-degree "depraved heart" murder and several other violent crimes based on what her office believed happened soon after he left Stop 2. Alone with Gray, Goodson stopped the van twice. The state's theory in court was that Gray was fatally injured while the van was in motion between Stops 2 and 4, but probably before Stop 3. It was a theory that relied on a few pieces of evidence and a process of elimination. First, prosecutors determined that Gray was not yet injured at Gilmor Homes because officers described him as still yelling and shaking the van at the end of Stop 2.

Next, prosecutors relied on video evidence of the van leaving Gilmor Homes, heading along the quiet streets of West Baltimore in the direction of Central Booking. CCTV videos show a white van driving south from Gilmor Homes for two blocks after Stop 2, turning left on Riggs Street at the police station, and then, about a half mile down, making a right turn onto North Fremont Street. (See the map of the official BPD van route, page 3.)

The eight seconds of Goodson turning right onto Fremont were his "rough ride," according to prosecutors.[6] "At 8:56 and 51 seconds, the defendant driving the van makes the right turn from Riggs on to Fremont," Chief Deputy State's Attorney Schatzow argued in his opening statement in Goodson's trial. "And when he does that, he runs a stop sign that's on the corner. And he takes that turn at sufficient speed that when he turns on to Fremont, he can't stay in his lane. The vehicle crosses over the double yellow line on the road."[7] In the video, Goodson's left wheel lands slightly over the median lines in the street. He then straightens up into his lane. Prosecutors theorized the van might have thrown Gray forward at that point and broken his neck.

By itself, the video of Goodson's turn doesn't offer compelling evidence of a rough ride. He doesn't appear to speed; he takes as long as the other cars making turns on the CCTV video. He also doesn't make any sharp movements. Goodson probably didn't imagine that rolling through that stop sign would get him in trouble. He had made a full stop at an intersection about a hundred feet before. Fremont runs diagonally, so Goodson didn't have to make a full 90-degree turn. There were also no other cars on the road.

For prosecutors, Goodson's actions after his wide turn offered additional evidence that Gray was injured during that turn. Two blocks south, Goodson stopped at the corner of Mosher Street, where he got out to check the back of the van. This became known as Stop 3. It wasn't revealed to the public until April 30, the day before Mosby announced charges. Deputy Commissioner Kevin Davis said, "We discovered this new stop based on our thorough and comprehensive and ongoing review of all CCTV cameras and privately owned cameras. And in fact this new stop was from a privately owned camera."

The video came from CR Market, belonging to Jung Hwang, who told *Undisclosed* that the officers visited his store twice in one day. It was April 23, according to case files. He described two detectives showing up first, and one of them saying "bingo" as he watched the security video. Later that day, Hwang said, two technicians came and took his hard drive and camera with them. The backup was looted during the riots on April 27, and police didn't return his equipment.[8]

In court, prosecutors played the security video. The footage was grainy. Capturing the front left of the police van at 8:57 a.m., it shows a driver stopping, getting out, and walking behind the van for about nine seconds. Mosby said Goodson "proceeded to the back of the wagon to observe Mr. Gray . . . for the purpose of checking on Mr. Gray's condition." It's not clear from the video that the driver opened the back door of the van. Goodson later told internal affairs investigators that he didn't check on Gray; he only checked to make sure the door was secure, given that Gray had been kicking and making noise in the back while he was driving.

While the video of Stop 3 doesn't, by itself, confirm that Goodson checked on Gray at Stop 3, prosecutors based *that* assumption on what happened next. Three minutes after Stop 3, while driving east in the direction of Central Booking, Goodson radioed for someone to meet up with him to check on Gray. His radio conversation was as follows:

GOODSON: 91 [his unit number]
DISPATCHER: 91
GOODSON: Yes, ma'am, can I have a unit 10-11 meet me at Druid Hill and Dolphin? I need to check this prisoner out.
DISPATCHER: Let me have a unit, Druid Hill and Dolphin.
PORTER: 43 [his unit number]. I am headed over there.

The intersection of Druid Hill Avenue and Dolphin Street, or Stop 4, was in the Central District, just over a mile from Central Booking. It provided the state with the last piece of evidence for its theory of the timing of Gray's fatal injury. While prosecutors theorized that Goodson's wide turn was the *likely* cause of Gray's injury, they were *certain* that his neck was broken by the time Goodson got to Stop 4. Yet the only evidence for that allegation came from the statement provided by Officer Porter, and he specialized in confusion.

* * *

At the time of Gray's arrest, Porter lived in Owings Mills, a majority-Black suburb just northwest of Baltimore, and he had family still in the city. Before he faced trial, the *Washington Post* published a profile, "Freddie Gray and William Porter: Two Sons of Baltimore Whose Lives Collided," reported by Michael A. Fletcher.[9] The article outlines how Porter and Gray started their lives in the same place, living in poverty in West Baltimore and raised by single mothers. They both got into trouble and struggled with school as children. Porter dropped out of college and joined the police force in 2012.

"If I had made different choices, I would have been Freddie Gray. If he had made different choices, he could have been an Officer

Porter," Porter told the *Post*. One of the key choices that saved Porter, according to Fletcher, was actually made by his mother. She moved the family out of West Baltimore to a safer area when he was still a child. Porter's father also came home from the military around that time. Porter didn't end up like Gray in part because he was no longer in the same circumstances.

The *Post* article benefited Porter in the lead-up to his trial. The article supported the police union's portrayal of the officers as well-intentioned, passive victims of unfortunate events. Porter "maintains he did nothing wrong," Fletcher writes. The two men's paths "collided" and "intersected" at the corner of Druid Hill and Dolphin on April 12, as if guided by fate. Fletcher even frames Porter as the more beleaguered party, an unusual take for a homicide story: Gray is considered a "symbol," he writes, while Porter "has heard few such accolades."

Porter was the first officer to face trial, and his defense was a continuation of the same public relations campaign. His lawyers highlighted that he was a son of Baltimore who worked foot patrol in his old neighborhood. "During my shifts, I frequently walk Gilmor Homes, and I'm a familiar face, and I know people by first names, and I talked to them a lot," he testified.[10] Porter gave a few chatty anecdotes on the stand about his experience policing.

The older witnesses at Stop 1 recognized Porter as the cop who looked like them but refused to intervene to help Gray. Jamel Baker also remembered Porter from the neighborhood: "He was always pulling up, stopping, saying 'move' or something."[11]

Porter's role in the Gray case is marked by some dualities. He went to the academy with Miller and was a member of a text chain with Miller, Nero, and Novak, but he had a somewhat different approach on the streets. He was far less likely to make arrests for zero tolerance crimes and, in the year before Gray's death, never made one arrest for marijuana possession. While on suspension, he watched *The*

Wire for the first time, texting his colleagues about how little had changed in BPD. "The push for stats, therefore you get half-assed police work," he texted. "I never cared about stats anyway. I did my own thing lol."[12] Porter's own personal permissiveness around marijuana aside, he was no political progressive. He joined Miller in celebrating Minneapolis's right-wing Sheriff David Clarke as a favorite politician.

* * *

On April 14, FIT Detective Syreeta Teel, who was assigned as lead detective, was reviewing the dispatch calls and heard Goodson ask for Porter to meet him at Druid Hill and Dolphin. She knew Porter personally from their working together at the Western District, so she called him on the phone the next day to discuss his involvement in Gray's arrest. He was driving at the time. She wrote about the call in her notes:

> *Porter confirmed that he responded to Dolphin and Baker St for to assist Unit 7B91 Goodson. . . . He observed Mr. Grey [sic] lying on his stomach, head facing the front of the wagon with his feet towards the doors, saying "Help." Officer Porter advised that he asked Mr. Grey what he needed at which time he stated that he couldn't breathe. Officer Porter asked Mr. Grey if he needed a medic in which Mr. Grey stated "Yeah."*

Teel's notes locate Stop 4 at Dolphin and Baker, two streets that don't intersect. But if she transcribed the rest of her conversation with Porter correctly, then Porter was the first officer in the case to acknowledge that Gray was in medical distress before Stop 6. Two days later, on April 17, Porter went downtown to give a taped statement to FIT detectives. Like most of the officers, he waived his rights and spoke voluntarily.

Porter stands more than six feet tall, with a broad build. In court, he seemed mostly confident, but during this interview, he sounded like a child or adolescent constantly working his way out of a lie. When he got tripped up, he gave himself away with a nervous stammering of his syllables, as well as the repetition of an extended, trailing off "eh" sound with vocal fry. It's the kind of sound one might make to deflect the importance of a thought—to throw away words. As the interview went on, these vocal habits took over his speech.

Porter met his foil in Detective Charles Anderson, the investigator with a habit of pushing his subjects relentlessly on whichever details preoccupied him. Anderson began grilling Porter about what he saw at Stop 2. The beginning of Brandon Ross's video captures Porter leaving his car and approaching the van just as Rice climbs in to pull in Gray's body. Porter told detectives he saw only one officer put Gray in the van, but he struggled to describe how and couldn't say which officer. It was "either Miller, Lieutenant Rice, or Novak," he said at first. Novak wasn't on the scene yet. Later, Porter said it wasn't Miller but a "skinny white guy" on a bike. That left Rice or Nero.

"How long you been working with these gentlemen?" Anderson asked. They went back and forth for several minutes on the question.[13]

The conversation took a dark turn when Porter discussed Stop 4. Goodson opened the van's door, he said, and the officers found Gray lying on the wagon's floor, which is how he was left at Stop 2: "He says, 'Help.' I was like, 'What's your deal? What's wrong with you? Why do you need help?' And he just—he just keeps saying, 'Help.' He was like, 'Can you help me up?' So I help him up." The first time through the story, Porter said he sat Gray up on the floor. Later, he said he lifted him up onto the bench. "You need a medic or something?" he recalled asking.

"Yeah, I need a medic," Gray responded, according to Porter. Then Porter discussed with Goodson what to do next:

> *So I look at Goodson and said, you probably have to take this dude, um, to the hospital. We're going to need to call a medic. 'Cause we've got a transport vehicle and you transport him there. We look at each other and are like, yeah, he's probably not going to pass medical down at Central Booking.*

Yet the officers didn't call a medic, and Goodson didn't take Gray to the hospital. Instead, they both answered a request from Lieutenant Rice at 9:07 a.m. for backup and a wagon back on North Avenue in the Western District, in the opposite direction of Central Booking and more than two miles from the nearest hospital. Over and over again, Porter sounded like he was confessing to a crime, with no remorse: "I was like, 'You need a medic or something? You need to go to the hospital?' And he would say, 'Yes.'" These statements would be followed by Porter admitting he didn't help Gray.

Detective Anderson asked Porter why he didn't get medical attention for Gray. Porter offered a few reasons. First, he said, Gray wasn't really injured. "Everyone plays the 'I need to go to the hospital thing' when they get arrested," he said. "He couldn't tell me that he was hurt in any way shape or form. He just wanted a medic." But calling a medic was Porter's own idea that he said he proposed to Gray.

Porter diagnosed Gray as having an "adrenaline dump" from all of the van shaking and banging since Stop 2. "You get your adrenaline pumping and pumping, you're kicking around and everything and eventually . . . you get lethargic and tired after that, the adrenaline is gone," he said.

Porter gave another reason for refusing Gray medical attention: "Medics don't really want to transport prisoners if we already have a wagon available," he said. "If a prisoner needs to go to the hospital, you transport them in the wagon." This was neither policy nor practice. Medics provide on-scene equipment, medication, and life-saving procedures.

At trial, Paramedic Angelique Herbert was asked, "In your seventeen years of experience, have you ever declined to come to the aid of a prisoner when called by a police officer?"

"No," she answered.[14]

After Porter wrapped up his statement, FIT Detective Anderson brought him back into the interview room and asked him again, more directly, why he didn't get a medic for Gray. "Is there any way that it's possible that he needed medical attention right then and there?" It was a pertinent question—Gray was found to be in a coma a half hour later—but Porter gave the same responses as before. All of the officers gave statements that set off various bells, but Porter set off a symphony of alarm.

* * *

At 9:07 a.m., Lieutenant Rice called for backup and a van on North Avenue near the Penn North metro station to help with their second arrest of the day, Donta Allen. Porter and Goodson responded to the call with Gray in the van, still without medical attention. This became Stop 5 in the official narrative.

At Stop 5, Porter again checked on Gray. He told FIT detectives that Gray was "kneeling" on the floor of the wagon, facing the bench, and leaning over the bench with his head over his arm. Gray would answer to his name and not much else, Porter said. "If you asked him what was wrong with him, he couldn't tell you what was wrong with him. He never said anything. I said, 'What's wrong with you?' 'I need a medic.' He just didn't say anything." Gray didn't say anything, except, "I need a medic," apparently.

According to Porter, Sergeant White, who was on the scene at Stop 5, commanded him to follow the van to Bon Secours hospital after Goodson dropped Allen off at the police station. Officer Nero also mentioned this in his first-day statement: "I know Sergeant White, I believe, was talking to our suspect, the first one. And I don't know exactly what transpired from there, but after that at the North Ave, he was—I guess Goodson was supposed to take him to the hospital, I believe."

There is a rotating CCTV video of Stop 5 showing the back of the van.[15] After Porter checks on Gray by himself, five officers stand looking into Gray's side of the van. Sergeant White is on the step that leads into the van and stays there for about a minute, with Porter and Goodson behind her, as well as Wood and Gladhill, who had provided backup at earlier stops. SAO did an extreme close-up and enhancement of this moment. The officers appear to be looking downward into the van, but the inside of the van isn't clear.[16]

The officers' defense team insisted Gray wasn't injured until after he left Stop 5. It was the only theory in which no officers were to blame. If Gray was perfectly fine at Stop 5, why were so many officers staring at him during the supposedly routine arrest of another suspect? It's surprising that BPD released this footage to the public, although none of the bike cops—Rice, Miller, or Nero—are implicated in it. They stayed away from the back of the van until the door to Gray's side was closed.

* * *

The only woman working the Western District Baker patrol shift on Sunday, April 12, Sergeant Alicia White was left to handle various supervisory duties when Lieutenant Rice went on bike patrol. Technically, he was still the shift commander, but she oversaw inspections in his absence, including checking her officers' clothes and vehicles. She also monitored the police radio and reviewed and submitted reports.

Like Goodson and Porter, White was born and grew up in Baltimore City. She joined the force in 2010 with a college degree. Even more than Porter, she received a saint-like spin in the press. The *New York Times* described her as a "thirty-year-old churchgoing black woman with a reputation as a rising star."[17] The article quoted a neighbor who insisted White would never even jaywalk, let alone hurt someone.

White's colleagues described her to internal affairs investigators as professional and by-the-book, someone who might write you up for not having your boots shined but also would help you get time off. Officer Gladhill recalled her punishing Miller and another officer who were doing something in a vacant house without telling her. She made them do foot patrol. "That was pretty comical," he told investigators.[18]

Things became complicated for White when she got involved with what the bike cops were doing on April 12. She said she headed up to North Avenue in response to Rice's backup request, but she was also tasked with looking into Brandon Ross's first 911 call, in which he reported "an altercation between a police officer and a citizen" at Stop 1. The call had been marked by the dispatcher as a "supervisor complaint," meaning a complaint that would be handled initially by a shift supervisor. That should have been Lieutenant Rice, but he was on bike patrol.

According to Carrie Everett, "The complaints shouldn't have been left for her to handle, because he was still the 09," or shift commander. "She can't. She's not in charge." Everett would have called for someone in another district. She also points out that White was still on probation as a new sergeant. The stakes were high for any choices she made.[19]

Within the department, White became a symbol for officers who believed Mosby was pursuing a malicious prosecution. For no more than one minute of interaction with Gray a half hour after his arrest, she was charged with manslaughter and second-degree assault and faced up to twenty years in prison. On May 13, the Vanguard Justice Society, a membership organization for Black BPD officers, held a news conference in response to the charges against the six officers. Ken Butler, Vanguard's president, offered "our full support in reference to the officers that have recently been charged and one officer in particular, a Vanguard member, Sergeant Alicia White."[20]

Captain Lisa Robinson, who was Vanguard's vice president at the time, also spoke, saying, "The stop snitching culture is prevalent on the streets of Baltimore as well as within the Baltimore Police Department." It was a provocative statement, one of very few moments when the possibility of tension among the officers came to the surface.

Years later, Robinson doesn't remember making the statement but repeats the sentiment: "That's the fear that a lot of Black officers have," she says. "If I say something or I do something against what they're doing that's corrupt, then then they are coming for me."[21]

The Vanguard Justice Society was established in 1971 in Baltimore to advocate for the interests of Black BPD officers outside of the Fraternal Order of Police (FOP). BPD didn't accept Black officers until the late 1930s, and it took decades for Black cops to receive basic privileges like wearing uniforms, carrying guns, advancing in rank, and being allowed to arrest white people. Vanguard has filed lawsuits on behalf of Black officers around hiring, promotions, discipline, and racist practices. The FOP historically opposed Vanguard in several actions, meaning that Black officers who wanted to be in the police union had to pay dues to an adversarial group.[22] Vanguard won a lawsuit in 1979 around the height and weight requirements for officers, which made it possible for White—at five feet, one inch tall—to become an officer.[23] More recently, Robinson led a complaint against BPD to allow Black officers to wear their natural hair.

White's promotion to sergeant at age thirty, four months before Gray's arrest, was supported by a Vanguard initiative aimed at mentoring and advancing younger Black officers. Leading up to the promotional exam, she attended study sessions about twice a week. According to Robinson, she excelled at the academic portion. "She was one of those people that I saw really one day becoming a commander. I mean, that's what her heart, you know, her goals were." Robinson also worked with White on strengthening "her little bird voice," her high-pitched, soft voice. "The guys are definitely not trying to listen to you and hear you, because they're not trying to do that anyway," Robinson says.

After Gray's arrest, Robinson found out White had given a statement without talking to a lawyer. She later discovered that nobody had paid White's bail. Robinson found an attorney she trusted for White—Ivan Bates, who is Black and was not on the FOP's usual list of attorneys—and says she pushed the FOP to cover his legal costs. Bates filed a motion to separate White's case from the other officers before the judge ruled to separate all the cases.[24] Robinson also checked in on Goodson, who had the experience to know not to give a statement and to find his own lawyer. "This is what happens on a regular basis," Robinson says. "You know that you're not going to get the representation that you need. A lot of Black officers just simply accept punishment for things that they didn't do. It's no different than, you know, the African Americans on the street."

Everett had that experience herself. "I went out and got my own attorney when they charged me," she says, referring to an IAD case. "Because they always want you to plead."

* * *

Sergeant White ended up giving two statements to FIT detectives during the week after Gray's arrest. She was first interviewed as a witness on the afternoon of April 12. Then, on April 17, she was interviewed as an involved officer under suspicion of possible guilt. According to Porter, she knew Gray wanted medical attention at Stop 5, but she didn't immediately call for a medic.

White had a sincere manner in her interviews and, more than some of her colleagues, seemed to grasp when to stop talking. When she got to Stop 5, she said, Rice pointed her to Gray's side of the wagon. She hoped that he might be responsive to her "as a female." "Hey what's going on?" she recalled asking Gray. He wouldn't respond, but he appeared to be breathing, she said.[25]

Like Porter, White initially described Gray as seated on the floor, with his head bent into one of his arms. Gladhill gave the same description, calling it a "praying" position. All three officers described a position that was impossible, as Gray's hands were restrained in flex cuffs behind his back. White seemed to remember that by her second statement, in which she described him leaning on the bench with his hands behind his back.

In her first statement, on April 12, White left open the possibility that Gray was injured at Stop 5 when she checked on him and she just didn't realize it:

> The only thing they kept saying—they always like, "Oh he just has jailitis." You know that was the kind of words that they used, like, they said "jailitis" because he doesn't want to go to jail, and I'm like, "You don't know that." But once we got to the district and I see how he was, so . . .

White trailed off. "Jailitis" was police-speak for faking illness to avoid prison. By her second interview on April 17, White no longer gave any hint of a suggestion that Gray might have actually been injured at Stop 5.

During White's second interview, FIT Detective Teel informed her that she had been brought back for a reason. "We were given information that on North Avenue, a conversation was held in reference to a unit being advised . . . if he needed a medic to drive him straight to Bon Secours. Is that usually . . . how it's done, instead of calling for a medic?"

"That I'm not familiar with, no," White replied.

"Have you had any other contacts, any other conversations, about him needing a medic with any of the officers on scene?" Teel asked.

"No," White answered.

"None whatsoever?" Teel asked.

"No," White answered. "The whole medic conversation didn't come up with me until I got back to the Western District."[26] She also told detectives she left Stop 5 quickly after checking on Gray, but CCTV video shows her and Porter still on North Avenue for about four minutes, talking to the bike officers on the sidewalk.

Although White wasn't part of the text chain with her colleagues in the Gray case, she did speak on the phone with and text many of them in the days that followed. "You're doing a good job," she texted Novak after Gray's arrest, in relation to a work assignment. On April 21, after she was administratively suspended, she texted Novak, "Hey just checking on you." Novak wasn't suspended. He let her know that he'd spoken with someone at FOP who would set them up with attorneys and offered that person's name. He asked how she was doing. "I'm doing good," she answered and said she was on top of her legal needs.[27] White didn't give away much to detectives or to her colleagues. Her phone records indicate that she had her own confidants, other Black BPD officers with whom she spoke often after Gray's arrest.

In November 2016, no longer facing any charges, White gave an interview to a local television station. Her life as a well-intentioned public servant was now defined by a mug shot, she said. She lost income from being suspended without pay after she was charged. Her engagement fell apart. "I'm not that officer that was seen on TV," she said. "It's not like I'm from somewhere else and came to Baltimore. This is home." White expressed sympathy for Gray's loss of life. Asked if she would do anything differently, she answered with a characteristically succinct "no."[28]

CHAPTER 9

ROUGH RIDE

BPD WAITED UNTIL APRIL 20, the day after Freddie Gray died, to reveal information it had withheld from the public for the previous week, including the knife arrest and the van's journey that morning. Officials held a grander-than-usual press conference as national media began to arrive in Baltimore, with speeches by Baltimore Mayor Stephanie Rawlings-Blake and BPD Commissioner Anthony Batts. It was during this press conference that officials established a new way of talking about the Gray case, shifting attention from whatever happened at Gilmor Homes during Stops 1 and 2, to the rest of the van's journey, as well as setting the stage for the case to be an unsolvable mystery.

Mayor Rawlings-Blake spoke first. The Black daughter of a state delegate, she was Baltimore City Council president when her predecessor as mayor, Sheila Dixon, was found guilty of fraudulent misappropriation of gift cards. Dixon resigned, and Rawlings-Blake took over and then won the 2011 mayoral election. Her star rose on the national stage during her first three years in office. She became the secretary of the Democratic National Committee, visited the White House to discuss urban affairs, and made appearances on TV news talk shows. Meanwhile, in Baltimore, she closed more than twenty public recreation centers, citing budget concerns, while increasing police spending. BPD's budget soared by more than $120 million while she was mayor. Spending on police overtime and other public safety also increased significantly.

Rawlings-Blake often had a dry, robotic manner when reading from scripts at press conferences. She injected a bit more dynamism into her speech on the morning after Gray's death. "I understand the community's frustration," she said. "I'm angry that we are here again, that we have had to tell another mother that their child is dead." She expressed her own desire for answers to the mystery of Gray's death. "I wanna know if the proper procedures were followed. I wanna know what steps need to be taken for accountability."

Commissioner Batts spoke next. He was appointed in 2012 after leading police departments in Long Beach and Oakland, California. He called himself a "reform commissioner."[1] Batts announced that BPD would put together a task force to investigate Gray's death, made up of investigators from various internal departments including homicide, accident reconstruction, the crime lab, training, and more. He promised the investigation would conclude in two weeks, on Friday, May 1, and then he would turn over the case to Mosby's office. "We guarantee transparency and, as the mayor said, we guarantee accountability."

Putting investigators on the spot to solve a homicide case in two weeks and then shifting the case to another department is not how traditional law enforcement works. Detective Lakishna Lewis, who was part of the task force, says, "You can't say when we're going to finish our investigation. I was heated about that." She describes the investigators feeling "rushed" and says she never experienced that kind of a deadline before in her career, unless it was related to a policy or statute of limitations. "You don't know when my evidence is coming back. You don't know when I'm gonna find my witnesses," she says. Lewis assumes the deadline was an effort to manage the growing protests.[2] Batts earned the nickname "Hurricane Batts" inside the department for the chaos he introduced.

Finally, Deputy Commissioner Rodriguez spoke. He had been brought over from the Los Angeles Police Department to lead Batts's new Bureau of Professional Standards and Accountability. He oversaw the FIT investigation that had been going on for the prior week. This was already BPD's seventh press conference addressing police force concerns in the prior six months. By April 2015, Baltimore locals were accustomed to the dance officials performed when someone was harmed in custody—the solemn statements of concern, the promises of independent investigations, the subtle smearing of victims—but this time the country was watching. "I want to make this very clear," Rodriguez told the audience on April 20. "We go wherever the facts, wherever the evidence take us." Rodriguez had announced his retirement five days before this press conference, and he left four days after. The leadership of the case shifted to Deputy Commissioner Kevin Davis, who oversaw criminal investigations.

Rodriguez shared for the first time the rest of the van's known stops except Stop 3, which still wasn't known. The public had already learned about Stops 1 and 2, generally, as well as that a medic was called to the Western District police station around forty-five minutes later. Rodriguez filled in the long gap in time with a trip to Central Booking and a summary of Stops 4 and 5. He offered some time stamps along the journey and played CCTV video from Gilmor Homes, which didn't show anything remarkable.

The effect of the press conference was to flood the public with platitudes and data but no apparent answers. "What we don't have at this point is how Mr. Gray sustained those injuries," Rodriguez said. Officials seemed to know so much, just not the one thing that mattered. But while officials insisted Gray's cause of death was still a mystery, they were already making some early determinations of blame. Batts described the arresting officers as appearing calm on video and not using force. Rodriguez also denied any evidence of force, even any "statements" describing force. By that point, Kevin Moore,

Jamel Baker, Sierria Warren, Brandon Ross, and Kiona Craddock had given taped statements describing excessive force in similar ways. As the press conference wore on, the subtext became more explicit: "I know that when Mr. Gray was placed inside that van, he was able to talk, he was upset. And when Mr. Gray was taken out of that van, he could not talk, and he could not breathe," Rodriguez said. It was a framing of events that ignored what happened at Stop 2. Gray was placed inside the van more than once.

In case Rodriguez hadn't made the point clearly enough, Mayor Rawlings-Blake stepped forward toward the end of the press conference to interrupt Batts, who was in the middle of discussing future plans to require body cameras. She interjected:

> *I just want to add to that that it's clear that what happened happened inside the van. And it's—we don't have any procedure that would have an officer riding in the back of the van with the suspect. So even if the officers had body cameras, it would not cover that period of time.*

It was a defining moment in the Gray case. BPD hadn't yet interviewed the four backup officers, the medics, or many eyewitnesses. The medical examiner hadn't made a determination of the cause and manner of death. Still, city and police leaders were already pushing an agenda about what happened to Gray—in the van, out of sight of any people or cameras.

Two days later, FOP Attorney Michael Davey gave a press conference at which he emphasized the same message: "Our position is, something happened in that van, we just don't know what," he said. "What we don't know and what we are hoping the investigation will tell us is what happened in the back of the van."

Davey's statement on April 22 kicked off a wave of speculative stories about "rough rides," a practice in which drivers abuse prisoners as punishment for being difficult. Baltimore had some history of prisoners paralyzed or killed in this manner, including Dondi Johnson Sr., whose family won a jury award of $7.4 million in 2010. Even though none of the city leaders used the phrase "rough ride" in their press conferences, the rough ride theory of Gray's death appeared in headline stories in the *Daily Beast, Chicago Tribune, New York Times, Atlantic, Buzzfeed*, NBC, and many other outlets.

In an April 24 press conference, Batts said, "We know he was not buckled in the transportation wagon as he should have been—no excuses for that, period. We know our employees failed to get him medical attention in a timely manner multiple times."

These press conferences provided the blueprint for Mosby's charges announced on May 1 and influenced media coverage. News outlets eventually stopped reporting seriously on witness accounts of force at Stops 1 and 2. Both police and prosecutors agreed that whatever happened at Gilmor Homes was irrelevant to Gray's death, and they were on opposing sides of the case. With the facts of the case now being defined within parameters set by the two chief adversaries in the evolving public drama, other possible explanations for Gray's injuries steadily left the media conversation.

* * *

During the April 20 press conference, Batts and Rawlings-Blake begged the media to report responsibly and be careful of rumors. Yet in the following weeks, neither expressed any concern about the speculative rough ride stories, which put the focus on the van driver.

Behind the scenes, Officer Goodson was an early and consistent target of the police investigation. On April 16, investigators delivered to SAO a case book containing evidence titled "Officer C. Goodson." This was the Freddie Gray case file, and it focused on Goodson. (The case book was renamed "Freddie Gray" when the task force took over.) Goodson's refusal to give an initial statement may have hurt him, though he may well have had an inkling of what was to come. Van drivers are understood to be the custodians of the prisoners in their care.

Early on, officials and investigators tried to put everything on Goodson. FIT sent a 24 Hour Report memo up the chain of command. It attributed the decision to pull over at Stop 2 to Goodson, even though all of the officers reported it as Rice's decision. Shadowy stories circulated implying Goodson's general culpability. Both Porter and FIT Detective Anderson reported hearing Goodson say, on April 12, "Things like this only happen when someone is working overtime."[3] Investigators made note of this statement and of the fact that Goodson was the only officer working overtime, as if the statement were a confession.

A story leaked to the media that Goodson got in trouble once for losing a patient in the hospital, which was his most serious sustained IAD complaint. Notably, it was reported just one day after Rice's issues with his ex-girlfriend first appeared in the *Guardian*.[4] In fact, Goodson's internal disciplinary file contained only seven complaints over sixteen years, about half as many as Miller acquired over three years.

Officials put a public target on Goodson's back when they unanimously agreed that Gray's injury "happened in the van." Commissioner Batts was explicitly interested in focusing blame on Goodson. On April 23, in front of a *Baltimore Sun* reporter, he revealed that Goodson was the one officer who hadn't given a statement. The FOP had already told the public that there was one holdout. Batts asked his commanders why they couldn't force Goodson to speak. He said only two people knew what happened to Gray: "It's him and the victim."[5]

There was a performative quality to some of the investigation's focus on Goodson. On April 28, investigators executed a search-and-seizure warrant at his home and on his locker at the police station. The *Baltimore Sun* was invited to videotape the search of Goodson's locker and added the footage to a big story on the investigation.[6]

On April 30, Deputy Commissioner Davis announced a single discovery from the two-week task force investigation: Goodson's unreported stop at Fremont and Mosher, or Stop 3.[7] The media didn't entirely know what to make of this anticlimactic revelation. The van previously had made five confusing stops, and now it had made a sixth. The officers on the text chain weren't confused, though: "They're going to try to turn it into this rough ride thing," Porter texted his colleagues on April 30.

The security footage of Stop 3 was hardly the task force's only finding in the case, and it was barely mentioned in the case files. Investigators also learned, for instance, what witnesses saw and heard at Stops 1 and 2. Yet Stop 3 was chosen as the only result BPD shared publicly from the investigation. It paved the way for Mosby to charge Goodson with murder the next day.

Goodson's family members knew where this was going, so they kicked off their own media campaign. His loved ones appeared in multiple news stories, their identities sometimes shrouded. They put the blame on the arresting officers and acknowledged racism in the department.[8] One of Goodson's family members gave an interview to the *Daily Mail*, describing him as a family man, "haunted by images of the dying prisoner," and "crying uncontrollably."[9]

* * *

By the end of April, BPD's official timeline of Gray's arrest became media canon, contributing to acceptance of the police narrative. Media outlets began printing timelines and maps of the van's reported route uncritically. Not everyone bought it, though. "They wanted to find another way to cover up what they had done," witness Harold Perry says. "They came up with a solution that kept him in that wagon moving him around."

BPD did not provide independent verification for every part of the six-stop journey, which should have prompted journalists to examine the police account skeptically. There is a gap of evidence to support what really happened between Stops 3 and 5 in particular, a gap of about thirteen minutes. BPD insisted that, in departing Stop 2, the van was heading to Central Booking to have Gray booked for a crime and that Goodson met up with Porter to check on Gray at Stop 4. There is as much evidence to contradict as to support this part of BPD's story.

That Goodson was bringing Gray to Central Booking after Stop 2 was important to the official six-stop narrative. It explained the van's journey east, and it gave the impression that Gray wasn't severely injured yet at Gilmor Homes. The journey to Central Booking was so foundational to the official story that the *Baltimore Sun* gave it a separate slide in an interactive slideshow of the stops.[10] The public never learned about the missing toe tag and band or the officers' statements and other evidence suggesting that Gray's arrest wasn't so clear-cut.

Goodson did announce on the radio that he was headed to Central Booking as he left Stop 2, but he took a long time to get there. He added about four to five minutes to that journey by taking side streets that cut at angles. A couple of the backup officers mentioned this in their statements. Then, for about eight minutes, he was reportedly delayed at Druid Hill and Dolphin, or Stop 4, only about a mile from Central Booking. BPD said Goodson waited several minutes for Porter to meet up with him to check on Gray. That alone was an unusual choice: Goodson told internal affairs investigators he had never made such a stop before in his career.[11] Also, Central Booking has medical staff that can check out prisoners.

Goodson was nearly at his reported destination when he turned around to pick up Donta Allen at Penn North. BPD said there was just one van working the district that day, so the bike officers had to call Goodson immediately for their second arrest. Yet police also had available to them what are known as "cage cars," which are police cars outfitted to safely transport prisoners in the back seat. In court, Police Academy instructor John Bilheimer testified about cage cars being a routine way to transport prisoners.[12] He also said prisoners could be transported in regular police cars provided that two officers rode with them.

As for Stop 4, there was no evidence to confirm that Porter met up with Goodson except the dispatch calls framing their meeting, which were played during the trials. Goodson requested a prisoner check at 9:00 a.m. at Druid Hill and Dolphin. Porter responded he was on his way. Then, at 9:07, Lieutenant Rice requested backup and a wagon on North Avenue. Goodson responded quickly, "I'm gonna turn around, coming up there." About thirty seconds later, Porter responded, "Okay, I'm coming behind 91," meaning Goodson. It sounded like Porter was following Goodson from Stop 4 to Stop 5.

If that was the case, he must have flown there. CCTV shows Porter's car arriving at Stop 5 by 9:09 a.m., two minutes before Goodson got there, even though Goodson drove with lights and sirens on. (That was, incidentally, a policy violation with a prisoner on board.) Porter also took a longer and less direct route than Goodson to get to Stop 5, arriving on North Avenue from Carey Street, a curvy street to the west of where the van parked. Did Porter lie on the radio about "coming behind" Goodson from Stop 4 to Stop 5? In his statements and court testimony, he was inconsistent as to whether he followed right behind Goodson or left Stop 4 before Goodson closed the van doors. Was Porter even at Stop 4? If so, it couldn't have been for long. Goodson told investigators he waited several minutes for Porter to arrive.

The dispatch radio calls framing Stop 4 are further suspect because, by the time the officers got on the air, they were already having unrecorded conversations on their cell phones, in violation of BPD's communications policy.[13] Rice called Porter twice at 8:57, before Goodson's call for a prisoner check. Nero called Goodson at 9:04, and Goodson called Nero at 9:06, both during Stop 4. The officers were supposedly handling separate cases after Stop 2.

The narrative of Stop 4 is particularly shaky when it comes to the video evidence. The intersection of Druid Hill and Dolphin is in the middle of McCulloh Homes, a public housing development. Like Gilmor Homes, McCulloh is filled with cameras. There are twenty-four CCTV cameras within a couple of blocks of the Stop 4 intersection and five cameras right on that block. BPD released footage from only one of those five cameras. Stop 4 is at one of the most highly surveilled intersections in Baltimore, yet BPD couldn't produce one video of the van or a police car parked at the scene.

BPD did share two videos showing an unidentified white police van approaching Stop 4 at 9:00, heading south on Druid Hill, and two more videos showing the van around the corner from Stop 4 eight minutes later, headed north. Those could have been Goodson. One of the first videos also shows an unidentified police car, with lights and sirens on, heading south on Druid Hill toward Stop 4 three minutes after the van. If that was Porter's car, it didn't appear in any other videos around Stop 4.[14]

It was always odd that Porter would be the one to respond to Goodson's call for backup, given that his sector was around Gilmor Homes, at the northern end of the district. There were other Western District officers posted closer to Stop 4. Officer Novak was also nearby. He told FIT detectives that, after Stop 2, he went to get gas at Front Street and drop off some reports to BPD headquarters. Both are in the Central District, about a mile southeast of Stop 4.

In fact, Novak seemingly disappeared for more than twenty minutes, just as he had gotten in trouble with IAD for doing the day before. He left Stop 2 at 8:52 and reappeared at the police station at around 9:20. Before his disappearance, Novak had diligently updated the dispatcher with his every move. After Stop 2, he didn't even let the dispatcher know he was going downtown.

Novak popped up briefly on the radio during his absence. At 9:10, Nero radioed Novak directly, asking him to provide backup on North Avenue to help with Allen's arrest. Novak responded, "10-4, coming from downtown," but he didn't end up going to Stop 5. He also didn't tell the dispatcher that he had decided against it.

Novak explained what happened during his absence when he spoke to internal affairs investigators in 2016. He said he was getting gas that whole time and never even made it to BPD headquarters to drop off paperwork. Novak told investigators he was still "at the pumps" when he got a call from Nero on his cell phone at 9:13, three minutes after the backup request. He said Nero asked him to debrief Allen at the police station—another conversation that, by policy, should have happened over the radio. Novak headed to the police station, neglecting once again to tell the dispatcher his destination.[15]

There are many possibilities for what really happened between the van leaving Gilmor Homes after Stop 2 and picking up Allen at Stop 5. Goodson, Porter, and Novak could have been anywhere. The evidence is partial and inconclusive, and the officers' actions and statements about what they did during that interval raise questions.

BPD had a special interest in promoting the story of a nearly eight-minute Stop 4. It provided an explanation for why Goodson never made it to Central Booking and would have bought the officers time after Stop 2. In their statements, most of the officers mentioned hearing about the stop and its location on the radio. During Nero's FIT statement, Detective Michael Boyd asked, "You said you heard on the air at some point Goodson had to stop the wagon?" But up until that point in his statement, Nero hadn't mentioned Goodson stopping; it was Detective Boyd who brought it up out of nowhere.

"Yeah," Nero replied. "I think he said Druid Hill and Dolphin. He just wanted to make sure the prisoner was okay because he continued just flailing around."

Further complicating the canonical six-stop narrative is Ross's statement about seeing the van behind the police station after Stop 2. He told detectives the same thing he told a reporter on April 19: "On Sunday, we came down here and knocked on this door round like nine o'clock. They pulled off around 8:49. That wagon was in there. Why didn't anyone come to the door when we was banging on the door, kicking on the door?"[16] Is it possible that the van just went back to the police station after Stop 2 and stayed there for a while? It's possible. None of the evidence of the van's journey east is that conclusive. It is just seconds of footage of a white van in another district.

* * *

The media might not have asked hard questions about the van's route, but the task force investigators, who took over from FIT after Gray's death, were questioning it. A map of the van's route that appears in the case files shows a different path after Stop 3, one that was never discussed publicly. Investigators theorized that Goodson was driving to the hospital. The map includes a mixture of solid lines for the van's confirmed path and dashed lines for what it calls the van's "most likely course of travel." A dashed line sends the van hypothetically through Stop 4 and then southwest, out of frame, before turning it around. There's a note: "Most likely course of travel of Wagon after Dolphin on Druid Hill Avenue to Bon Secours MLK to Baltimore." Bon Secours is the hospital where Western District cops generally brought prisoners who needed medical attention, though it wasn't the closest hospital to Stop 4.

If Goodson was on the way to the hospital, then he would have been doing exactly what prosecutors claimed he refused to do: pursuing medical help for Gray before being summoned back to North Avenue by his supervisor. For this trip to be possible in thirteen minutes, though, the map sends Goodson right through Stop 4 without stopping. The task force was so serious about finding evidence that Goodson was on the way to Bon Secours that investigators canvassed for security footage along the presumed route. The files don't show any recovered footage of the van near the hospital.

The task force route map doesn't by itself explain what actually happened after the van left Gilmor Homes. Neither does BPD's official public account. What the map does make clear is that the van's route wasn't firmly established within the department during the last two weeks of April. The actual route was a mystery to investigators too—or a work in progress.

* * *

While the van's journey was still being worked out internally in BPD, the public story solidified. All of a sudden, just after Gray's death on April 19, multiple city leaders were expressing the same idea before the investigation was half completed. BPD leaders, FOP representatives, and the mayor jointly insisted it "happened in the van," while insinuating Goodson was to blame.

At the same time, SAO was quietly playing a major role in shifting the focus away from the bike cops and any questions of excessive police force at Gilmor Homes. The first explicit mention in any case materials of the idea that Goodson drove roughly *on purpose* appears in notes handwritten by Chief Deputy State's Attorney Schatzow during meetings right after Gray died.[17] Schatzow was number two in Mosby's office and co-prosecuted the case in court.

Schatzow's notes about a rough ride appear within the context of multiple conversations discussing a settlement for the Gray family. First, indicating "potential litigation," Schatzow mentions calling Gary Nilson, who was the city solicitor. From 2011 to 2015, the city solicitor's office paid about $5.7 million to more than one hundred victims of police brutality or civil rights violations.

Schatzow notes an "initial mtg," undated, with "Billy and Hassan to discuss a framework for restitution." That would have been William H. "Billy" Murphy and his partner (and son), Hassan, who were representing the Gray family in any civil action. "Didn't get to #s," Schatzow writes, "did discuss ground rules, approach." The ground rules were a likely reference to the gag orders that infamously went along with city settlements in police brutality and other cases in Baltimore. The gag orders usually forbid anyone who accepted settlement money to speak out about the case. The practice of buying the silence of police brutality victims and their families in Baltimore finally ended in 2020.

Schatzow made a list of things still needed to finalize a settlement, which was extensive: the "entire police report," "entire SAO investigative report," and the "ME medical examiner's report." He also listed some historical topics for research, including brutality settlements and "prior comas in vans."

The next page of Schatzow's notes record a meeting dated April 21 attended by himself, Mosby, Deputy State's Attorney Janice Bledsoe, Billy Murphy, and Zach McDaniels, who was assisting Murphy's firm with public relations. "Pinballing, tossing, tossing the salad," Schatzow writes, "subject prisoner to worst kind of jostling." It sounded like a description of a rough ride, aside from the reference to a sexual act ("tossing the salad"). Even in court, Schatzow had a tendency toward malapropisms. SAO seemed to have the rough ride story before knowing what evidence had been collected: "Any DNA done of inside of vehicle?" Schatzow asks. "GPS analysis?"

The "tossing the salad" meeting notes contain an obscure but telling reference: "Don Giblin—Hubbard—brought in all 23 witnesses to tank a case." Giblin was the chief homicide prosecutor in SAO. Larry Hubbard Jr. was shot and killed while in the custody of two BPD officers in 1999. BPD tried to exonerate the officers, claiming Hubbard fell on an officer and tried to grab his gun. But witnesses came forward describing an unprovoked shooting of someone begging for his life. The witnesses "tanked" the case by telling the truth of what they saw. The Gray case also involved a large number of witnesses who could "tank" any framing of his death around a rough ride.

SAO's meetings with Murphy are notable beyond the discussion points. It is surprising that these two parties were acting so cooperatively, especially early on. Joshua Insley is an attorney in Baltimore who handles police brutality and other civil liability cases, including many of the cases resulting from the notorious Gun Trace Task Force scandal. He sees a conflict of interest in involving prosecutors in a civil case. "I have never had a state's attorney involved at any level, at any time, in settling or even negotiating a brutality case. As far as I am concerned, at most they are potential witnesses to any documents the cops may have filed or anything they said to the prosecutors about the case."[18]

It is likewise surprising that prosecutors were so concerned with civil liability, which is outside of their usual domain, especially before they had investigated the case criminally. One explanation for why Schatzow was so involved in the settlement may be the benefit to city officials of having the family commit to "ground rules," or a gag order. Both Gray's family and Billy Murphy were speaking out ardently right after he died, galvanizing the public against the police. "The officers who did this need to be arrested now, locked in jail, and

charged with murder," Gray's sister Carolina said. "And this all needs
to be investigated by separate police. How can Baltimore police look
into their own?"[19]

Murphy's firm issued a press release on April 19: "We believe the
police are keeping the circumstances of Freddie's death secret until they
develop a version of events that will absolve them of all responsibility."[20] Murphy appeared on CNN on April 20, stating, "The witnesses'
stories, at this point, are not as critical as the video, which will show
everything." He also said he had information not widely known.[21]

Both Murphy and Gray's family effectively went silent after the
April 21 settlement discussion. The next time Gray's family spoke
out, Freddie's twin sister Fredericka was standing beside the mayor
asking for the demonstrations to remain peaceful after a riot downtown on April 25: "My family wants to say, can you all please, please
stop the violence? Freddie Gray would not want this."[22] A $6.4 mil-
lion settlement for the Gray family was worked out that summer and
announced on September 8 by the city. The city solicitor's request for
that amount mentioned "complex and hotly disputed" facts without
acknowledging specific liability.[23]

Billy Murphy's involvement in the Gray case was controversial.
A former judge and legendary figure in local politics, he appeared
as himself in the last season of *The Wire*. His "personal and professional" relationship with Mosby was mentioned in a defense motion
demanding she recuse herself from prosecuting the case based on
conflicts of interest. Murphy was previously Mosby's own attorney. In October 2014, he represented her against a claim before the
Attorney Grievance Commission of Maryland. He supported her
election for State's Attorney and was also part of her transition team
after she won.

Murphy spoke positively of Mosby soon after Gray's death. "Well,
we're enthusiastic about the new prosecutor. She's newly elected and
she comes to the office with a belief in the integrity of these kinds

of investigations," he said.[24] After he met with SAO on April 21, he mostly stopped discussing the case itself, but he continued speaking highly of Mosby. After her third trial with no convictions, he referred to her as "one of the most courageous prosecutors in the United States."[25]

Of all of the people attending these settlement meetings, Murphy's firm stood to profit the most from a favorable agreement. By working with Murphy, Gray's family obtained one of the largest pretrial police brutality settlements in history. Yet the family also tied the fate of justice for its loved one to Mosby and her political goals.

It is common to hear unease about the settlement among Gray's friends and neighbors. "They hadn't even started the case or find out if anybody's guilty or innocent, and they gonna offer money?" Alethea Booze says. "They bought things off right there. They gave that money up so fast!"[26]

Before he died, Booze's brother Tobias Sellers expressed a similar sentiment. "Billy Murphy should have gotten the witnesses before any money was exchanged, so they could put the officers away," he told *Undisclosed*.[27]

Sierria Warren took the way the settlement and criminal trials unfolded personally. "I just felt that me and my young activism was used for nothing, because no justice ever was served," she says. "We out there protesting. 'No justice, no peace.' Our feet hurt. We thirsty. We doing that because he our friend. We're not trying to get anything. We're just trying to get justice for that man," she says. At the same time, she has sympathy for Gray's mother. "She wants something out the deal for you killing her son."[28]

Asked about Billy Murphy, Kevin Moore spits out the words "rat snake" with anger. "I felt like he was just in it for the money. I don't feel like he cared about them people," he says. He recalled meeting the attorney in person. "Our conversation didn't last long at all. He barely wanted to hear what I had to say."[29]

* * *

Schatzow's notes suggest that finalizing the settlement was related in some way to the rough ride theory. But who initially came up with the idea that Gray's injury "happened in the van"? Within a day of Gray's death, there was extraordinary coordination across BPD, FOP, SAO, and City Hall around some kind of a rough ride, whether purposeful or accidental. At the same time, officials from each of these agencies took active measures to turn attention away from civilian witness statements.

Whoever its original architect, the rough ride theory proved extremely convenient to city leaders. It gave the public someone to blame without implicating almost the entire Western District squad. Goodson was Black, which offered a seemingly self-evident response to protesters crying racism, as if racism is never implemented by non-white enforcers.

Still, BPD was not aligned from the top down in letting Goodson take the fall. As the department shared Stop 3 as the official result of the task force investigation, unofficial stories were being leaked to the media. One of those was the idea that Gray's injury was self-inflicted.

CHAPTER 10

CONFIDENTIAL INFORMANT

TOWARD THE END OF APRIL, speculation in the news about what could have happened to Freddie Gray was supplanted by coverage of the massive demonstrations in Baltimore, beginning on April 23 and culminating in major riots on April 27. While the city was under a curfew, on the evening of April 29, a story popped up that brought back questions about how Gray was killed. For the next twenty-four hours, the news cycle was dominated by the account of Donta Allen, the man who rode in the van between Stops 5 and 6 while separated from Gray by a metal partition and who may or may not have heard Gray banging his head.

Behind the scenes, Allen's story was important because it marked where prosecutors diverged from BPD's recitation of the facts. BPD insisted the van's fifth stop, to pick up Allen, was unrelated to what happened to Gray. But prosecutors believed Gray was already injured by that point and suggested that Allen's arrest was a part of a conspiracy to cover it up.

As always, most of the witnesses to Gray's arrest already knew. "Everything was a setup," Kevin Moore says. "They was trying to cover their asses from the shit that they did. It was no reason to go looking around and try to lock somebody else up or try to go to another site when you got a man bleeding into the back of your fucking paddy wagon. It's no need to or reason that you wouldn't go straight to the precinct to try to get this man some help."[1]

* * *

For the thirteen or so minutes that Goodson was on his reported journey east toward Central Booking, from 8:54 to 9:07 a.m., the three bike cops were involved in their own business back on North Avenue, where they had started that morning. They called it "proactive policing." On CCTV video, the bike cops are seen circling the commercial block around the Penn North metro station. They stop to talk to a group of people in front of A & Z Grocery Store, a convenience store. The video rotates away from the block. When it rotates back a minute later, the bike officers are arresting Allen in front of the store at 9:06 a.m.[2]

Miller offered a short description of Stop 5 to FIT detectives: "We stopped another gentleman, which became another scuffle with that gentleman, where we called for a 10-16, other units, and a wagon run."[3]

"10-16, 1600 North," Rice radioed the dispatcher, asking for backup. He sounds breathless, with noise in the background. "And a wagon, and a wagon!" Rice directed some of the backup officers to block foot traffic at Carey Street.

Two CCTV videos of Stop 5, from Citiwatch cameras 727 and 728, offer a relatively clear view of most of the action, except for exactly where the bike cops arrested Allen. Both videos are so blurry over the same one hundred or so feet of the sidewalk that the activity is obscured. That is, footage from two separate cameras, located at two different places, has a nearly unwatchable view of the same specific area. Only the bike cops' yellow shirts are readily discernable through the fog, and the videos do show a lot of fast and aggressive movements while the cops take Allen down.

Miller's brief explanation of Allen's arrest left out a couple of suspicious details captured on the CCTV video. For one, Lieutenant Rice seems to disappear at some point after the van arrives at 9:11 a.m. The van leaves at 9:16, and Rice bikes back to the scene from Carey Street at 9:20.

Also, after arresting Allen, Miller walks down the block for a full minute, staring at the gutter and sometimes bending down to pick up something from it. He told detectives he was busy "picking up some CDS controlled dangerous substances that Allen had thrown." He checks the gutter all the way down at the bus stop at Penn North, about 250 feet from the convenience store.

Officer Wood later told detectives that Allen had thrown drugs into the gutter and they "floated" away. The videos show puddles and water stains on the curb, but in forty minutes of footage, the water doesn't appear to flow in any direction. Miller later submitted marijuana bags and suboxone strips, which the officers claimed to find on Allen's person, to ECU.

In many respects, Stop 5 played out like a repetition of Stop 1: a seemingly rough arrest over a minor infraction, a hunt for evidence after the arrest but nowhere near the prisoner, a disappearing lieutenant, and almost the entire Western District shift showing up as backup.

The first officer to provide backup was Alvarado-Rivera. He parked his car inside the intersection of North Avenue and North Carey Street at 9:08 a.m. and was ordered by Rice to stay on that corner and restrict foot traffic. Someone who looks like an undercover officer also talked to Rice and stood watch on the other side of Carey. Sergeant White and Officers Porter, Wood, and Gladhill arrived over the next few minutes. They all stayed on North Avenue for about ten minutes.

At 9:13, as Sergeant White and the others looked into Gray's side of the van, Nero began pacing in front of the van while on his phone.

He was talking to Officer Novak, reportedly asking him to meet the van at the police station and speak to Allen. Was his call prompted by Sergeant White checking on Gray? Before she arrived on scene, was there another plan for what to do with Gray and Allen?

Goodson then closed the right side of the van and opened the left side. Nero and Miller escorted Allen into that side. BPD's police transport vans are designed with two compartments in the back in order to separate prisoners by gender.[4] Though Allen and Gray were both men, they were put in separate compartments. Novak explained the rationale for this to investigators by saying Gray was "agitating" and "kicking and yelling."[5] Novak wasn't at Stop 5, though. Everyone who did witness Gray at that stop described him as lethargic.

As the van drove away from North Avenue, Goodson radioed he had "two males on board, North and Pennsy, headed to the district." According to the officers' defense attorneys, Gray was fatally injured during those two minutes on the road to the police station, and Allen was the only witness to it.

* * *

The *Washington Post* published a breaking news story on the other prisoner in the van on April 29, originally headlined "Prisoner in Van Said Freddie Gray Was 'Trying to Injure Himself,' Document Says." The *Post* reported that the other prisoner in the van could hear Gray "banging against the walls of the vehicle" and "trying to injure himself." The reporter, Peter Hermann, didn't provide a name for the other prisoner, only that he was a thirty-eight-year-old male in jail for violating a protective order. The prisoner's statement came from an affidavit in a search-and-seizure warrant for clothing belonging to the van driver. Hermann's source was an investigator working on the case. Within a day, most major media outlets had picked up the story.

The very next day, on April 30, two Baltimore TV stations had a breaking news story about the *Washington Post* article from the day before. The other van rider came forward. He was twenty-two, not thirty-eight, and he was angry. He first spoke to WJZ's Mike Schuh:[6]

> *I am Donta Allen. I am the one that was in the van with Freddie Gray. All they did was go straight to the station, but I heard a little banging like he was banging his head. . . . And they trying to make it seem like I told them that Freddie Gray did that to hisself. Why the fuck would he do that to hisself?*

Later that day, Allen spoke to WBAL's Jayne Miller, repeating the same message. "All I heard was like a little banging for like four seconds." He added, "There's no space where a man can hurt himself."[7] A few days later, speaking to CNN's Don Lemon, Allen offered a critical rebuttal to the insinuations in the *Post*: "I know for a fact that he did not hurt hisself," he said. "A man cannot hurt hisself with three fractured bones in his neck, a crushed voice box, a spinal cord messed up, and a broken leg. . . . You probably can hit your head and have a little headache."[8] Allen was repeating some popular rumors about the extent of Gray's injuries; Gray never suffered a broken leg or crushed voice box.

Porter texted his colleagues about Allen's TV interviews: "It's crazy how the news can report false information without ever investigating."

"What he tells the media is one thing, what he was taped saying is another," Miller texted. More than once, the officers suggested they knew the details of Allen's statement to FIT detectives.[9]

After local media broke Allen's identity, the *Washington Post* printed a correction to its article, with a new headline—"Prisoner in Van Heard 'Banging against Walls'"—that no longer suggested Gray tried to harm himself. The media didn't know what to make of

Allen's story or the whiplash of his apparent sudden half retraction, so there was almost no reporting on him again for the next year.

Hermann wasn't wrong in his reporting about the police document. The language in the affidavit was copied and pasted from the FIT 24 Hour Report, that short narrative based on the first-day investigation. "According to Donta Allen," the report states, "during the transport from North/Mount he could hear Mr. Grey [*sic*] banging against the walls of the wagon compartment. Donta Allen went on to say that it is his belief Mr. Grey was intentionally trying to hurt himself." Allen was the only civilian witness mentioned in that report, despite several other interviews conducted that day.

Hermann's reporting in the *Post* demonstrates the intrinsic power of a police story. Once FIT committed the idea that Gray injured himself to paper, it became reproducible. It influenced investigators, the judge who approved the warrant, and the media. It became something Hermann felt he could report, more powerful than a dozen Gilmor Homes witnesses who got very little attention in the *Washington Post*. Yet Hermann's reporting was derived secondhand from a police document that was describing the shakiest of interviews.

* * *

On April 12, at 12:40 p.m., Allen sat down with FIT Detectives Boyd and Poremski for a videotaped interview. He was the first person they interviewed that day, before any of the officers. He was slim and medium height, with short braids in his hair. Boyd took the lead and established rapport. He learned that Allen's nickname was "Twin" and that he had just started a new job at Checkers, was pursuing a GED, and lived with his girlfriend, who was newly pregnant. As with Moore, the detectives chatted with their subject about tattoos. Allen's mood was initially upbeat and cooperative, but he became distracted and impatient during some of the questioning.[10]

"Take me back to that point, and what was going on, you know, without saying what happened beforehand. See what I'm saying?" Boyd asked. Allen wasn't supposed to talk about his own arrest. He was being interviewed as a witness in the Gray case.

Allen jumped right into it: "Well, when I was in the police van, we were just riding, and I heard some—I didn't know somebody was on the other side at first. You know what I mean? But I heard him telling—banging himself," he said. "It sounded like he was banging his head against the metal, like he was trying to knock himself out or something. . . . It sounded like he was crazy. Like he was a crazy man or something. I don't know."

"And you didn't know anyone else was on the other side?" Boyd asked.

"Nobody was in there," Allen said. "I heard banging. I still didn't know if there was somebody in there."

"Was he saying anything when he was banging his head?" Boyd asked.

"No, he was just banging his head," Allen answered. "And I thought it was a fiend, like a dope fiend or something like that." Boyd asked Allen if Gray was banging with a lot of force. Allen responded, "Like a loud bang. . . . It wasn't like he was doing it hard and shit, but he was definitely banging himself in the head. I know he was."

At first, Detective Boyd seemed to be pulling an interrogator's trick of accepting his subject's terms in order to build trust and openness before challenging him. Yet Boyd never broke through that surface layer. He not only went along with Allen's story but reinforced it: "Do you feel like he was trying to knock himself out?" he asked. "He is banging his head and banging his head, and you guys are just continuing down the road, and then he just stops?"

Allen responded, "Mmm-hmm. And then we got there and I realized, I was like, man, he probably knocked himself out. They said he was unconscious."

Allen was unable to answer any other questions about his experience accurately. He said he was on the right side of the van when he was on the left side. He wasn't sure what happened when he got back to the station. He remembered the van ride being smooth apart from riding over some train tracks. There are no train tracks on Mount Street. If there wasn't CCTV video of Allen entering the van at Stop 5, wearing the same clothes he wore during this interview, one might wonder if it really happened at all. Whenever Allen was insecure about what he was saying, he pivoted back to his main point: "But, yeah, he was definitely banging his head. I know he was."

Jeff Noble, a former deputy police chief and author of two books on police accountability, analyzed the transcript of Allen's statement and found fault with Boyd's interview techniques: "There is no clear explanation for how he knew Gray was banging his head if he could not see him," he says. "I would expect much more detailed questioning on these facts as they are so important to the investigation." Noble also pointed out contradictions in Allen's statement that the investigators let slide, including inconsistency about whether the banging was hard or not.[11]

The article in the *Washington Post* didn't misconstrue Allen's statement to investigators. Allen did say Gray was banging his head and trying to injure himself. But by rushing to print based on the affidavit alone, Hermann missed all of the nuance and context from Allen's actual interview. The missing nuance was that Allen wasn't specific or believable in any of his recollections. The missing context was that the "banging his head" story wasn't Allen's unique observation. Lieutenant Rice and Novak were telling investigators and medics the same story on April 12.

Once Allen discovered he was in the van with Freddie Gray, he no longer wanted to be associated with this cover-up and publicly retracted, immediately reducing the power of the *Post's* story. He risked a lot to do this, considering the willingness of some BPD offi-cers to find a charge where one doesn't exist.

* * *

When Deputy Commissioner Kevin Davis discussed the other passenger in the van, in a press conference on April 24, he would reveal only that he was part of an "arrest scenario." His phrasing sounded like overwrought police-speak, but it turned out to be a good description of what happened. As Allen later testified, "They didn't charge me with nothing."[12]

Allen walked away from his interview with FIT detectives a free man on April 12. That evening, the officers handled the paperwork for the arrest "to keep our ducks in a row," Novak told FIT detec-tives, rather bluntly. Novak wasn't involved in arresting Gray or Allen, but he helped his colleagues wrap up their work for the day. Nero requested a CC number from the dispatcher at about 5:00 p.m. and wrote the number on a ticket for a "CDS violation." He checked the box on the ticket for "investigative stop" instead of a criminal or civil citation, essentially documenting contact with Allen rather than an arrest. Miller submitted six marijuana bags and two suboxone strips to ECU under Allen's name that evening.

At some point, Nero typed up a separate incident report on the arrest, which he left undated. It states that Allen left the convenience store without any purchases. The officers apparently found that sus-picious, so they questioned him. Allen told them he bought a loose cigarette, which is illegal. According to Nero's report, Miller then noticed a "bulge" in Allen's front right pocket, and "due to recent crime in the area," the officers concluded he might have a weapon. Allen was ordered to put his hands above his head to submit to a pat-down, during which the officers reportedly discovered the drugs later submitted to ECU.

* * *

In June 2016, after more than a year out of the spotlight, Allen appeared on the stand at Goodson's trial in handcuffs and prison-issued clothing. He was serving ten years for violation of probation. It was his first appearance during these trials. His mood was sullen, angry, and resistant. He was called as a defense witness, but he was reluctant to respond to Goodson's defense attorney, Matthew Fraling. "Mr. Allen, I'd like to direct your attention to April 12, 2015. Were you arrested in Baltimore City on that day?" Fraling asked.

"What day?" Allen asked.

"April 12, 2015," Fraling answered.

Allen mumbled, "I don't recall." Fraling was unable to get a substantive response from Allen to the questions that followed, but he did manage to get the video of Allen's April 12 statement into evidence.[13]

When cross-examined by the prosecutor, Deputy State's Attorney Janice Bledsoe, Allen was suddenly cooperative. He answered all of her questions. He acknowledged his statement from the year before but qualified it, saying he was "guessing" about Gray banging his head. "It wasn't very, very loud, but it was loud enough," he said.

Bledsoe focused next on another conversation Allen had just before his FIT statement. Allen said he was brought into the police station and interviewed by what he described as a "white police officer," elsewhere identified as Officer Novak. That interview wasn't recorded.

"Did you guys have an agreement that he would be called Danny?" Bledsoe asked about Novak, whose real first name is Zachary.

"We had an agreement that he would let me go if I took his number," Allen responded.

"And the code name was Danny if he called you or texted you?" Bledsoe asked.

"That *was* his name," Allen answered, confused. "I thought it was his name."

"Were you on probation for armed robbery at the time you gave that information?" Bledsoe asked. "Were you backing up fifteen years, sixteen years?"

"Seventeen," he answered. By "backing up," Bledsoe meant Allen would face a more serious charge of violation of probation on top of the drug possession charge if he were arrested. Allen had been convicted in 2013 for armed robbery. He received a suspended sentence and three years of probation. Bledsoe seemed to be dancing around some kind of conspiracy claim involving Novak.

Chief Deputy State's Attorney Schatzow laid out the claim explicitly in a hearing before Goodson's trial started. He told Judge Barry Williams he believed Allen had a "motive to fabricate" the statement he gave to police after talking to Novak. "So, in our view, given the . . . fact that he was opining about things that he couldn't possibly tell, he couldn't possibly see, he couldn't possibly know what part of Mr. Gray's anatomy was being used to bang . . . but it sounded remarkably like what some of the officers were saying, we had a suspicion about where he got that story," Schatzow said.[14]

"You believe that Officer Novak told Mr. Allen what to say on April 12?" Williams asked.

"Right," Schatzow replied. "That's what we believe . . . if you ask for my personal belief." As often during this case, the prosecutors' various theories didn't always fit together logically. If Goodson alone caused Gray's death by driving roughly after Stop 2, as they argued, why would the bike cops and Novak have gotten so involved in this cover-up?

* * *

Novak's private meeting or "debrief" with Allen at the police station was a subject of concern inside BPD after Gray's arrest. FIT detectives interviewed Novak about it three different times during April 2015, and his story evolved considerably over those three interviews. At first, on April 12, Novak minimized his conversation with Allen: "I was like, 'Hey, do you know anything to, like, help you, that would be worth tell—calling a detective for?' But it didn't seem like he really knew anything." He told detectives he was asked to debrief Allen because his colleagues were out on bikes and the District Detective Unit, which normally handled debriefs, was on call Sunday morning.

On April 21, Novak was interviewed again about Allen. He provided more details this time. He remembered asking Allen specifically about two recent shootings and gave the addresses for them. "He didn't have anything but said he could be useful because he was outside a lot," Novak said. After that interview, prosecutors began inquiring skeptically about a claim that Allen was a registered confidential informant (CI). They subpoenaed Allen's CI records from the district major.

Novak was interviewed one more time about Allen, on April 27, during which the CI issue came up. This time, he was in a testy mood, without his usual Eddie Haskell mask. Detectives asked if he ever talked to any of the other officers about registering Allen as a CI. "No, not at the time," he said. Minutes later, in the same interview, he was asked the same question and answered, "Yeah, I think I mentioned it to Miller and probably Nero." By the end of the interview, Novak said, "Yeah, we were pretty interested in making him an informant." He described the steps he was beginning to take to register Allen before the Gray situation upset his plans. "Normally, we'd sign you up to make it more official, not just under-the-table kind of CI," he said. In court, Novak used Allen's potential to be a good CI to justify why he needed to be debriefed at the police station while Gray was supposedly sent straight to Central Booking.

Often, Novak came off as so steeped in BPD culture and lingo that he didn't realize he shouldn't share so much. More than once, he was quite open about using Allen's probationary status as a reason to see if he might talk. This was against BPD policy, which states, "Interviewing officers shall not coerce or intimidate an arrestee/informant into responding to any debriefing questions."[15]

Novak revealed a bit more about his relationship with Allen when he testified before the grand jury on May 19. He read through their text messages and turned over his phone to jurors. Novak had saved Allen as a contact on April 12 under the name "Donta Allen Intel By Monday Noon."

The day after Gray's arrest, a Monday, Allen texted Novak at 3:58 p.m.: "Still on it Danny."

Novak replied, "Thanks for checking in."

On April 20, Allen texted, "Danny I'm still trying. Please bare [sic] with me and I got u."

Novak replied, "I trust you—no worries." Prosecutors never asked Novak what intel he was expecting from Allen.

Novak's testimony before the grand jury was offered in exchange for immunity from prosecution, but during the trials he appeared as a regular witness for the defense. During Porter's trial, Bledsoe asked Novak if he recalled talking to Allen about Gray banging his head. "I don't recall any discussion between myself and Mr. Allen regarding anything in the van," he testified.[16]

Novak characteristically changed his mind a year later when he spoke to internal affairs investigators. He *did* talk to Allen about the van ride, he said, but he shared a new and clever twist on their conversation. He explained that the reason he told medics that Gray was banging his head was because Allen gave *him* the idea. "He said something to, like, to the effect of, like, 'He did that shit to himself,'" Novak claimed.[17] It was his sixth interview on Allen—after

three FIT statements, a grand jury appearance, and an examination in
court—but it was the first time he offered this explanation.

* * *

While Novak was being repeatedly questioned about his "debrief"
of Allen, Allen was lying low in Baltimore after his television appearances. Case files show BPD investigators tried to get hold of him
throughout the spring of 2015. They finally got his phone number
from a family member, but he wouldn't speak to them and requested
a lawyer.

Though Allen avoided the police, he did meet with prosecutors.
He was a free man when he met with them on May 7, 2015, but
they had considered charging him with obstruction of justice for
his involvement in the Gray case.[18] The next year, during Goodson's
trial, prosecutors were sanctioned for not disclosing this meeting to
the defense or turning over notes. Deputy State's Attorney Bledsoe
insisted there weren't any notes. Allen was "consistently inconsistent," she claimed.[19]

Allen stayed out of trouble after the meeting with prosecutors. His
probation was due to end on March 18, 2016. Then, his life spiraled
out of control. Lower-level offenses made him guilty of higher-level
offenses, and his witness status may or may not have played a role in
how those cases unfolded.

It started on August 29, 2015, when Allen received a citation from
a Baltimore transit officer for "failure to exhibit payment." The officer
must have run Allen's name in the National Criminal Information
Center database because that same day, an officer filed a fugitive
declaration against him. There was an active warrant against him in
York, Pennsylvania, an hour north of Baltimore, for a check forgery
incident on July 3. On September 2, York County filed its own fugitive declaration against Allen and locked him up in Pennsylvania.[20]

For York County prosecutors to decide Allen was a fugitive from Pennsylvania and not just guilty of check fraud, they had to believe he had purposefully fled the state to avoid charges, even though his residence was in Baltimore.[21]

On December 23, 2015, Allen agreed to a plea deal in the forgery case and was sentenced to three years of probation. That deal didn't clear him of the violation of probation charge he faced in Maryland stemming from the forgery case—the seventeen years he had been "backing up."

Being incarcerated in Pennsylvania, however briefly, appears to have created additional problems for Allen. As part of his probation, Allen was responsible for checking in every six months with BPD's Gun Offender Monitoring Unit. He had been consistently compliant, but he missed his January 2, 2016, check-in, which was just a week after he got out of prison in Pennsylvania. The detectives from the Gun Offender Monitoring Unit tried to locate him, calling various phone numbers and paying a home visit before filing charges. On January 11, 2016, BPD issued an arrest warrant for Allen for "failing to register as a gun offender." He was served with that warrant, together with a warrant for the violation of probation. He found himself back in prison in February 2016.

On May 2, 2016, Allen appeared in court on both charges. His public defender introduced a "global plea agreement," which would give Allen ten years instead of seventeen. The prosecutor handling the case at the time told the judge she wasn't consulted on the agreement, but Allen's attorney said it was approved by someone else at SAO, whom she didn't specify.

Two days after Allen's plea deal was settled, he met with prosecutors in the Gray case, who also happened to be the second and third most powerful people in SAO. A few weeks later, Allen testified in Goodson's trial, where he was cooperative with the prosecution and uncooperative with the defense attorney.

Allen's public defender submitted an application for a "modifica-
tion and/or reduction of sentence" for Allen on May 27. She wrote
that he was twenty-three years old with a seven-year-old daughter
he actively supported. "Petitioner has a long-standing drug problem,
for which he is requesting treatment," she wrote. "Petitioner's efforts
to address his drug addiction were exacerbated by the stress of being
unwillingly placed in the national limelight as a witness to the events
leading to the unfortunate death of Mr. Freddie Gray, on April 19,
2015."

* * *

From media reports, the theory that Gray caused his own death by
banging his head seemed associated with, and limited to, the Donta
Allen story. The public never learned how important that theory
was to BPD's investigation. A plethora of evidence shows that FIT
had initially considered blaming Gray for his own injury. Once the
April 19 autopsy examination revealed there were no contusions to
suggest Gray had banged his head repeatedly, let alone enough to put
himself into a coma, BPD leaders pivoted to a vaguely conceived
rough ride theory. But there were still investigators making notes
about Gray banging his head after the autopsy.

Gray wasn't the first person BPD would accuse of battering his
own head in police custody and causing catastrophic damage. In
1997, Jeffrey Alston's spine was broken in the back of a police van,
and he became a paraplegic. "The officers contended that Alston
freed himself from a seat belt in a police van and repeatedly rammed
his head into a plastic window that separates police from passen-
gers," a *Baltimore Sun* article reported.[22] A trauma surgeon said Alston
didn't have the types of injuries that would result from hitting one's
head. Alston won a $6 million settlement in 2004, which came with
a gag order. BPD admitted no specific fault.

Like Gray, Alston is often included on lists of BPD's rough ride cases. Yet he survived and told his own story. In his lawsuit, he stated he was "handcuffed, put in leg irons, strip searched, put in a head-lock/choke hold, and then thrown headfirst" into a police van.

In the Gray case, Mosby made the point that her charges brought attention to police issues and led to reforms, including the mandatory seat-belting of prisoners. However, city officials failed to reckon with another pattern and practice when they effectively buried the story of what happened to Gray at Stop 2 by not telling the public that numerous witnesses saw Gray thrown headfirst into the van. In lawsuits, case files, and videos from the uprising, there are many stories of prisoners thrown carelessly into police vans in Baltimore. Abdul Salaam was one more. As he told a reporter during a protest for Gray, "On July 1, 2013, I was brutally beaten by Baltimore police officers, thrown in the van, violently thrown on my head, hogtied, handcuffed."[23]

CHAPTER 11

INJURED ARM

OFFICERS NOVAK, PORTER, AND GOODSON stared at an obviously unconscious Freddie Gray in the back of the police van sometime after 9:20 a.m. Sergeant White was standing nearby. None of them had arrested Gray. None of them was in charge that morning. But now they were back at the Western District police station, and there was no place else to go.

The van's last stop at the police station, known as Stop 6, was presented to the public as the least controversial of the stops. In reality, it was a prolonged fiasco. There were delays and issues in getting Gray appropriate medical care, which were later blamed on the dispatcher.

According to Deputy Commissioner Rodriguez, "At approximately 9:24 and 32 seconds is when a medic is called."[1] Goodson announced his arrival at the district at 9:18, and a medic was called six minutes later, police said. The *Baltimore Sun* reported that the medic call happened "within national response standards."[2] Prosecutors apparently had no problem with this version of events and played audio of Novak making the request for a medic in court:

NOVAK: Hi, yes ma'am, can we get a 10-38 [medic] to respond to the district for a, uh, approximately twenty, uh, twenty-year-old number one male Black male. Appears to have lost consciousness.

DISPATCHER: 10-4, 32 [Novak's unit number]. Male uncon-scious at the district.[3]

In the above exchange, the dispatcher sounds clear about an unconscious male at the police station. That type of call would receive the highest priority in the CAD system and result in the immediate dispatch of an ambulance and support personnel. That didn't happen. Instead, what happened over the next fifteen minutes was the fol-lowing: An ambulance showed up back at Stop 5 on North Avenue, where the bike cops were still hanging out. An ambulance eventually responded to the police station, but the medics didn't know Gray was unconscious. The full medical team needed to assist an uncon-scious person didn't show up until after 9:45, twenty-five minutes after Goodson had arrived at the station. And a mysterious patient with an "injured arm" played into all of it.

There are two primary explanations for what happened: Either the dispatcher profoundly messed up to a negligent degree, or police were engaged in another messy cover-up in order to distance them-selves from Gray's injuries—or perhaps run out the clock.

* * *

Officer Novak described Stop 6 to FIT detectives on the afternoon of Gray's arrest. He said he met up with the van and immediately brought Allen into the police station to debrief him. "There was no problems [*sic*]" on Gray's side of the van, he said. "There was no yelling or banging at this point."[4] There were no problems, yelling, or banging, because Gray was unconscious, which Novak soon discovered.

Novak said he checked on Gray at Goodson's request after debrief-ing Allen. Goodson had a different story for internal affairs investiga-tors: "Novak said that Lieutenant Rice wanted Mr. Gray also brought into the station. I guess to sit down or cool off or whatever."[5]

Porter also took credit for checking on Gray: "I opened up the other door," he told FIT detectives, "and I looked in and I called Freddie Gray's name. He doesn't say anything. I pick him up and he looks unconscious. He's not breathing. I call for a medic." Porter and Novak both often presented themselves as proactively helpful in their stories.

After one or all of the officers opened the door to the right side of the van and found Gray unconscious, Novak put on gloves and tried to do a "sternum rub" to wake him up. He then sat him up in what he called a "recovery position," but nothing helped. "So I said let's call for a medic just to be on the safe side," as if one wouldn't always call for a medic for an unconscious person. Unlike Nero, Novak had no background as a medic. Prosecutors gave Novak a hard time during the grand jury for moving Gray's body around without medical training, as well as for speaking about these maneuvers as if they were protocol. He explained that he was trying to do things he'd seen medics do successfully.

Novak was usually a smooth operator, even as his stories constantly evolved, but he showed cracks in his polish when describing Stop 6 to FIT detectives. Handling Gray's unconscious body was his most consequential involvement in the case, but he couldn't remember Gray's position when he was interviewed later that day. "I think his head was facing the door, if I remember right, but I can't say with 100 percent certainty," he said. He said he "flipped him over," prompting Detective Anderson to grill him on Gray's original position. "I don't know," he answered. Novak was far clearer on what happened at the stops where he wasn't present.

According to the audio played during the trials, after several minutes of waiting for a medic, Sergeant White placed a follow-up call to the dispatcher: "Yeah, do you have a medic en route to the district in reference to this person that they have?" she asked. She didn't mention Gray's injury.

"I made the request for the, ah, district," the dispatcher responded. According to BPD's timeline, this call happened at 9:28. By 9:33, despite two reported requests, there still wasn't a medic on the scene. Two fire departments are very close to the Western District station, one only four blocks away. Again, an unconscious person is a highest-priority call.

Asked by FIT detectives how long it took the medics to get to the station, Porter answered, "It seemed like a really long time."[6]

* * *

While all of this was happening at the police station, an ambulance had already arrived back at Stop 5, exactly where the van was before. All three bike cops were still at that location. At 9:21, after Goodson drove the van away from Stop 5, Officer Nero called for an ambulance for a fifty-year-old man with a "possible broken arm . . . unrelated to what we had previously" and "in serious pain." Two minutes later, the fire department dispatched a medic. Nero reportedly made this call just after Sergeant White left Stop 5 and just as Lieutenant Rice returned to the scene.

Officer Miller later told internal affairs investigators that the officers were planning to go out again on bikes after the van left, "but Nero's bike chain popped off," he said. "And while we were standing, a guy just appears. His left arm is broken. He said he fell off his bed, I think."[7] None of the officers mentioned this man in their first-day statements.

On the way to treat the man with the injured arm at Stop 5, the medic got a call from the dispatcher. "If you don't have a patient there, I think police took him to 1034 North Mount Street," which was the Western District police station.[8] For some reason, the fire department dispatcher thought the injured arm call was moved to the police station, despite Nero saying the call was "unrelated to what we had before."

The medic soon responded at North Avenue, around 9:28, parking exactly where the van had been parked at Stop 5. "We're on the scene, patient's still here," he announced. The rotating CCTV camera shows the ambulance parked at Stop 5 for five minutes. A patient doesn't come into view, but Miller climbs out of the back of the ambulance at one point.

Back at the police station, Goodson called Nero on his cell phone at 9:31 a.m., while he and the others were still waiting for a medic. Novak and Porter also took credit for calling the bike cops to let them know about Gray's condition, but only Goodson's phone records show any such call.

A medic finally arrived at the police station around 9:35 a.m., more than ten minutes after Novak's reported call. She came from a mile away. Gray received treatment at the police station for about the next fifteen minutes before being taken to the hospital. He arrived at the hospital around 10:00 a.m., an hour and twenty minutes after he was arrested.[9]

As for the medic who responded to the injured arm call on North Avenue, he announced that he was at the hospital at 9:51 a.m. "My patient just walked away, refusing to go in," he said. "So I guess mark this as a verbal refusal."[10]

BPD never included in the case files anything about the fifty-year-old injured arm patient, whose name is therefore not recorded. BPD has cited medical privacy in refusing to share more detailed records. Although investigators created the impression that the injured arm patient was unrelated to the Gray case, both the fire and police dispatchers seemed to think the same patient was moved from Stop 5 to Stop 6. The police and fire department CAD reports reflect that understanding too.[11] In fact, there was a patient moved from Stop 5 to Stop 6, namely Freddie Gray.

* * *

The medics who treated Gray at the police station also seemed convinced that the injured arm call was related to the Gray case. That's because they showed up to treat an injured arm, not an unconscious person. At 9:30, the fire department dispatcher put out a call: "Medic 43 respond 1034 North Mount Street. Cross street of Moses Street. At the district police station. For an injured arm." So, several minutes apart, fire department dispatchers sent medics to two locations for injured arms. From the available evidence, the police dispatcher repeated "unconscious male" back to Novak and then told the fire department dispatcher about a second injured arm instead, several minutes later.

The paramedic, Angelique Herbert, and the EMT, Thurman White, arrived at the police station at 9:35 expecting to treat someone with an injured arm and found an unconscious patient. Herbert called the dispatcher: "Can I have, um, company here? We've got a non-breathing." Gray was without a pulse. He was given CPR and shocked twice with a defibrillator. His pulse was eventually revived by the time he was treated at the hospital.

Showing up for the wrong kind of injury created several problems for the medics because they weren't prepared with the right equipment, medicine, or supplies. EMT White had to run back to his ambulance to get a backboard and stretcher to move Gray. They also had to call for an emergency medical services (EMS) supervisor and a fire engine truck with additional support staff to maintain chest compressions, intubate Gray, ventilate him, and give him needed medications. It took the dispatcher another five or so minutes to locate an EMS supervisor in service. He was far downtown at the time.

Asked about the medic confusion, Officer Miller told internal affairs investigators that the dispatcher switched up the two calls by mistake. That is, she mixed up the twenty-year-old unconscious male with the fifty-year-old with the injured arm. Yet there was no initial response for an unconscious male at all on the radio, just two medics responding to injured arms.

The issues around the medic calls make far more sense if Novak did not actually call for a medic for an unconscious male at 9:24, as BPD told the public. There is audio of Novak's call, played during the trials, but none of the CAD reports reflect that it happened. The first medic call from the police station isn't logged on the CAD reports until 9:26:51, and the reports don't show who made the request.[12] If Novak had placed his medic call at 9:24, as BPD insisted, then the dispatcher waited more than two minutes to log the high-priority call and also logged it incorrectly, as a patient with an injured arm moved from North Avenue.

As with all of the dispatch audio played in court, there is no way to independently confirm the time stamps. Baltimore fire department dispatchers announce the time at the end of their calls, but BPD dispatchers announce the time only in certain circumstances.

The question of the medic call time was briefly explored by WBAL's Jayne Miller. On April 24, she reported a "mix-up" that caused delays in Gray's treatment, citing unnamed sources and "records the I-Team obtained," meaning her station's investigative team. She wrote, "When that call was dispatched, it was not for that type of injury, an unconscious male, but for a broken arm." Miller also wrote that an officer requested a medic for Gray at 9:26, two minutes later than BPD claimed but more in line with the CAD reports. Other media outlets failed to pick up on Miller's story, though she didn't provide any evidence or name her sources.[13]

The officers themselves gave very mixed messages as to who called for a medic. Novak told FIT detectives, "It's me and Porter and Goodson there, and I think Sergeant White came along a little bit later. She was there at least when we called for the medic."

Porter initially told detectives, "I called for a medic," but he also said in the same interview that Novak "might have" called for a

Rough ride billboard. (Sharyn Blum)

Freddie Gray and Jamel Baker.
(Jamel Baker)

Freddie Gray, Jamel Baker, and Donzell
("Zelly") Canada (deceased June 2016).
(Jamel Baker)

Inside of van that transported Gray. A view of the right side. (Baltimore Police Department, Freddie Gray case file)

A view of the metal partition divding the back of the van into two separate compartments. (Baltimore Police Department, Freddie Gray case file)

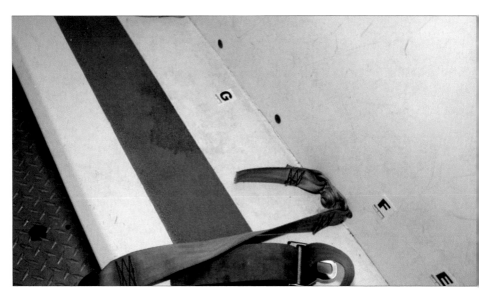

Blood smears identified as belonging to Freddie Gray on bench and seat belt.
(Baltimore Police Department, Freddie Gray case file)

Still image from Stop 1 cell video:
Gray yells, "Get off my arm."
(Videographer Kevin Moore,
with annotation by author)

Still image from Stop 1 cell video: Lieutenant Rice threatens to lock up bystanders at Stop 1,
with Brandon Ross. (Videographer Kevin Moore)

Still image from Stop 2 cell phone video.
(Videographer Brandon Ross)

*Still image from CTTV of Stop 5: Officers check
on Gray.* (CitiWatch camera 728)

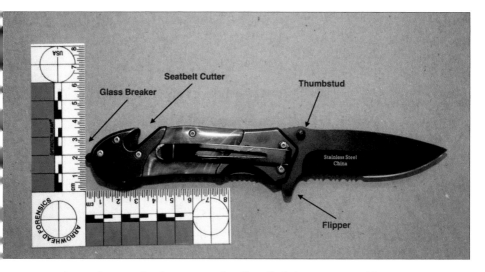

Assisted opener knife, rescue-style, allegedly belonging to Freddie Gray.
(Baltimore Police Department, Freddie Gray case file,
with annotation by author)

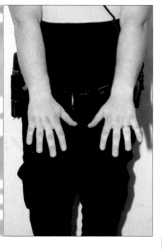

Officer Garrett Miller's hands on the
afternoon of Freddie Gray's arrest.
(Baltimore Police Department,
Freddie Gray case file)

Still image from April 20,
2015, press conference:
Officials whisper about case
evidence. From left:
Commissioner Anthony
Batts, Deputy Commissioner
Jerry Rodriguez, and Mayor
Stephanie Rawlings-Blake.
(Baltimore Police
Department YouTube)

"Purge" flyer.
(Fairness and Accuracy
in Reporting)

Protest at Western District police station, April 24, 2015. (JM Giordano)

Penn-North start of rioting, April 27, 2015:
Young people build a barricade to line of cops. (JM Giordano)

Penn-North start of rioting, April 27, 2015:
Police vehicles on fire. (JM Giordano)

July 27, 2016, press conference at which Marilyn Mosby drops charges against the remaining officers at Stop 1. From left: Marilyn Mosby, standing at the podium; Michael Schatzow; and Janice Bledsoe. (Steve Burns)

Sergeant Alicia White and Officer William Porter, official staff photos. (Baltimore Police Department, Freddie Gray case file)

Caesar Goodson, Crime Scene Unit photo after Gray's arrest. (Baltimore Police Department, Freddie Gray case file)

medic and he might have followed up. On May 5, Porter texted his colleagues, "I'm not trying to go to jail, seeing as though Novak and I rendered medical attention and I called for the medic." Novak didn't challenge his claim.[14]

In her first FIT interview, on April 12, Sergeant White told detectives she got to the station while her colleagues were pulling Gray out of the wagon. She asked if he was breathing and told them to call for a medic if he wasn't. "So then I get on the air and I like—so Novak calls up for a medic," she said, catching herself. "And then I get on the radio, and I'm like, when they—after they said, do you think, you know, is he breathing? So they're all like, I don't know. You know, I can't really tell." In her second interview, on April 17, she was clearer: she said Porter told her they had already called for a medic when she arrived.

BPD's raw, unedited dispatch from the morning would certainly clarify who called for a medic and for what injury, but BPD declined to share it. The CAD reports also show that Lieutenant Rice apparently used the CADAPP mobile system to notify the dispatchers of something at the exact times the two medic requests were logged, to North Avenue at 9:21 and to the police station at 9:26.

Whatever actual requests were made for a medic, case files show BPD investigators put very little effort into sorting it out. Only one BPD investigator, FIT Detective Lakishna Lewis, seemed curious. "You said you got the call for an injured arm," she said to EMT White. "Was there another medic that was also dispatched?"[15]

"There is a closer medic," he replied, meaning the fire department a few blocks from the police station. He couldn't recall another medic being dispatched.

"So there's a closer medic to the police station that could have responded," Lewis said. "The injured arm. Did anyone ever go to that?" He wasn't sure. "Was there ever a call dispatched for a non-breather?" she asked.

"No," he responded.

Years later, Lewis remembers the mix-up as likely the fault of the dispatcher. "This reminds me of Lemony Snicket's *Series of Unfortunate Events*," she says. "It was all these different things just kept happening that, in my opinion, contributed to his death. If any one of those things had been a little different, maybe he would have survived this."[16] If the mix-up all boils down to dispatcher error, then it was a very serious error, leaving an unconscious male untreated. That still wouldn't explain why so many officers couldn't get their stories straight about who requested a medic for Gray.

* * *

The fire department medics who showed up to help Gray did not hide their misgivings about how everything went down. "The only thing I felt was out of the ordinary was we got the call for an injured arm and he was non-breathing," Herbert told FIT detectives. "I mean, that was the biggest joke of the whole case."[17] Her colleagues also shared their honest confusion and dismay.

James Irons was the EMS supervisor who finally made it to the scene after Herbert realized the seriousness of the problem. He was surprised to see "an otherwise healthy twenty-five-year-old man having a cardiac event."[18] He sounded baffled by the whole event and contrasted Gray to the types of unconscious patients he usually sees, with outward signs of injury.

After Gray died, FIT interviewed Herbert, EMT White, Irons, and three other fire department employees who arrived at the police district in a fire truck. Even though the medics were busy trying to save Gray's life—and weren't interviewed until more than a week later—they provided more detailed information about what happened than the officers interviewed on the day of the arrest. Herbert was especially clear and informative in her statement and was a strong witness for the state in court.

The medics told FIT detectives they saw Novak and Porter holding Gray's head as it hung out of the van, faceup, with almost half of his body out of the van and his legs folded under him. If Novak "flipped" Gray into that position, he may have been facedown, in the same position he was put in at Stop 2. For all of the officers' claims of Gray standing, sitting, and kneeling during the van ride, there's ample reason to suspect he stayed facedown on the floor the whole time.

"He was dead," Herbert said, meaning Gray had no pulse. Herbert and White described a little "pinkish" blood coming out of his nose and a little spit around his mouth but nothing to indicate someone punching him in his face. Based on her training, she identified the blood out of the nose as "basal skull fracture" with "some type of trauma." She also noticed that the back of Gray's neck didn't feel firm. "It was almost like a baby," she said. "It was, like, crunchy like." Herbert later testified in court that she could smell fecal matter, which was found in Gray's underwear.

The medics struggled with treating Gray for two reasons. Besides not having the appropriate equipment for an unconscious person, they didn't know what had happened to the patient. "I remember asking several times, you know, 'What happened?'" Herbert said. "And they kept on saying, one said, 'I don't know.' He said, 'I'm not sure. I'm sorry, I'm not sure. But I think he was banging his head up in the paddy wagon.'" She said this statement was made by the white officer on the scene, which was Novak.

Irons, too, emphasized that he tried urgently to "get the story" out of the officers. "They said he had been banging his head against the wall, and that's the only thing they had." The medics ended up treating Gray for both trauma and an overdose.

Herbert remembered one other thing Novak told her: "I was like, 'Man, I can't believe this. What's going on?' He was like, 'All I know is he was complaining of his arm.'" This was something Novak mentioned in his statement to FIT detectives as well; he said Gray was complaining about the handcuffs being too tight. In Moore's cell video of Stop 1, Gray does complain about the handcuffs: "My wrists, yo, my wrists," he says. The handcuffs are "tight as shit," he says.

At one point in Moore's video, as Novak is bending down to pick up Gray off the ground—when his face is almost right next to Gray's face and they make eye contact—Gray says, "Get off my arm. Yo, tell him to get off me." It begs the question: Was Gray the original "injured arm" patient? The media demonstrated that they loved a mystery in the Gray case, but most reporters never learned about this one.

III

INVESTIGATIONS

CHAPTER 12

THE AUTOPSY

DAVID SIMON, THE CREATOR OF HBO's *The Wire*, wrote in a May 2015 blog post on his website about the juking of police stats in Baltimore under former Mayor Martin O'Malley, a storyline on season three of *The Wire*. "Is there anyone still actually willing to believe that Martin O'Malley somehow made violent assaults go down by 30 percent in the same city where murders increased by six percent?" he asked.[1] Simon argued that homicide stats can't be juked. More recently, he summarized the point on Twitter: "No one has figured out how to hide bodies. Homicides are determined by state health department, not local PD; murder rate is a clean stat when all others juked."[2]

Tawanda Jones might beg to differ. Her brother Tyrone West was choked by police officers in 2013, but the state medical examiner (ME) declared his manner of death "undetermined" and his cause of death "Cardiac Arrhythmia due to Cardiac Conduction System Abnormality complicated by Dehydration during Police Restraint."[3] Jones paid to send her brother's body to Texas for an independent autopsy, which determined he died from positional asphyxiation, or choking, as a result of police restraint. Her attorneys later ordered yet another independent autopsy, which produced the same result.[4]

Tyree Woodson's family might also question Simon's faith in homicide numbers. Woodson was found dead from a gunshot wound inside of a police station. The ME ruled it a suicide, even though Woodson was searched for a gun before entering the station. Police claimed he was hiding the gun in a medical boot he was wearing following surgery, though the "boot" was more like a sandal, with less foot coverage than the New Balance sneaker he wore on his other foot.[5] A detective who visited Woodson's mother to share the ME's results wrote in a memo, "She believed the police officers from the Southwestern District killed her son. . . . She believed the ME's Office is working with the Police Department."[6]

It may be harder for police to downgrade crimes resulting in death in order to juke stats, but it can happen, and not just with police killings. Political careers have been made and lost based on the total number of homicides annually in Baltimore. All it takes to downgrade a homicide is to secure an alternate ruling about the manner of death—suicide, natural, accident, or undetermined in most states. Police and politicians play a role in how that can happen. Autopsies carry the sheen of objectivity and science, but in 2011, the National Association of Medical Examiners found that about one in five of its members were pressured by a public official at some point to change a cause or manner of death determination.[7]

Freddie Gray's death was ruled a homicide. The ME's office determined the cause of death to be "acts of omission," namely the police's failure to seat-belt him and call for timely medical help.[8] The homicide ruling by itself seemed favorable to people who sought accountability in Gray's death, yet the trials exposed a seemingly corrupted and haphazard process in arriving at those findings.

The Gray case provides a window into how determination of cause and manner of death is affected by subjective factors. These include what evidence detectives collect, what evidence and information detectives share with the ME, political pressures, and even the passage of time. Gray's body wasn't available for an autopsy until he died, a week after he was fatally injured.

* * *

At 10:02 a.m. on April 12, the University of Maryland Medical System (UMMS) R. Cowley Shock Trauma Center made its first note about Gray upon admission: he was "found unresponsive in the back of a police van," medical staff reported.[9]

For more than twelve hours, Gray's family and loved ones weren't notified that he was hospitalized in a coma, though the police knew his name and had his identification. Tawanda Jones says the same thing happened to her when her brother suddenly went missing. She found out he was killed from a relative watching the news. Police had her brother's wallet and identification too but failed to notify any of his family. Gray's girlfriend, Jamia Speller, told the *Baltimore Sun* that his friends guessed he might be in the hospital when she didn't hear from him late that afternoon. She started calling different hospitals and finally found him at UMMS, where the doctors said his condition was critical.[10]

The next day, a social worker met with Gray's family and made notes: "Parents seem to be high but hopefully understood all the information. Mom and Dad are primary and the girlfriend is a secondary spokesperson. Police were here to ask questions and physicians were not able to speak with them."

Gray underwent a number of tests and scans after he arrived at the hospital. A trauma scan quickly identified that he had suffered cardiac arrest, a "C4–C5 fracture/dislocation with jumped/locked right facet joint," which is a type of broken neck, and a related spinal cord injury. Doctors also identified a contusion behind Gray's left ear with internal bleeding. His other scans were largely normal.

The day after Gray was admitted, he underwent complex spinal surgery. Hospital records show he suffered a serious seizure condition and developed diabetes while in the hospital. He was put into a medically induced coma to control the seizures. For the rest of the week, hospital staff sought to keep Gray stable. The last days of his life are told in hundreds of pages outlining labs, medications, and scans, which indicate swelling up and down his spinal cord and into his brain. On the morning of April 18, Gray's condition worsened. Speller and Gray's mother, Gloria Darden, spent his last night alive by his bedside talking to him. He suffered another cardiac arrest episode, and doctors were unable to revive him. He was pronounced dead on April 19 at 5:59 a.m.

* * *

Gray's fatal injury was identified by trauma staff and later confirmed by the autopsy. "The type of fracture/dislocation documented in imaging studies on admission is a high energy injury most often caused by abrupt deceleration of a rotated head on a hyperflexed neck, such as is seen in shallow water diving incidents," Assistant ME Dr. Carol Allan wrote in the autopsy report. Gray had a unilateral "jumped facet," which happens when a rotated head slams into a surface so hard that it causes one neck vertebrae to jump over another. It is also known as a locked facet because the joint gets "pushed so far forward" that it gets "jammed into the bone below," according to Dr. Morris Marc Soriano, a witness for the state.[11]

Soriano outlined in court all the injuries that happened as a result of the jumped facet, including a torn artery, impinged spinal cord, swelling of the spinal cord, fractures in the C4–C5 bones and joints, and tears in every ligament in the area and "hundreds of little muscles that keep your neck stable." The torn artery prevented blood from going to Gray's brain and supplying oxygen to the damaged spinal cord, which also affected his ability to breathe. Ultimately, what killed Gray was a lack of oxygen to the brain, Soriano explained. The defense's medical witness agreed with most of this description.

Dr. Adam Lipson, a spinal cord expert and neurosurgeon, sees jumped facet injuries frequently in his practice. After looking at Gray's hospital records and autopsy report, he agreed with Soriano's analysis. "Usually you see this from car accidents, and it's usually someone who hits their roof or hits the window with their head flexed," he told *Undisclosed*. "It does take a lot of force to make that occur." If Gray had survived, he would have lived as a quadriplegic.[12]

According to the autopsy, the only external injuries to his scalp were small abrasions on both of his temples. When the ME dissected Gray's scalp, however, she found a "subscalp hematoma on the lateral aspect of the left side of the back of the head just superior to the neck region," or a pool of blood behind the left ear. She concluded this was the point of impact for Gray's jumped facet injury. Dr. Leigh Hlavaty, University of Michigan forensic pathologist and Chief of the Wayne County Medical Examiner's Office, also reviewed the medical records and autopsy for *Undisclosed*. She speculated that the smaller abrasions to the sides of Gray's head were from the cervical collar in the hospital.[13]

Early on, misinformation spread about Gray's specific injuries. Richard Shipley, Gray's stepfather, told reporters on April 13 that his stepson suffered "three or more broken vertebrae." The *Baltimore Sun*, citing Shipley, reported that Gray had "double surgery on three broken vertebrae and an injured voice box."[14]

Billy Murphy, the Gray family's attorney, told CNN on April 20, "He died of an 80 percent severed spinal cord and three broken vertebrae in his neck." He said he learned this from his "own sources."[15]

To this day, it is often incorrectly reported that Gray suffered three broken vertebrae, a crushed voice box, and a nearly severed spinal cord. Gray's medical records indicate he had only one major injury to his cervical spine, the C4–C5 jumped facet. His voice box and the rest of his spine remained "intact." An MRI performed at the hospital did report his spinal cord was 80 percent severed, but Dr. Allan testified otherwise in court. From the surgical autopsy, she discovered that Gray's spinal cord was "anatomically intact," though severely bruised and kinked.[16]

* * *

Gray's body was transferred to the Office of the Chief Medical Examiner for the autopsy examination on the morning of April 19, after he was pronounced dead. On April 20, Dr. Allan met with seven BPD commanders and investigators before performing the autopsy examination. Many of them were newly assigned to the task force and learning the case themselves. They shared with her their understanding of video evidence and statements before watching her perform the exam.

From there, Dr. Allan was tasked with determining the cause and manner of Gray's death, relying in large part on the stories she was told. Todd Oppenheim, a longtime public defender in Baltimore, says it is standard practice for MEs to base their findings on what the police tell or give them. "You would think that they're medical professionals and they're trying to be as unbiased as possible. And that if they're going to take evidence from one side that they might do their own independent investigation and take evidence from the other side, but it doesn't happen," he explains.[17]

In the Gray case, there was the added involvement of prosecutors. On April 23, Dr. Allan met independently with a few prosecutors and her boss, Chief ME David Fowler. Prosecutors gave Dr. Allan the videos filmed by eyewitnesses on their cell phones and "taped witness statements" by the officers. More than once during the trials, Dr. Allan referred to the defendants in the case as "witnesses." She did not mention ever receiving or even hearing about civilian witness statements, besides that of Donta Allen. Dr. Soriano also told the court he reviewed only the statements given by officers.

Dr. Allan attempted to make sense of the warring voices. On April 28, she met with a large group of BPD officers and Deputy State's Attorney Bledsoe. After the meeting, she got to see the actual transport van, which had been going through forensic testing. Two days later, on April 30, she turned over her autopsy report to SAO. One day after that, on May 1, Mosby referred to the autopsy in her speech outlining charges against the officers.

The medical examiner's office originally told CNN that the autopsy report could take up to ninety days. Dr. Allan got it done within nine days. Handwritten notes from SAO's investigation suggests where the pressure likely came from: "Medical Examiner—report won't be done for 60 days but MM wants it done faster."[18]

Porter's defense attorney, Joseph Murtha, asked Dr. Allan about the speed of her findings in court. "Do you recall being told that SAO wanted you to expedite preparing your opinion?"

"Absolutely not," she replied.

"And you're telling the ladies and gentlemen of the jury that no one said, 'Hey we need this before May the 1st?'"

"Absolutely not," she repeated.

There is strong evidence contradicting Dr. Allan: Mosby concluded her May 1 speech by thanking Governor Hogan for "expediting the autopsy report."

Mosby could have filed charges without an autopsy determination, according to Oppenheim. "There is no statute that says you need a doctor to come in and make a ruling that it's a homicide," he says. He discusses how the COVID-19 pandemic especially caused delays in the ME's office while cases proceeded, forcing lawyers to work without autopsy findings. "If you're leaning so heavily on the medical examiner, you probably don't have enough evidence yet," he says.

* * *

Dr. Allan had much less time than usual to complete her autopsy report, but she ended up writing a much longer-than-usual "opinion" section. She confirmed in court that it was the longest opinion she had ever written. Most autopsy reports include sections that deal strictly with the physical evidence and conclude with an opinion, in which the ME or coroner outlines the cause and manner of death. Anthony Anderson was killed by Baltimore police officers in 2012. The opinion section of his autopsy was brief:

> *This 46-year-old, Black male, ANTHONY ANDERSON, died of BLUNT FORCE INJURIES OF TORSO, which caused multiple left-sided rib fractures, left lung contusions, and splenic lacerations, leading to extensive intra-abdominal bleeding. The manner of death is HOMICIDE.*

Many opinion sections are even shorter. Sandra Bland died in a police station in Waller County, TX. The autopsy report's opinion states: "Cause of death: hanging. Manner of death: suicide."

Dr. Allan seemed to redefine the genre in the Gray case, writing a dense, three-page opinion. It begins with Gray being chased by police and recounts the entire six-stop narrative, including many details that have no relationship to his injury. Her story is drawn from various evidence and police statements, but much of it has no source at all. About Stop 1, she writes, "After the inner and outer doors were closed, it is reported Gray could be heard yelling and banging, causing the van to rock." In court, she testified that "every witness statement" confirmed rocking at both Stops 1 and 2. In reality, while Rice, Miller, and Porter mentioned Gray shaking the van at Stop 2, not one of the defendants said that about Stop 1.

Dr. Allan's written opinion also tells a revisionary story about Stop 2, one that prosecutors replicated during the trials: "He was removed from the van and placed on the ground in a kneeling position facing the van door, while ankle cuffs were placed and then slid onto the floor of the van, belly down and head first." Yet according to officers and civilians alike, Gray's ankles were shackled when he was flat on his belly on the ground outside of the wagon. Dr. Allan seemed to be combining what she was told happened at Stop 2—namely that Gray's legs were shackled—with what she saw in Ross's video—Gray's legs hanging out of the back of the van before Nero lifts them into the van. The autopsy report erases a near minute of activity before Ross began filming, during which witnesses saw Gray tased and thrown headfirst into the van.

Dr. Allan's determination of Gray's cause of death relies mostly on what she claims happened at Stop 4: "Reportedly he was asking for help, saying he couldn't breathe, couldn't get up and needed a medic." she writes. The only source for Gray not breathing at Stop 4 was what FIT Detective Teel wrote in her notes after her phone call with Porter. Porter never stated it on the record.

Finally, in the autopsy report and during her testimony in court, Dr. Allan described Gray as "slumped" over and unable to bear his weight at Stop 5, another claim for which there was no source. The officers who checked on Gray at Stop 5, including Porter and White, explicitly described him as "leaning" and *able* to bear his own weight. That Gray kept changing positions at all was a police story without corroboration.

Dr. Allan's opinion statement works toward a conclusion that is explicitly speculative: "Therefore, the time the injury most likely occurred was after the 2nd but before the 4th stop of the van, and possibly before the 3rd stop," she writes. "He would have been hunched over with his neck in a flexed position if he had risen off the floor," she explains. Dr. Allan theorized Gray must have gotten up at some point after Stop 2 based on her own theory of when and how he was killed—thrown forward in the van while it was in motion. Her written opinion is rife with the conditional tense and qualifiers such as "possibly" and "most likely."

While Dr. Allan's homicide ruling benefited prosecutors, giving them the leverage to file charges, her opinion statement left their case vulnerable. Defense attorneys grilled her during all four trials about her speculative findings. "You have no factual basis or information to believe, other than speculation, that Mr. Gray had gotten up from the position he was on the floor. Is that correct?" Murtha asked.

"That is correct," she said.

"Do you have any facts that you can tell the ladies and gentlemen of the jury about—about anything that's documented between Stops 2 and 4 that Freddie Gray moved in any way, any fact, any information, at all?" he asked.

"Other than he was injured, no," she answered. "It's an opinion," she said.

Dr. Allan's responses in court were often soft-spoken and tentative. Sometimes, she mumbled as if talking to herself. The judge had to ask her to speak up several times. She was more confident when responding to Murtha's criticism of her homicide determination. She explained the difference between "volition," or will, which is necessary to an ME's homicide determination, and "intent," which is not.

Dr. Allan referred to the guidelines published by the National Association of Medical Examiners (NAME) as an authority, but the guidelines gave her other options besides homicide for her manner of death determination. NAME prefers that MEs rule a death an "accident" for any motor vehicle fatality, "even if by law the death may be ruled as vehicular homicide." Another option was "undetermined," which might have befitted all of the "likely/possibly" language in her written opinion.[19]

The autopsy's uncertain conclusions aside, a vehicle accident is a common cause of jumped facet injuries. "It's feasible," Dr. Lipson told *Undisclosed*, "but it's unlikely, at that velocity, unless they were doing a forty-mile-an-hour sudden stop or something like that." Goodson's wide turn isn't mentioned in the autopsy report at all.

Dr. Allan arrived at her conclusion within nine days, but notes from detectives suggest she had it sooner. According to Homicide Detective Cory Alston's notes from April 23, "Dr. Allan indicates that the victim sustained his injuries during the time when he was in the prisoner transport vehicle alone. . . . The victim could have been injured as he attempted to stand."[20]

* * *

Dr. Allan seemed to have arrived at a cause of death determination by a process of elimination, hence her discussion of the six stops. She ruled out that Gray was fatally injured at Stop 1 because he "exhibited both verbal and some physical resistance, bearing weight on his legs" and "actively speaking" on Moore's video.

In speaking to *Undisclosed*, Dr. Hlavaty agreed that Gray couldn't have been fatally injured by Officer Miller's restraint technique at Stop 1, even if he put a knee right into Gray's neck, as some witnesses reported. "It simply is just a different or wrong type of force," she said. She offered an alternative scenario for the jumped facet injury occurring during Stop 1: "If he was thrown to the ground and in being thrown to the ground, he's headfirst, like he's diving into a pool, and that is causing his chin to go down and his head to turn." Witness Shawn Washington told detectives he saw an officer just about to do that to Gray at Stop 1 before he left this scene. Dr. Hlavaty still ruled this out, as Gray didn't have abrasions to his head or face from impact with concrete. She suggested Gray's apparent difficulty walking to the van at Stop 1 could have resulted from Miller's prolonged restraint pinching nerves and/or cutting off circulation.

Police and prosecutors used evidence that Gray wasn't *fatally* injured at Stop 1 to argue he wasn't injured at all during his arrest. Yet Dr. Allan didn't examine Gray's body until a week after his arrest. One CSU photo of his body in the hospital, taken on the day of the arrest, shows a fresh and deep gash on Gray's left shoulder about two inches long. It was still bright pink in the hospital hours later. Layers of skin appear missing, as if Gray's shoulder had scraped roughly against pavement. It was described only as a "healing abrasion" in the autopsy report. Another photo shows the two circular marks just below Gray's kneecap, where Moore remembered seeing him tased.

Dr. Allan also ruled out that Gray's fatal injury could have happened at Stop 2. He was "still yelling and shaking the van," she wrote, and "reportedly still verbally and physically active" after being put back inside the van.

"We didn't see or hear no damned van shaking," Moore says. "That's bullshit. That man, he was not moving. . . . Yo, like the whole time. You could hear him complaining about not being able to breathe, up until the second stop."[21]

Stop 2 witness Sierria Warren agrees. "Hell no, and my eyes? I was looking. The van had my full attention at that point, so you know if that was happening, I would've seen it."[22] Jamel Baker also denies seeing the van shake at Stop 2.

When Dr. Lipson first learned about the case and Gray's injuries, he said, "The only way I could see this happening, without a major car accident, is if they shoved him into the van . . . say if his head was tilted or flexed and you pushed someone into a wall, and they don't have use of their hands to protect themselves." Dr. Lipson didn't know yet about the Stop 2 witnesses when he made this statement. He didn't know that Jacqueline Jackson described Gray's head as flexed forward when he was thrown headfirst into the van.

There is no indication Dr. Allan knew about those eyewitnesses either, but the type of injury came up in a conversation. Detective Teel took notes from a meeting in which detectives asked Dr. Allan about different scenarios for how the jumped facet could occur. "No way that this could have happened from lack of air," Teel wrote. "If he was forcefully placed in the van—yes."[23]

* * *

Defense attorneys performed a tricky dance in court, impugning Dr. Allan's credibility without entirely undermining her theory that Gray's injury happened in the van while it was in motion. So the medical debate during all four trials was not about *how* Gray was killed but *when*. Experts agreed that, without oxygen, the brain begins to die within minutes. The question was whether the injury itself caused a lack of oxygen immediately. Defense experts argued that Gray's spinal cord injury was "instantaneous and catastrophic" or "complete," meaning he would have lost oxygen quickly after the jumped facet. Therefore, he must have been accidentally thrown forward at some point between Stops 5 and 6 for him to survive by the time he got to the hospital. The state's primary expert, Dr. Soriano, argued Gray's injury could have been "progressive," meaning he could have been able to speak or move a little if he was already injured at Stop 4.

The defense's theory of a sudden catastrophic injury was undermined by the long delays in medical care. Even if Gray was thrown forward just before Stop 6, he still wouldn't have had appropriate care to restore oxygen intake for nearly twenty minutes.

According to Dr. Lipson, jumped facet injuries can be either progressive or instantaneous, making it hard to judge exactly when Gray stopped breathing. "It's not an all-or-nothing thing," he told *Undisclosed*. He has seen this type of injury lead to loss of life immediately, in fifteen to twenty minutes, or over hours. He did believe Gray's condition was made far worse by not being immobilized as soon as he was injured: "Say you have an acute fracture, the trauma happens, you don't have cervical precautions, you're not in a collar, you're not immobilized, all of the sudden the spine gets gradually a little more unstable and the little function you have progresses or gets lost."

* * *

Gray's autopsy was performed under the leadership of Chief ME Dr. Fowler, who ran the state's medical office for seventeen years, retiring in 2019. He met with Dr. Allan and prosecutors during the Gray investigation. Fowler became a notorious national figure after he retired. He appeared as an expert for the defense in the 2021 trial of Derek Chauvin, the officer who was convicted of murdering George Floyd in Minneapolis. Fowler suggested that Floyd might have died from a combination of a heart condition, intoxicants, and exhaust from a nearby car instead of Chauvin's knee pressing into his neck, as the world saw on a cell phone video. After his testimony, a group of 431 medical doctors and pathologists signed an open letter demanding a review of his prior rulings.

Dr. Fowler was an influential figure in forensic pathology, not just in Maryland. From 2015 to 2016, he was president and then chairman of the board of NAME. He was on the editorial board of several journals, including the *American Journal of Forensic Pathology*. Fowler was also a leading academic promoter of the "excited delirium syndrome" determination for deaths in police custody. He published several articles about it in the late 2000s, around the time that Axon, the company that manufactures Tasers, was funding such studies. The company, formerly known as Taser, was concerned about lawsuits from deaths or severe injuries caused by Tasers.[24] Many of the Stop 2 witnesses described Gray no longer screaming just before he was thrown into the van, after some of them saw or heard him being tased.

Excited delirium syndrome is a controversial cause of death explanation with no clear definition. It is not accepted by the medical establishment as an actual condition.[25] It emerged in the 1980s and was associated early on with cocaine usage. The author of the first book to explain the syndrome, Vincent DiMaio, testified for the defense in the Gray case. A 2020 study of deaths that were ruled to have been the result of excited delirium syndrome revealed that police restraint, usually positional asphyxiation, was involved in almost all of those cases.[26]

In Maryland, under Fowler, excited delirium was a somewhat common cause of death determination for people who were fatally injured in police custody until 2012. After that, his office stopped using the language of excited delirium as much, but they continued using other language to describe the same phenomenon, such as the explanation given for Tyrone West's heart complications in 2013. In 2018, Fowler's office determined "sudden cardiac death" caused eighteen-year-old Anton Black's death on the Eastern Shore of Maryland in September 2015, despite extensive evidence of brutal police force. The autopsy opinion cites "the stress of his struggle" and his bipolar disorder as contributing factors. The opinion sections in the West and Black autopsy reports are both longer than usual, at about a page each.[27]

The officers in the Freddie Gray case described him banging and flailing, excitedly and deliriously, which could have been a preliminary effort to support an excited delirium–type of finding. The literature on excited delirium, including pamphlets used to instruct police officers, describes its subjects falling into a state of fatigue or "adrenaline dump" after the delirium phase.[28] This precedes heart failure, according to the literature. "Adrenaline dump" was the precise language Officer Porter began using five days after Gray's arrest for how Gray seemed at Stops 4 and 5.

CHAPTER 13

MISSING FOOTAGE

CITY LEADERS DEBUTED SOME CCTV video from Gray's arrest during their major press conference on April 20, one day after he died. "We're going to show you the closed circuit TV that the police department has," Deputy Commissioner Rodriguez said, "and I want you all to listen to what I'm about to say: It is our video that has been unedited, that is raw. We are not in the business of hiding facts." It took a minute or so for the video to load up, so Rodriguez made a light joke: "We have only the very best equipment."

While the CCTV video was loading, a camera was filming the press conference stage where Mayor Stephanie Rawlings-Blake, Commissioner Anthony Batts, and Rodriguez whispered among themselves. BPD was filming the press conference to upload to its YouTube page. The microphones on stage picked up the conversation, though not loudly enough for the media in the audience to notice. It was a hot mic moment.[1]

"Besides these three, they can't be out there. Is that right?" Mayor Rawlings-Blake whispered to Rodriguez.

"Yes ma'am," he answered.

"What about the other one?" she asked.

Rodriguez responded, "It would just be better for no one else to know unless we have to." (The last four words aren't entirely clear.)

Commissioner Batts then jumped into the conversation: "State's Attorney," he said, smirking. They exchanged a few more whispered comments that made them laugh.

Finally, the video played. It showed a few minutes of footage from CCTV camera 2108 in the CityWatch numbered system, which looked over Mount and Baker Streets, or Stop 2. The video showed the cops biking over to the van as well as the top of the van. For those few minutes, it didn't show anything else of note.

After the video played, Rodriguez reinforced BPD's commitment to transparency. Reporters asked about other cameras. "This is the only one that I am aware of that we know that we have found that has captured any of the incident, and it was very little," he said.

A reporter asked, "But there are other cameras out in that area, correct?"

Rodriguez replied, "There's approximately six hundred cameras—over six hundred citywide, yes, ma'am. . . . We only had one camera that captured any of it, and that was this camera here." It wasn't an accurate statement. Two days later, BPD quietly uploaded to its YouTube page an eighteen-minute video titled "Gilmore [sic] Homes Surveillance Footage April 12, 2015," a compilation of footage from a few cameras at Stops 1 and 2.[2] FIT detectives started putting that video together two days after Gray's arrest. Then, on April 24, BPD uploaded to YouTube eighteen additional CCTV videos from the morning of Gray's arrest, each from separate cameras.

As for the "other one" "beside those three" that the mayor didn't want "out there," there is a strong candidate. There were three main videos capturing Stops 1 and 2 that were included in the Gilmor Homes compilation video: cameras 2101 and 2016 on Presbury Street at Stop 1 and camera 2108 on Mount Street at Stop 2, which was played during the press conference. The "other one" could be camera 2107, which is affixed to a Gilmor Homes building on Presbury Street. BPD didn't upload to YouTube the footage from 2107. Yet one minute of footage from that camera was included in the compilation video. It shows Davonte Roary running down Mount Street ahead of the cops.

Prosecutors obtained the rest of the footage from 2107 and included it in the discovery evidence, never sharing it with the public. The footage doesn't verify or disprove that the officers used force, but it does show the van driving right past Gray's arrest, with lights and sirens on, and parking up the street for more than a minute in front of 1707 Mount Street, while Gray was restrained and screaming around the corner. It also shows backup officers searching the ground for something. If released, the footage could have raised public suspicion about whether the officers were looking for a reason to arrest Gray—or a better reason than a knife.

As for Rodriguez's claim that the CCTV footage was "raw" and "unedited," prosecutors also discovered and documented evidence that BPD manipulated the footage on the publicly released videos. The manipulations weren't always subtle, but BPD depended on the media and the public not being used to how raw CCTV footage normally appears.

* * *

More than thirty CCTV cameras surveilled the Gilmor Homes community in 2015. Sierria Warren, who witnessed Stop 2, remembers one camera catching her "rolling a blunt" on her porch. "I didn't even get to light the blunt and they was swarming out to get me," she says. "Y'all really ran through all the drug dealers to get to me rolling my one little blunt." The same camera was less helpful when it came to protecting the community from violence. "The same place I was caught rolling my joint, my homeboy got shot seven times, in the summertime, broad daylight, people outside. The shooter didn't even wear a mask," she says, but he was never charged. "They see what they wanna see with those cameras."[3]

Warren expresses a common theme among Sandtown-Winchester residents. "If there's a drug arrest on that corner, they bring those videos out to convict these people, you know," Harold Perry says. "But for their officers, it was a cover-up."[4]

Sandtown residents didn't always live in the kind of dystopian video surveillance state predicted in 1953 by Ray Bradbury in *Fahrenheit 451*. The rise in the technological surveillance of Baltimore's poorest communities was a product of the overall increase in street surveillance in the ten years before Gray's arrest. In 2004, at the height of the zero tolerance era, Mayor O'Malley visited London, England, to gather information to improve policing. London was recognized worldwide for its extensive CCTV security system.[5] After visiting London, O'Malley obtained a multimillion-dollar grant from the Department of Homeland Security (DHS) to implement the CitiWatch program. The technology was created by DVTel, a company whose CEO was a former head of the Israeli army. Baltimore was the first city to use DHS funds for this purpose, and it soon had one of the most advanced CCTV systems in the country.

O'Malley's CitiWatch program kicked off with fifty cameras in 2005, mostly targeting high-profile tourist areas. His successors continued to expand CitiWatch in the 2010s, adding hundreds of cameras around housing developments and other high-crime areas. As happened in other major cities, a surveillance program that emerged out of post-9/11 fears of terrorism was shifted to focus on poor Black neighborhoods, where international terrorism was least likely to occur. By 2015, the city was budgeting about $13 million annually for "homeland security," which included CitiWatch and the gang and cyber crimes squads.[6]

CitiWatch cameras are operated out of a central command center, where retired and off-duty BPD officers are contracted to work as monitors, communicating with cops in the field and panning and zooming into activity as needed. Data is maintained for twenty-eight days and then destroyed, unless it becomes part of a case file. The CitiWatch program set the stage for ten years of other surveillance systems in Baltimore, including a network of private security cameras; a secret plane circling over the city obtaining mass location data (employed by the FBI during the uprising after Gray's death); a program called Stingray that simulates cell phone towers and tracks calls without warrants; and Geofeedia, which was used to monitor social media during the uprising. With its high crime rate and proximity to DC, Baltimore is a frequent site for the testing of surveillance equipment that has military and other applications on a mostly poor Black population. The US Army tested surveillance blimps over Baltimore during 2014 and 2015.

* * *

On April 24, 2015, BPD uploaded eighteen CCTV videos from the morning of Freddie Gray's arrest to YouTube and promoted the videos as a ramped-up show of transparency. Each video was from one camera only, giving the impression of raw footage. Protests were exploding, and Commissioner Batts promised that the investigation was progressing. Like when you "go to an ophthalmologist," he said, "the picture is getting sharper as we move forward."[7] The picture wasn't sharper in most of these YouTube videos. Some of the videos from Stops 1, 2, and 5 did confirm parts of BPD's official timeline, but the majority of the videos showed very little of note—a few seconds of a white van passing in footage that runs up to five minutes long.

The overload of data seems to have been the point. Journalists and other investigators had to wade through more than five hours of dizzying and challenging footage without any guidance. CitiWatch cameras are preprogrammed with rotation patterns that move in a 360-degree circle in one direction while also constantly panning up

and down, zooming in and out, and jumping back and forth at seemingly random angles and speeds. With a few exceptions, the videos
catch glimpses of Gray and the officers from a distance, not always
clearly, and then pan away from the relevant action. Camera 2106
overlooks the entrance to Bakbury Court, where Gray was held by
Miller and Nero. The video pans back and forth quickly over the
arrest and then zooms in to the second-floor window of someone's
row house and holds for a few seconds on each pass. Even if that
row house were the home base for a criminal enterprise, the video
doesn't get a clear look in the window. Someone sat on the stoop of
that row house observing the first minute of Gray's arrest. He was
never interviewed by police, but the bedroom window of that house
ended up in evidence.

The hard-to-decipher CCTV videos gave the impression that the
CitiWatch system was no longer up-to-date or useful, despite millions spent on the program annually. Rodriguez fed into that impression with his joke about "only the best" equipment and by asserting
that numerous cameras were not working, including all of the cameras around the police station.[8]

By uploading so much barely useful video footage, BPD diverted
public attention away from what the videos did reveal. The *Baltimore
Sun*'s Catherine Rentz reported on a few issues with the videos,
including freezes.[9] In fact, the most important videos of Stops 1 and
2 have several moments when the screen freezes but the time stamp
continues running. If these were just technical snafus, the time stamp
would freeze with the video footage, or there would be a moment
when the video jumped ahead to sync up with the time stamp. That
never happens. These moments point to either a magical disruption
in the space-time continuum or footage that was edited out.

BPD left some other clues along its trail of evidence manipulation. The YouTube videos look different from police videos typically
released to the public. Instead of downloading the raw footage into

a conventional video file format for easy sharing on YouTube, BPD created screengrab videos of the videos playing within the DVTel's "control center" viewer. The control center has a "timeline tab" that allows for viewing "clipped" or curated video selections,[10] so this was an easy way to capture edited footage.

Anyone closely watching the CCTV video during the April 20 press conference might have noticed that the video from camera 2108 suddenly skips over the top of the van in one rotation.[11] BPD initially uploaded this video to YouTube as part of its big evidence dump and then immediately removed it, leaving an error message. BPD officially told Rentz there was a "technical glitch" with its upload, though the same video was working fine during the press conference four days earlier.

A month later, with some pressure from the media, BPD restored the camera 2108 footage to YouTube. This time, it was inexplicably cut up into nine short videos of one minute each.[12] The short videos look different from the other CCTV videos on YouTube. They aren't framed inside of the DVTel player; the time stamps are directly on the bottom of the screen. The local media described the short Stop 2 videos as new footage, but here's the rub: the full video from camera 2108 was already online, as part of the little-watched "Gilmore [sic] Homes Surveillance Footage" compilation.

So, by late May, there were two versions of the same video from Stop 2 camera 2108 online. The differences between them give away the video manipulation game. Both start by showing the camera completing the same one-minute clockwise rotation a few times, panning west across Baker Street before panning over the top and back of the van, parked on the corner. The videos don't show much of the back of the van, but at 8:48 a.m., Rice, with his black helmet, and at least one other officer have the van doors open and are doing something physical, likely pulling Gray out of the van. The camera rotates away. At 8:48:54 on both videos, a man and boy start tossing a ball back and forth down the street on Mount.

What happens next on the two online versions of camera 2108 is edited differently. In the compilation, at 8:49, the video suddenly freezes on a man running across Baker Street, his arms and legs stuck mid-stride. The time stamp keeps going for seven seconds. The video then cuts to the other side of the van, skipping the top and back of the van altogether. Brandon Ross is now across the street from the van, filming on his phone.

The same freeze-and-jump happens again twice more in the compilation video. There's another frozen man at 8:51 and a frozen car at 8:52, both on Baker Street. The video holds on them for seven seconds each and then skips the top of the van both times. The rest of the camera 2108 footage from the compilation is like the original pattern, panning over the top of the van. It is no wonder BPD immediately took down its camera 2108 video from YouTube. The frozen men and car are glaringly obvious. BPD benefited from news outlets never analyzing the compilation video, in which the frozen moments still existed online.

BPD did a slicker job of hiding the manipulation in the set of videos from camera 2108 released in May and cut into one-minute bits. At 8:49, instead of the video freezing on the running man, it cuts immediately from him to the other side of the van, but this time, *the time stamp jumps ahead*. It says 8:49:04, and then it says 8:49:10. That happens again at 8:51 and 8:52.

So BPD removed about six to seven seconds of footage at three moments during Stop 2 and found two different ways to cover its tracks. The manipulation is more effective in the one-minute videos because there are no frozen people in the middle of the screen. In addition, the time stamps are harder to read on those videos. They're in a dark faded font at the very bottom of the screen. The one-minute videos were also uploaded at lower pixel resolution, so they appear grainier in general. Either of the videos from camera 2108 would seem suspicious alone—with the screens freezing or the time stamps jumping—but both versions make it clear that Rodriguez was not telling the truth about "raw" and "unedited" videos.

There was another camera, 2113, filming Stop 2. It captured the front of the van from a block south on Mount Street. Instead of manipulating the footage, BPD just started the YouTube video about three-and-a-half minutes into the stop, after the van doors were already closed on Gray. The missing footage from camera 2113 is included in the discovery evidence and, while not totally clear, does show the officers dealing with something on the ground. It also supports Miller's claim to FIT detectives that he was "standing off to the side" of the van when his colleagues "put" Gray into the van.

Warren remembers when BPD first uploaded video of Gray's arrest to YouTube. She and her neighbors were doing their own investigation. "We trying to figure out, where is the footage from Mount and Baker that I seen with my own two eyes? Why is the camera showing all up and down Mount Street, but when you get to Mount and Baker, you can't see what's going on?"

These kinds of shenanigans—together with BPD lying to the public about the existence of witnesses like Warren—contributed to the Baltimore Uprising. "They tell us, cameras don't work in the projects," one of Gray's friends shouted during a protest at the Western District station. "But when we shooting dice, they see all that!"[13]

* * *

During trial preparation, SAO staffers discovered how to recover the missing seconds of footage from camera 2108 by "rewinding back from after the frozen parts," as mentioned in their notes. The recovered footage is included in SAO's own video compilations. At

8:49, the recovered video shows some activity at the back of the van, including Goodson and two bike cops seeming to handle something. Jamel Baker can be seen looking right down on them from his window, with the screen removed. By deleting this footage, BPD removed any video evidence to support what witnesses said about officers throwing Gray into the van. The recovered footage from camera 2108 also shows a bit more of the top and back of the van than the one-minute videos. So, on top of cutting out footage, BPD also seemingly cropped the frame.

As for the recovered footage at 8:51 and 8:52, it shows only the top of the van and the van's back doors closed. Its importance may lie in what it doesn't show. As SAO's notes explain, "It shows the wagon not shaking." The video appears to contradict the officers' claim that Gray was causing the van to shake at the end of Stop 2, which was used to prove that he was still in good health leaving Gilmor Homes.

SAO had knowledge of this missing footage but never shared it in court. Baltimore public defender Todd Oppenheim has an idea why: "Think about the potential can of worms that could open up from exposing the ease in which manipulation can occur and the questions that could come out of every case that includes footage."[14]

It appears that BPD also manipulated the YouTube footage from three videos of Stop 1.[15] There are frozen men, a frozen car, and moments when the screen holds longer on a wall or scene than in any previous rotations, while the time stamp keeps running. There are also subtle alterations to one camera's rotation pattern. The Stop 1 editing is trickier to analyze because the freezes and other alterations don't all happen at the same time across the three videos. If anything was removed from one video, there were two other videos that needed to be synched up to match it.

So what is missing from the video evidence of Stop 1? At times, the officers' actions appear extremely fast, suggesting footage was removed. At 8:40:11, Nero is biking over to the ramp in Bruce

Court to stop Gray. Only eight seconds later, he is climbing *back onto his bike,* which is parked at the other edge of the long ramp. About fifteen seconds after that, he is suddenly about a hundred feet away, now walking both his bike and Miller's bike back toward the ramp. He doesn't move that fast when he is on screen. In the midst of all of that, Lieutenant Rice is captured biking *away* from where the officers are arresting Gray, yet the videos never show him at the scene.

The whole first two minutes of Gray's arrest happen fast like that. As with Stop 2, these videos are most likely missing what witnesses observed. Ross, Perry, and Yolanda White, among others, told investigators similar stories about police using excessive force on Gray at the beginning of Stop 1, just before he began screaming.

* * *

In 2016, Reynaldo Chavez filed a lawsuit against the City of Albuquerque, New Mexico, alleging that he was fired from the local police department after he blew the whistle on video tampering in the police department. As records custodian, he claimed he was instructed to withhold video evidence from attorneys and media outlets. He knew of others in the department who tampered with evidence in cases in which officers had shot civilians. He gave detailed testimony in multiple civil cases as to how footage could be manipulated.[16]

Chavez used a software known as Evidence.com, owned by Axon, which BPD uses to store Taser download information and, since 2016, body camera footage. Axon's website promotes the "ability to redact" even while watching videos. "Redacting video shouldn't be an endless cycle of processing, reviewing, and re-blurring footage," it states. The ACLU, upon learning about how "clips" can be made of body camera footage, revised its policy to demand that police turn over entire cameras and not just video files.

In the last few years, a number of lawsuits and complaints have involved police editing video, including by slowing down footage or blurring officers' identifications.[17] Several of the videos in the Gray case are too bright, dark, or blurry to see the action clearly. It's easy to change the contrast on a video to make it brighter or dimmer, but these kinds of edits are harder to prove than missing footage. Sunlight and shadows exist in the real world and can obscure the visual plane. Videos can also seem blurred in places because of smudges on the glass windows surrounding the CCTV cameras.

That said, BPD does use its technology to purposefully blur video footage, such as when it hides the faces of children or license plates. At Stop 5, BPD purposefully blurred out the top of the ambulance that showed up for the injured arm patient. In most of the frames, the top appears white and opaque, but the video editors missed a brief moment. Suddenly, "Medic 8" appears on top in bold black letters as the van is leaving the scene. BPD may have been concerned about showing the lettering because it was Medic 15 that had responded to the scene on the radio. Also, as discussed earlier, the two Stop 5 videos from two different cameras (727 and 728) are both unintelligible over the same part of the sidewalk where Donta Allen was arrested. It's as if an impossibly thick fog covered only a small part of that block.

BPD once again gave away its own evidence-manipulation game by posting too many videos online, making it possible to contrast footage. On July 10, BPD shared on YouTube two hours of video from camera 728 that was shot during the April 27 riot at Penn North metro station. The footage from Gray's arrest on April 12 looks like a badly lit home video from the 1980s, with smudges and shadows all over the place. The footage on April 27, from the same camera, is clear and easy to watch up and down the entire block of North Avenue. BPD chose to provide less-clear footage when the investigation involved its own officers and more-clear footage when it involved civilians.

CHAPTER 14

FORCE INVESTIGATION

On July 27, 2016, as Marilyn Mosby gave a speech announcing that she was dropping the remaining charges against the officers in the death of Freddie Gray, she railed about perceived misconduct within BPD's investigation. "What we realized very early on in this case was that police investigating police, whether they're friends or merely their colleagues, was problematic," she said. She described "a reluctance and an obvious bias" among some BPD investigators:

> *There were individual police officers that were witnesses to the case yet were part of the investigative team. Interrogations that were conducted without asking the most pointed questions. Lead detectives that were completely uncooperative and started a counter investigation to disprove the state's case.*[1]

BPD leaders were aware, early in the Gray case, that the public might have qualms about the department handling this investigation. So they immediately started promising other investigations to come. One day after Gray was arrested and hospitalized, Deputy Commissioner Rodriguez said BPD would "empanel a blue-ribbon commission" to investigate the case, whatever that meant. On April 20, Commissioner Batts promised an "independent review board," not to be confused with the "task force" he promised on the same day, which he said was part of the Force Investigation Team (FIT), another entity that was already investigating the case.[2]

BPD never established an independent review board or blue-ribbon commission, but it did set up a task force for the rest of April after Gray died. A peek behind the curtain of the two internal investigations—FIT and the task force—reveals a moving line between investigating and covering up.

* * *

When Commissioner Batts announced a thirty-plus-member task force on April 20, he didn't admit FIT was bungling the use-of-force investigation that was under way. It was failing to collect key evidence and was enabling major conflicts of interest. In fact, during the Gray case, FIT developed a negative reputation and was disbanded later that year. A 2021 report investigating BPD corruption following the Gun Trace Task Force scandal described FIT as "staffed with mediocrities" who were cast off by other departments.[3]

The squad's low level of experience came up during the trials. Detective Syreeta Teel was new to the squad when FIT Sergeant Tashawna Gaines put her in charge of the Gray investigation. It was one of her first serious force investigation cases. In interviews and case files, she comes across as a diligent company woman who takes detailed notes but is short on follow-up questions during interviews.

Retired BPD Detective Lakishna Lewis was part of FIT and helped Teel on the case. "Because the unit was so small, it was always all hands on deck," she explains. "The unit was not as efficient as it could have been," she admits, but it was a "pilot unit" that had to "learn as we went along."[4] While Lewis characterizes FIT fondly as a "team of misfits" and "underdogs," some of the FIT investigators were very experienced. Lewis herself had investigated police misconduct for fifteen years in the Internal Affairs Division (IAD), in addition to working in robbery and domestic violence units. She recalls the Gray case at first as "just another in-custody, not different from the other ones we had," until it blew up.

Inexperience was only part of the story of what went wrong with the FIT investigation into Gray's death. Conflicts of interest and cut corners pervaded the investigation. Both Teel and Michael Boyd, who led the first-day interviews, were recent colleagues of the officers under investigation. Without compunction, Teel testified that she gave Officer Porter a hug before interviewing him as a murder suspect.[5]

Lewis recalls being required to investigate her friends in IAD too, against her protests. She ended up handling those cases ethically, she believes, and lost friendships over some of them. She also remembers higher-ups seeking to influence her investigations by protecting their own friends. "I left internal affairs three times," she says, over what she calls "this favoritism crap."

Lewis wasn't working on the first day of the Gray investigation, a Sunday. At around 9:54 a.m., medics took Gray to the hospital. The officers involved in the arrest spent the next two hours around the police station, unsequestered, having conversations with each other and the investigators. Crime scene photos show some of the officers talking outside of the van. Seth Stoughton, law professor and expert on police force, says involved officers should be "separated and instructed not to communicate with each other" during force investigations.[6]

Detective Teel testified that she entered the police station and passed Officer Novak hanging out in a hallway with Donta Allen, the other van passenger, who was not handcuffed. She gave Novak a hug and told Novak and Allen to stand by. By this point, Novak and Allen had had more than an hour to chat after the medics left. Teel also saw Lieutenant Rice talking with FIT Detective Charles

Anderson in another part of the police station. Anderson later drove Goodson around the neighborhood to identify the homes of possible witnesses.

After day one, some of the FIT investigators continued to have relaxed boundaries with the officers. Lieutenant Rice talked on the phone with FIT Lieutenant Michael Norris that afternoon and the next day. Novak passed on Detective Teel's contact information to Miller, and he called her the next day.[7] Novak texted his colleagues on April 15: "She said she's not really supposed to discuss it, but she said she'd call me back and give me some more details."[8] Teel shared the knife with Novak on April 27. According to Stoughton, "Communications between an officer being investigated and the investigator conducting that investigation should generally be limited, and those that occur should be formal and documented." None of these conversations was documented.

In addition to mishandling the suspects, FIT mishandled the main piece of evidence. Just before noon on April 12, a CSU technician, Jennifer Anderson, arrived at the police station. As she later testified, FIT Lieutenant Norris ordered her to take photographs of the outside of the van only. He did not ask her to photograph the inside nor to swab the van for any fingerprints or DNA.[9] Norris then let the van go back into service, even though some of the officers were saying Gray had banged his head against its walls.

Unlike on television shows, CSU technicians in Baltimore and many other cities do not have expansive or prodigious powers. They are usually told what evidence to collect and document by police investigators. Sandra Guerra Thompson of the University of Houston Law Center and author of *Cops in Lab Coats* advocates for independent, civilian crime labs: "There are an awful lot of labs, whether they are medical examiners or others, who have for a long time viewed their role as helping the police, helping the prosecution, and it's very dangerous," she says.[10]

* * *

At 12:35 p.m. on April 12, several hours after Gray's arrest, the bike officers and Goodson arrived downtown at the homicide unit to give statements. Except for Goodson, all of the officers gave voluntary statements that day. FOP attorney Michael Davey said in a press conference that, if he had been around, he wouldn't have allowed the officers to give statements.[11] The officers in similar cases, including those of Tyree Woodson and Tyrone West, gave statements weeks or months later, with their attorneys present.

"I ignored my attorney," Rice told internal affairs investigators. "I had nothing to hide, I hadn't done anything wrong. I'm—I had a very minimal role."[12] Lewis says that officers more commonly gave statements to FIT when the cases seemed straightforward.

Novak later told internal affairs investigators that he and others felt implicitly coerced to give statements. "They were like, 'You're just a witness in all this. We're just trying to keep it sorta straight.'" Initially, Novak checked a box requesting an attorney. He was brought back in after his interview to say on tape that he checked that box in error.[13]

* * *

On the day of Gray's arrest, Novak, who keeps popping up around the margins of this case, was involved in an even bigger conflict of interest than hugging Teel when he was named "primary officer" by FIT Sergeant Gaines. "Primary officer" is a specific and short-term designation that plays a role in the first-day investigation. The assignment usually goes to the first officer on the scene of an incident. According to BPD policy, the main job of the primary officer is to "make critical observations of the crime," as well as to write the initial report. It was an emblematic role for Novak. He often sounded like the officers' unofficial narrator. As it turns out, he was their official narrator.

Stoughton had a strong reaction to the discovery that Novak, a named witness, was the primary officer: "That is bat-shit crazy. You don't have an officer who is involved in the officer-involved homicide as the primary or play any sort of investigative role into that officer-involved homicide. Anyone who is involved in the underlying incident is a witness who needs to have their information taken by an investigator." Teel testified that Detective Anderson was concerned about Novak being made primary officer and called their sergeant to warn her, but she kept Novak in the role.

Novak did a lot as primary officer. He spent the afternoon taking FIT investigators and the CSU technician to selected scenes around Gilmor Homes. He joined the FIT detectives going door-to-door to speak to witnesses. In a few CSU photos, he is standing behind Detective Teel while she knocks on doors. Eyewitness Jamel Baker remembers Novak at his door. "One of the officers that came and knocked on my door was already out and about when the situation first happened," he says.[14] Baker wasn't at Stop 1, but he was told later by his neighbors that the "white guy" that participated in his interview helped arrest Gray. One can imagine the witnesses' confusion at seeing an arresting officer ask about the incident hours later, not to mention the intimidation factor. Indeed, Novak helped the FIT detectives find Kevin Moore, who had just filmed Novak carrying Gray into the van at Stop 1.

After they were finished canvassing, Teel, Anderson, and Novak returned downtown, where Novak gave a taped witness statement to the other two, as if he hadn't just been shaping their perceptions for hours. He then wrote a narrative report that had Gray's arrest starting at 9:11 a.m., a half hour after it really started.[15]

When Novak testified before the grand jury in exchange for immunity, he revealed how much his involvement in the door-to-door interviews could have compromised the case: "When I went around with the Force Investigation Team afterwards to interview some citizens in the area, some had made the comment they thought that Gray was thrown in the wagon headfirst," he said. "And then when I brought that up with the officers who were there at the second stop, to my understanding, they said they guided Gray in the wagon. I think they said Lieutenant Rice led the way in and brought Gray in then."[16]

"Okay, so you were made privy to interviews regarding this case," one juror asked. "You were made privy to photographs regarding this case, and you have a really great idea of how this investigation took place because you were part of it. Correct?" Novak concurred.

During the grand jury, Novak seemed comfortable with, even prideful in, his temporary assignment as an investigator. More than a year later, when he was interviewed by internal affairs investigators from outside counties, he expressed a different feeling about the situation. He called the FIT investigation a "debacle," with unqualified and lazy detectives.[17] He said the investigators were focused on wrapping up work and getting "Joe's Squared Pizza." He also said he never wanted to be the primary officer and was coerced into writing his report, which would "have that taint regardless because of my involvement." Novak flattered the internal affairs investigators for doing a much better job than the FIT detectives. One can only imagine the conversations Novak had with prosecutors that earned him immunity.

The Gray case wasn't the first time FIT gave primary officer designation to someone with a conflict of interest. Officer Dale Mattingly was named primary officer after Tyree Woodson was found shot dead inside of the Southwest District police station bathroom in 2014. Mattingly had arrested Woodson months before on drug and assault charges. He claimed Woodson slammed into his car. Prosecutors wouldn't call Mattingly to the stand in that case because of "integrity" concerns, so the judge acquitted Woodson. Months later, Mattingly was at the scene of Woodson's mysterious shooting inside of a police station. He "rendered the weapon safe" at the scene, according to a colleague, and wrote the first-day report. Woodson's death was ruled a suicide.[18]

FIT investigators did a lot in one day to compromise the Gray case. To her credit, Detective Teel did listen to the police radio and pick up on the radio calls about Stop 4. She called Porter and then brought him in for a statement. His statement about Stop 4, in which he described Gray requesting a medic, changed the course of the investigation.

* * *

Before the creation of FIT, BPD homicide detectives would handle cases involving death or serious injury in police custody. Batts established FIT in 2014 as part of sweeping changes to the department. By then, many big-city police departments across the country had distinct force investigations squads. Yet BPD's FIT was put together in haste, without attention to how such squads are appropriately set up.

In a moment that escaped media notice, Detective Boyd revealed his understanding of his job while on the stand during Nero's trial. "Can you just generally describe what the duties of the FIT team would be?" one of the prosecutors asked. Boyd replied:

We would conduct an investigation of the facts, see where they fell as far as training and policy was concerned. We'd then present our findings to a board, which consisted of a few of the commanders, deputy commissioners, and they would determine if the officer was acting in policy or out of policy and if any training needed to be addressed.[19]

Boyd here described a textbook *administrative investigation*, exactly the kind of investigation IAD routinely conducted when officers faced complaints. Administrative investigations can lead to job-related penalties, like suspensions or firing, which are decided by a trial board. Boyd did not describe a *criminal investigation*, which is what most people think of as a standard police investigation, the type of investigation homicide would perform that can lead to prison time. According to Stoughton, administrative and criminal investigations have "extremely different functions and goals." For one, criminal investigators ask far more detailed questions of witnesses, parsing the microdetails of an event, he explains. Criminal investigations are also more time-sensitive and forensics-oriented.

Like Boyd, Lewis understood her role in FIT as a specialized extension of what she did at IAD. "I thought it was a policy review, because we had to decide whether a shooting or situation was within policy or not. The criminal part was left to the state's attorney's office (SAO), even at internal affairs."[20] Yet SAO was making decisions whether to charge criminally based on such administrative investigations.

It also matters who conducts criminal and administrative investigations of officers because, by law, they should be conducted separately. *Garrity v. New Jersey*, a 1967 Supreme Court decision, protects officers from their statements or anything derived from them being used against them. Deputy Commissioner Rodriguez articulated *Garrity* issues one day after Gray died: "We cannot interview an officer administratively and compel them, if an officer is the subject of the criminal investigation. Every person has the right against self-incrimination, so for us to compel an officer to provide a statement, that could potentially taint the criminal investigation."[21] Only officers identified as witnesses, not "involved," can be compelled to give statements.

FIT was based on a model out of Las Vegas that had two divisions to handle the two types of force investigations, like many big-city departments.[22] BPD only had one force investigation squad. Batts's policy establishing FIT was murky. It referred to "FIT or homicide" as leading force investigations, as if they were interchangeable.[23] It also had the FIT detectives handling both criminal and administrative paperwork.

"They never seemed to be able to figure that part out," one BPD homicide detective says. "At first, we were told it was all FIT. Then, at times, they wanted homicide involved," he says. "Bottom line is FIT would screw it up, and we would be asked to fix it." This detective also criticized FIT's capacity: "You just let people with no experience investigate what could be some of the most serious incidents a department can have."[24]

Asked for clarity on FIT's role, BPD officially responded in an email that, per the Chief of Professional Responsibility, "The Force Investigation Team (FIT) started the criminal investigation into Freddie Gray's death. After the criminal trials were concluded, Montgomery County was asked to handle the internal administrative investigation for BPD. As you can see the investigation was bifurcated."[25] If FIT was supposed to be doing a criminal investigation, Detectives Boyd and Lewis were not made aware.

Commissioner Batts gave several statements indicating he was unconcerned about the difference between the two types of investigations and *Garrity* law in general. The topic came up during a task force meeting attended by a *Baltimore Sun* reporter. Batts wanted to compel Goodson to give a statement. "Well, he's not talking to us already. He's already lawyered up, right? What do we lose by compelling him?" Batts asked.[26]

Deputy Commissioner Kevin Davis explained: "If the state's attorney finds out we learned something administratively that they can't use criminally, they would have a problem with that."

Batts replied, "They wouldn't know anyway." He said this in front of a reporter.

Batts was fired in July 2015. Davis took over BPD and disbanded FIT, while creating a new squad with a clearer approach, at least on paper. It called for "separate and concurrent criminal and administrative investigations," and it referred to *Garrity* rules.[27]

FIT's lack of clarity in its mandate may have been the point. Tawanda Jones calls FIT the "making shit fit" squad. She remembers detectives coming to her house after her brother Tyrone West was killed by police to make excuses for not notifying the family while at the same time trying to dig up dirt on his medical history. Someone raided her brother's house after he was killed, turning it upside down but leaving the photo ID he had on him when he was killed, she says.[28] The FIT file on her brother's case includes summaries of civilian witness statements describing brutal force. The summaries conclude with detectives dismissing most of the statements as partially or entirely untrue.[29]

* * *

FOR TWO WEEKS AFTER GRAY'S death, a large group of investigators assembled every morning and afternoon in a conference room as part of the Freddie Gray Task Force. The meetings were led by Homicide Major Stanley Brandford, who was overseeing the second phase of the investigation with Davis. Special guests gave demonstrations on topics like proper leg lace technique. The meetings were guided by a long to-do list of tasks, with a widespread division of labor.

The FIT detectives became part of the task force. Lewis was impressed by what she saw in the meetings. "You know, you see on TV how they have the war room and have the pictures on the wall with the timelines attached to it. And that was a real thing. I was blown away," she recalls. "We really got pictures of each person on the wall. And what officer did what at what time." She felt motivated and inspired. "It was about finding out what happened to this man. This was a mystery."

The task force put the investigation under the leadership of experienced homicide investigators, and for a spell, they seemed to be cleaning up some of FIT's mess. On paperwork, investigators started timing the beginning of Gray's arrest more properly at 8:38 a.m. instead of 9:11 a.m. The van was brought back for blood and DNA testing. The task force also interviewed the rest of the backup officers and the medics. The red carpet was rolled out for the medics. Some of them got to see a photo array to identify the officers involved, which civilian eyewitnesses never got to see.

In some cases, though, the task force was too late to retrieve uncompromised evidence. It was too late to recover black box data to reconstruct the van's acceleration and deceleration patterns.[30] Some of the backup officers seemed extremely well coached by the time they were interviewed. The inside of the van had been compromised by a week in service.

The quality of the task force's investigation was also affected by too many detectives working in silos on narrow assignments. There was an extensive effort to find "Rodney Clark," the name given by someone who called 911 and originally requested anonymity. Detectives called every Rodney Clark in town, yet Brandon Ross had already identified himself to detectives as the person who called 911 twice. At least some detectives could have recognized his voice from his taped statement.

Some of the task force's work looked like evidence gathering but stopped short of actual evidence gathering. For example, BPD's crime lab took samples from fifteen bloodstains on Gray's clothing, many of them likely from hospital procedures, and ran DNA tests on them. Yet it tested the stains only against Gray's own blood card. Not surprisingly, Gray's DNA was found all over his own clothing. BPD also analyzed blood and DNA in the van, finding Gray's blood on a seat belt in the middle of the bench and against the wall behind it. This information wasn't used by the ME at all. Indeed, she may not have received it. She theorized that Gray was thrown headfirst into the front of the van's compartment while the van was moving. (The interior of the van, incidentally, was covered in visible bloodstains, most of which matched a single male "undetermined.")

Lewis recalls being assigned under the task force to canvass for witnesses, conduct interviews, and generally "find out whatever I could add to the rest of the evidence." She doesn't recall seeing anyone jump to conclusions or cover up evidence, and she does seem sincere and passionate in her defense of the investigators. Yet she admits that she never got a chance to see a lot of the evidence herself, including witness statements and CCTV videos. Normally, she says, a case would be her "baby," and she would know it "top to bottom, inside and out, but that wasn't the case here," she says.

As much as the task force was an investigation, it was also a public relations effort. Its major public relations coup was in its courtship of the *Baltimore Sun*. A *Sun* journalist, Justin George, was invited to attend task force meetings, advertised to the public as transparency. George published positive articles, showing the investigators hard at work, relentless, not afraid of the truth, and ultimately arriving at a conclusion about Gray's injury: "Whatever happened," one detective told him, "happened in the van."[31] This was also the mayor's conclusion before the task force ever met.

* * *

The task force disbanded after Mosby filed charges, but one detective stayed on the case with a mission. Homicide Detective Dawnyell Taylor took over as lead detective in May, and she did not agree with SAO's charges. She took up space, as they say, constantly speaking her mind and pursuing her own agenda. She had fifteen years on the force, eight in homicide, and several years working undercover narcotics. Before that, she spent more than ten years in the military.

The investigative binders contain a few sets of Taylor's notes. The first were handwritten during task force meetings and show a preoccupation with FIT's errors. "What is our explanation for not processing the wagon," she wrote. "We need to show what was happening between the 12th & 19th as far as the investigation." Then, at some point, Taylor typed up nine dense pages of notes, but with all kinds of storytelling and editorializing.[32]

Taylor's blunt and personal notes include vignettes of officials fighting and of FIT Detective Teel crying. She "has been continuously crying since my arrival on this task force," Taylor wrote, in what could be described as a self-own.

Mostly, Taylor's notes draw a negative portrait of Deputy State's Attorney Bledsoe, who was overseeing the case at SAO, with language like "adversarial," "tantrum," and "screaming." While Taylor's notes can't be verified as an accurate account of events, she also included in the case files text conversations with Bledsoe over the same period.

Taylor and Bledsoe's relationship didn't start out badly. "I meant what I said about you being professional and loyal to the investigation," Bledsoe texted Taylor early on. They had an agree-to-disagree relationship when it came to the charges but promised to work together professionally.

The relationship hit a small bump when Taylor was asked to read from a script before the grand jury on May 19. "I did not feel comfortable reading that script," she texted. "Between us, I believe we omitted key things from their combined statements."

Bledsoe responded, "Understood. And you skipped some parts." Their issues escalated in late June after someone leaked the autopsy report to the *Baltimore Sun*. Only a few people, including Taylor, had access to the report.

Taylor began pursuing her own leads. She made a request for medical and disciplinary records for Gray.

"Why?" Bledsoe asked.

Taylor said there was an anonymous tip. "The information was simply a female caller that stated Freddie often feigned injury when arrested and once had to receive medical attention for hurting himself in the jail," Taylor explained.

"We need to talk," Bledsoe texted. Taylor was clearly on a mission to investigate Gray himself. She also looked into a "Cash for Crash" scheme in which Gray might have been involved in an accident for money the year before. It didn't pan out. Taylor tried unsuccessfully to get someone in BPD to break into Gray's phone. She wrote in her notes that Bledsoe accused her of doing "the defense job for them," arguably another self-own.

Bledsoe was thwarting Taylor's agenda, and vice versa. Taylor pushed back on some of SAO's demands that she felt were too broad, like a warrant for all of the officers' emails. Bledsoe became more distant, and Taylor became more assertive in documenting things, including requests from SAO to remove her from the case. Their tense relationship eventually dissolved into Bledsoe asking, "Why are you so angry all the time?" and Taylor asking, "What in the world did I do to you today?"

According to Taylor's notes, despite all of their challenges, she and Bledsoe consistently agreed on one thing: "We went over the fact that all of the witnesses in the case fit their story to whatever injury they believed Freddie had," she wrote. "Jan Bledsoe agreed that no officers had used force on Freddie." Asked for comment, Bledsoe responded through her attorney. A letter from her attorney calls Taylor's statement "false." "Witnesses were not selected to fit an incorrect narrative," the letter states, "and Ms. Bledsoe did not agree that no officers used force on Freddie." Yet the same letter also asserts, "No witnesses provided reliable statements that Mr. Gray was tased or was otherwise injured outside the van."[33]

* * *

Taylor's appearance during Goodson's trial on June 16, 2016, cut through some of the tedium of the trial to that point. In a blunt and unapologetic voice, she testified that Dr. Carol Allan was planning to rule Gray's death an accident, not a homicide. Her claims weren't supported by any statements or evidence in court besides her own notes. She stood by it, claiming Dr. Allan called it a "freakish accident," not caused by "human hands."

Lewis backs up what Taylor said in court. She was at the meeting when Dr. Allan talked to the entire task force about Gray's injury. She recalls with certainty that Dr. Allan described Gray's death as "accidental" and "like an accident." "And so it blew our minds when something different was said to the state's attorney," Lewis says.

Chief Deputy State's Attorney Schatzow, Bledsoe's cochair, cross-examined Taylor, and their exchange made news. He accused her of creating backdated notes and other evidence to support the defense, and he said she had personal issues with Bledsoe.

"And in fact, you're not particularly fond of me, are you?" Schatzow asked.

"I've never had any interaction with you until this moment," Taylor answered.

Schatzow then asked Taylor if she realized she was removed as lead detective from the case at his request. "I'm aware that you made a request," she answered, "but you don't have the authority to remove me from the case."

"You were never removed as a lead detective on this case?" he asked.

"No," she said.

Schatzow laughed, dumbfounded laughter to which the defense objected. Then he asked if, on or about August 11, Major Brandford had requested her removal, mentioning a letter he received.

"What we determined is that I would cease any contact with your office, but I still maintained all of the case files and everything related to the case," she said. "I am still the lead investigator." Media photographed Taylor walking out of court that day with a big smile on her face.

Before she became lead detective, Taylor interviewed Yolanda White, a witness to Gray's arrest. She found White in the neighborhood on April 24. Taylor's talents as an investigator come through in that interview. She was the only detective to nail down where a witness was standing when they observed the arrest. She gave White time to detail not only the brutal police violence she saw, including beating and tasing, but also all of the movements of the bikes and cars on the scene. White recalled those movements with impressive accuracy almost two weeks later. Taylor produced a piece of historical evidence that is as detailed and compelling as any in the Gray case. She even had it transcribed, turned over to SAO, and included in the files. It's the only civilian witness transcript in the publicly released binders. Taylor's interview with White gives a glimpse into how the detective might have handled an investigation like this if she weren't pursuing an agenda to discredit SAO's case.

Mosby took shots at Taylor in her press conference when she dropped the remaining charges on July 27, 2016. She condemned "detectives that were completely uncooperative and started a counter-investigation to disprove the state's case." She went on:

> By not executing search warrants pertaining to text messages among the police officers involved in the case, creating videos to disprove the state's case without our knowledge, creating notes that were drafted after the case was launched to contradict the medical examiner's conclusions, turning these notes over to defense attorneys months prior to turning them over to the state, and yet doing it in the middle of trial.

Taylor did create two videos. On May 27, she made a video with Major Brandford intending to prove that it would have been possible for Gray to cause the transport van to shake while he was in shackles. She recruited a police cadet named Lloyd Sobboh, who, at five eleven and 155 pounds, was taller and larger than Gray, to re-create Stop 2. Sobboh proved that it was possible for someone taller and larger than Gray to make the van shake while shackled.[34] A month later, Taylor made a video showing herself operating the knife in evidence, claiming it had a "spring assist."[35]

There was a widespread belief that Taylor was instrumental in helping cover up what happened to Gray by not obtaining the officers' personal cell phones in a timely manner, an issue Mosby mentioned in her speech. After the trials, prosecutors took the position that they were victims of a police cover-up that compromised evidence and harmed their case.

In fact, it was Detective Lewis who hesitated to serve the warrants after the first set was rejected by a district court judge based on insufficient probable cause. SAO had reviewed those applications. After that, a circuit court judge approved the warrants, but Lewis expressed concerns about a practice known as "judge shopping," in which prosecutors seek favorable judges without changing their strategy. It didn't matter because, within one day after that judge approved the warrants, Mosby filed charges against the officers. This created jurisdictional issues because warrants issued by the Baltimore Circuit Court do not have jurisdiction outside of Baltimore City.[36] The officers all lived outside of the city and could no longer be compelled to appear at work to be served after they had been charged. After the warrants expired, Detective Taylor tried again in district court, at SAO's request, and the warrants were rejected on probable cause grounds. Bledsoe was frustrated Taylor didn't try again in circuit court. "It would have been better to have a signed warrant and figure out how to serve it then [*sic*] not to have a signed warrant at all," she texted Taylor.

Regardless, prosecutors did obtain key phone and text records but didn't use them much in court. Rice, Miller, and White used their departmental phones during Gray's arrest, and BPD included those records in its case file. Novak also gave up his personal phone to SAO in exchange for immunity, which included the officers' text chain.

Taylor became a notorious figure from her trial testimony and her appearance in the 2017 HBO documentary *Baltimore Rising*, in which she cheers on Goodson's acquittal. After all of the charges were dropped, the local FOP shared a meme on social media showing Leonardo DiCaprio as Jay Gatsby raising a wineglass. "Here's to the Baltimore 6 defense team, the FOP and Detective Taylor."[37] The FOP may have bolstered the impression that Taylor did what was needed to stop the convictions, but her actual impact was much smaller. She got involved in the case fairly late. If anything, Officer Novak never received his due from the FOP for all of the work he put in on many fronts.

IV

SYSTEMS OF
ACCOUNTABILITY

CHAPTER 15

THE MEDIA

The history of Freddie Gray's death was written, like all history, by the victors. According to the Wikipedia page about his killing, "While being transported in a police van, Gray sustained injuries and was taken to the R. Adams Cowley Shock Trauma Center." It's the well-established narrative of his death: It happened in the van somehow. Those who controlled the narrative began authoring this version of events as soon as Gray was injured, with each dispatch call, statement, and report. The medical examiner and prosecutors contributed too. Getting buy-in from the media was the last important step in framing an explanation for Gray's death that sounded most like an accident.

Gray's death was one of the most reported stories in the United States during 2015. In addition to daily news reports, there were also longer pieces with titles including "The 45-Minute Mystery of Freddie Gray's Death"[1] and "The Mysterious Death of Freddie Gray,"[2] along with a CNN documentary titled *Who Killed Freddie Gray?* and the HBO film *Baltimore Rising*. These and other projects were aspirational in their artistic or journalistic intentions, but none really aspired to uncover what happened to Gray. Most seemed to want to do the opposite: to refract knowledge through a prism of unknowability and multiple perspectives, to tell Gray's story as if it were *Rashomon*.

The media coverage of the Gray case provides an opportunity to consider the premise of contemporary journalism. There is a huge gap between the amount of proverbial ink and video hours spent by news outlets discussing the case and the percentage of accurate content they reported, which can be judged in retrospect with evidence in hand. A case in point is the sheer number of stories that discussed rough rides in the context of Gray's death simply because officials decided it "happened in the van."

Eyewitness Jamel Baker recalls a shift in the coverage after Gray's death. "Before he died, it was like regular coverage. Like, that was cool. They were just keeping us posted on what was going on," he says. After Gray died, "It seemed like they was more focused on the police point of view instead of what really happened. It just seemed like it shifted the energy of the real story to what they wanted it to be."

Over two years and thousands of stories, the media never exposed that at least nine witnesses saw Gray thrown headfirst into the van at Stop 2, an action that could have caused his "shallow water diving accident" type of fatal injury. Every bad media habit at once was at work: a reliance on "police say" journalism; passive voice reporting; the fetishization of mystery, tragedy, and racial strife; and "both sides" reporting with shifting binaries. There was also gatekeeping by local reporters with arguable conflicts of interest in a town that is often called "Smalltimore."

* * *

Jayne Miller had been an investigative reporter for local WBAL-TV for more than thirty years when Gray was arrested. She reported live from the streets of Baltimore, often in a T-shirt or windbreaker, with short windswept hair, looking at times like a veteran war correspondent. Unlike David Simon, Sarah Koenig, and the *Baltimore Sun* reporters who usually leave for larger opportunities, Miller stayed local. When she announced her retirement in 2022, news outlets referred to her as "hard-nosed," "tenacious," and other complimentary throwback terms.

Miller was mentioned in an early motion filed by the officers' defense team, which demanded Mosby recuse herself from the case due to various conflicts of interest.[3] One of the alleged conflicts was the romantic relationship between Miller and Mosby's deputy, Janice Bledsoe, who was overseeing the Gray investigation at SAO. (They have since married.) Defense attorneys accused Miller of using her access to Bledsoe to arrange an on-camera interview with Donta Allen. The state replied that Miller wasn't the first local news reporter to interview Allen. The motion was denied.

Miller has always denied that Bledsoe was her source in the Gray case, citing her long record of criminal justice reporting in Baltimore and deep rolodex of sources. She agreed to stop reporting on the case after the indictments of the officers. There are still three weeks of her reporting before she stepped back, on TV and in articles online, that are packed with scoops, context, and intrigue. Miller had information that would take weeks or months for other reporters to find out, if they ever did, but her reporting wasn't always straightforward.

Miller was the first to report on Stop 2, before BPD acknowledged it happened. Three days after Gray's arrest, on April 15, she wrote, "Video at a different location shows Gray had been taken out of the van, police said, for additional restraint. Gray is seen on video on the pavement on his knees."[4] The header image is a photo still from Brandon Ross's video, with Gray's legs hanging out of the van. Nobody else had Ross's video. The *Baltimore Sun* wouldn't report on it for over a month. Miller didn't report on it either. The photo's caption doesn't attribute or explain the source of the image.

Miller's reporting style was sometimes oblique, dropping hints without full context. In this April 15 article, she considers two different explanations for Gray's death, but indirectly. First, she explores some kind of a rough ride: "Police are required to secure a prisoner who is being transported so they don't bounce around inside a police van while handcuffed, exposing them to injury," she writes. BPD hadn't shared yet that Gray wasn't seat-belted. "The key question is what happened inside the police transport vehicle where no camera was rolling?" she asks. She had a "key question" before BPD had shared anything about a van ride.

Miller's article then jumps to another subject altogether. It brings up the 1997 case of Jeffrey Alston, who was paralyzed in police custody. "He argued police threw him head first into a police van," she writes.

On April 17, two days after her first article on the case, Miller was more direct, providing the first account from an anonymous witness to Stop 2: "They threw him in the paddy wagon face first, you know, facedown, and mind you, his arms and legs are locked up," the witness stated. "They just threw him in the paddy wagon facedown, head first, ankles bound, arms bound."[5] Miller writes, "It is not known if Gray's injury—a broken neck—occurred at that point."

Miller continued to report on the anonymous Stop 2 witness in articles and television appearances, with no other outlets picking it up. On April 23, a few days after the big press conference by city officials, she appeared on MSNBC's *Morning Joe*.[6] Host Willie Geist asked, "What happened inside that van?"

She replied that "what didn't happen" may be more important, insisting the case "boils down to" lack of medical care. She and Geist discussed Gray being jostled around in the van, unrestrained. Briefly during this interview, Miller also mentioned that the second stop may be "the key moment," and discussed the witness who saw Gray thrown "headfirst." Geist didn't follow up. Information about Stop 2 always seemed to fall on ears that weren't listening. After her appearance on *Morning Joe*, Miller's reporting on the Gray case shifted, and she stopped mentioning Gray being thrown into the van.

At the end of April, Miller reappeared on network television with what seemed like a new agenda. First, she sought to refute the *Washington Post* story from that day about Gray banging his head after Stop 5. According to her unidentified sources, Gray was nonresponsive by the time the second prisoner was loaded. Second, she pushed the rough ride theory of Gray's death, though without specifying whether the driver drove roughly on purpose or not.

On April 29, Miller called in to Lawrence O'Donnell's *The Last Word* on MSNBC with a breathless urgency to her tone: "The medical evidence in this case, according to the autopsy that we know of at this point, is that he suffered a severe neck injury, very similar to what you suffer in a car accident.... An awful lot of energy, and energy is the key word in this kind of energy—in this kind of injury. Because energy is what the speed of a vehicle—and I don't mean that the vehicle was going eighty miles an hour, I just mean, the momentum of the vehicle in an—in an injury like this—"

O'Donnell then interrupted Miller: "Suddenly it comes to a stop."

"Correct," she responded.[7] Miller seemingly knew details from the autopsy report, which hadn't yet been signed by the medical examiner.

The next night, Miller appeared on Chris Hayes's show on MSNBC.[8] She furnished Hayes with the full video of her interview earlier that day with Allen. In return, she was given a spotlight on-camera interview as an expert on the case. She outlined the rough ride theory with confidence, based on her insider sources. Miller did not disclose to Hayes—or O'Donnell or Geist—that she was in a serious relationship with one of the lead prosecutors on the case. The next morning, Mosby announced charges against the officers based on the same theory Miller shared with MSNBC viewers.

Miller officially recused herself from reporting on the case after that, but her network did continue to get some scoops, usually ones that favored the prosecution. On September 4, WBAL broke the story that Allen was a fugitive in York, Pennsylvania, a few days after those charges were filed. The story discusses how Allen's "credibility" as a defense witness would be hurt by the charges.[9]

Miller's reporting could be as complicated and dimensional as any of the evidence in the case. To her credit, whomever she used as a source for her stories, she held the police accountable during the first ten days after Gray's arrest. She not only exposed Stop 2 but also reported on the injured arm confusion. For her work on the case, she won the Alfred I. duPont-Columbia Award for Excellence in Broadcast and Digital News.

Miller provides an explanation for why she pivoted away from Stop 2 at the end of April: "I was relying on neurologists who were not part of the case," she says. "And there was information available publicly at that time about his injury. And they told me, in their opinion, that you would need more energy . . . to create that kind of injury than could be generated just by people thrown in the back of the wagon." In the same conversation, Miller recalls the autopsy's description of the injury as like a "diving accident." Asked if she believes several people picking up Gray and throwing him could create more force than someone using their own body weight to dive, she replied, "No, I don't think so."[10]

Stop 2 eyewitness Sierria Warren remembers Miller taking a strong interest in her and being "super nice" after Gray's arrest. They talked and texted, she recalls. "She was saying stuff to make me not trust other reporters, like trying to get me to just talk to her. That's the vibe she was giving me, with a little cherry on top. She would sweeten it up."[11]

Around the same time, Warren recalls speaking to an "older white lady with short hair" at Mosby's office. From a picture, she identified the woman as Bledsoe. Warren recalls both Miller and Bledsoe making her feel important to the case. Then, she says, they both disappeared. "Media stopped coming around once they found out he was dead," she says. Warren received summons notices but was never asked to testify. She was surprised to learn that Miller and Bledsoe were in a relationship at the time.

* * *

During the last week of April, the news about Gray's death took a dark, absurdist turn. A slew of false theories about his cause of death popped up at a frantic pace, some of them reported in mainstream outlets as if from credible and official sources. If BPD was engaged in a coordinated distraction campaign, it was successful.

On April 27, a rumor appeared on a right-wing news website called the *Fourth Estate,* which no longer exists. "Exclusive," it stated, "Freddie Gray's life-ending injuries to his spine may have possibly been the result of spinal and neck surgery that he allegedly received a week before he was arrested." The local Fox affiliate also circulated the story. On April 28, conservative radio host Tom Marr repeated this theory on WCBM and suggested he heard from sources that Gray had jumped out of a window.[12]

The *Baltimore Sun* published an article on April 29 debunking the preexisting injury story. The *Fourth Estate* was looking at records related to Gray's lead paint settlement, it stated.[13] A number of media outlets followed suit. On April 30, the *Washington Post* published a story headlined, "Those Stories That Freddie Gray Had a Preexisting Spinal Injury Are Totally Bogus."[14] The *Post* was not immune from getting it wrong, though. The same day, the news outlet issued major corrections to its story from the day before about the prisoner who heard Gray banging his head in the van after Allen came forward.

Actually, the "banging his head" story first appeared on social media on April 26. The website *Photography Is Not a Crime,* or

PINAC, reported on a BPD detective named Avraham Tasher posting on Facebook that Gray faked his injury and broke his own neck by banging his head.[15] *Post* reporter Peter Hermann thanked *PINAC* for its lead.

Yet another explanation for Gray's death popped up on April 30. Brad Bell at WJLA in DC reported, "According to our law enforcement sources, an autopsy found on Freddie Gray's head, a mark on the top of his head that matched a place on the back of the police transport van, specifically a bolt."[16] The bolt story went viral for twenty-four hours, with headlines like "Freddie Gray Died after 'Head Slammed into Bolt in Police Van,' Reports Say," in the *Guardian*, which cited the "medical examiner's office" as its source.[17] The *Baltimore Sun*'s bolt story cited "sources familiar with the probe."[18] The *Washington Post* also published a story on the bolt that didn't mention Gray banging his head, the *Post*'s big story from the day before.[19] News was happening fast.

The ME's office denied the bolt story and insisted it doesn't release preliminary findings. The autopsy made no mention of a bolt. Dr. Allan later testified that she examined the van on April 28 to see if a bolt or a seat belt might match an abrasion on the side of Gray's head. She concluded the bolt was *not* responsible for the abrasion, let alone Gray's death.[20]

The bolt story arrived and disappeared within a day, but it was the winner of this bizarre week of leaks. Based on anonymous sources, it lives on in internet results as if it were an official finding. The only outlet to question the story was the *Daily Mail*.[21]

April 30 was an absolutely haywire day in Baltimore media. Three different stories about what caused Gray's death were in play—the preexisting injury, Gray banging his head, and the bolt—while Miller was on TV discussing Gray being thrust forward because of sudden deceleration in the van, a cousin to the bolt story.

That wasn't all. Commissioner Batts and Deputy Commissioner Davis held a press conference on April 30 announcing the end of the task force and the discovery of a "previously unknown" stop, which was Stop 3. It would appear that BPD was providing the official investigation results in a press conference while leaking a slew of unofficial and spurious theories around the same time. At no point did any reporter step back and take a wide-angle lens to the media chaos and disinformation.

The media campaign didn't end when Mosby announced charges on May 1. Someone claiming to be a BPD officer appeared in disguise on Fox News that day, suggesting Gray had overdosed, the sixth explanation for his death that week, counting the window jump and rough ride. He also said Gray was a known informant.[22]

On the same day, Sergeant John Herzog of the Western District Detective Unit wrote a memo to a higher-up with his own story about Gray being an informant. On March 31, 2015, he wrote that Gray "voluntarily responded" to the police station to share information about "several robbery cases." While there, Gray was "awkwardly sitting in the chair, leaning to the left" and "stated something to the effect of 'I hurt my back' or 'I have a bad back.'" In other words, Herzog claimed Gray had a preexisting injury.

Months later, Herzog was interviewed internally about the matter. According to the interview notes, he reiterated that Gray was a generous informant, but he gave a different story about how Gray ended up at the station on March 31. He said Gray was stopped by an officer when he took off running near Penn North—rather like the famous story of Gray's last arrest.[23]

The evidence does not support that Gray was an informant. He was constantly arrested for minor violations and often held without bail. If he were an informant, he was getting nothing in return. Also, in his last eight arrests, he was debriefed at the station only twice. He was usually taken right to Central Booking. "If you know Freddie, no, he's no snitch," Baker says about his friend.

Once Herzog committed this story to paper, it became evidence in the case. The state was required to turn it over to the defense. Just after Porter's trial, the *Baltimore Sun*'s Justin Fenton published a story that took seriously the claim that Gray had a preexisting injury, citing Herzog's memo in detail. Fenton's own outlet had debunked this same claim earlier that year when it was reported by a conservative website, but once again, police had only to write things down to give them journalistic credibility. In the same article about Herzog's memo, Fenton cited Detective Taylor's notes about an anonymous phone call claiming Gray injured himself in prison. He selected those two documents out of a "slew of other new court filings."[24] Within that slew, they were documents that cast Gray in an unfavorable light.

* * *

The *Baltimore Sun* was the paper of record in the Gray case, cited more than any other source as an authority. The news outlet did extensive work narrating the case more than investigating it, sharing documents and creating timelines and slideshows to support the police's narrative. Catherine Rentz's work was an exception: she exposed Ross's Stop 2 video, interviewed witnesses, and asked BPD about missing CCTV footage. But she didn't publish frequently or comprehensively on the story. The crime desk—including Justin George, Justin Fenton, and Kevin Rector—reported on the case with a decidedly strong bias toward the police and the officers' defense, both in how stories were sourced and in how they were written.

BPD allowed George to attend and report on the task force meetings. On May 2, the day after Mosby announced charges, he published an article titled, "Exclusive Look inside the Freddie Gray Investigation." Then, on October 9, 2015, ahead of the trials, he published a four-part series on the same subject, titled "Looking for Answers."

George's articles mostly read like a love letter to BPD. Police are the heroes, and protesters are the antagonists. George describes the investigators having to hide their identities while passing angry residents and a "Fuck the Police" sign. "They all realized the importance of their investigation and that they were part of a pivotal moment in Baltimore history. . . . Amid the allegations of brutality, they wanted to show that they would leave no stone unturned." Throughout his articles, George repeats what the task force members tell him without fact-checking the information, including about certain cameras not functioning.

Homicide Major Brandford is the main protagonist of these stories, "a former Marine who kept his gray hair shorn close and thin mustache tight on his round face," George writes. Branford has "a calm demeanor, quick wit, and an uncanny ability to memorize facts without taking notes."

In George's May 2 story, he described BPD leaders as shocked by Mosby's announcement of charges the day before. Yet, in his October series, George wrote that Batts called Brandford on the evening of April 29 and asked him to turn over the entire case file to Mosby's office the next morning. Batts made a big deal publicly about announcing the task force results one day earlier than promised, which made room for Mosby's press conference on May 1.[25]

George turned up the rhetorical dial in describing Brandford working through the night of his birthday to prepare the files and deliver them early the next day:

Brandford didn't finish copying the files until 3:30 a.m. He took the case file home, told his wife what he was about to do and snapped some photos of the file as a keepsake. The next morning, Brandford placed the thick file in a blue tote bag and returned to police headquarters.

It was less than a half-mile walk, but he felt the weight of history in
his hands. He waited for walk signs before he crossed streets, fearful a
car might hit him, scattering hundreds of important documents over
the street, he said later, recalling that morning's events.

Then, all of that emotional impact was destroyed in a casual
moment of cruelty from Deputy State's Attorney Schatzow:

"Good morning," Brandford said, adding that he had come to drop
off some "materials."
He recalled that Schatzow said, "Materials, huh?"

The next day, in her speech, Mosby referenced the files Brandford
delivered as "information we already had." George did not include
her statement in his reporting.

The online version of George's four-part series includes several
highly produced videos following Lamar Howard, a chatty, well-
dressed, and charming detective having a busy couple of days. He
hands out fliers to people in the street and stops by a school to collect
security footage. He also participates in a raid on Goodson's locker
on April 28. As papers and clothes are removed from Goodson's
locker, Howard looks toward the camera and shakes his head in dismay. Goodson is cast in a cloud of suspicion throughout George's
articles. The *Sun's* video editors added stirring music and artful stills
and jump cuts to its videos. The camera zooms in on big bolt cutters
forcing open the lock on Goodson's locker. It then cuts dramatically
to a close-up of a broken lock on the ground. Nothing of note was
found in Goodson's locker besides some dusty clothes.

After Mosby filed charges against the officers, Fenton and Rector
published several fully reported stories based on defense motions,
often just as the motions were posted to the court's website, suggesting they had advance access. Like the story about Herzog's memo,

these stories usually impugned Mosby or Gray himself. The reporters published very little about motions or replies to motions filed by the state.

In 2017, BPD finally released selected files from the Gray investigation to the public, including nine binders of paperwork and six sets of photos.[26] While police withheld a lot of incriminatory evidence, the binders still offer a gold mine of context and evidence. They include the transcript from Lieutenant Rice's statement, which was never played in court; the alternate map of the van's route, with Goodson heading to the hospital during Stop 4; Yolanda White's witness statement; and much more.

After two years covering the case, the *Baltimore Sun* didn't report on the files at all, except for one article. Rector wrote about some of the officers' text messages, which he described as "candid, even vulnerable." His story discusses the officers denying ever harming Gray and outlining the pressures they felt around so much "anti-police sentiment." In 2015, George had reported that the task force investigators left "no stone unturned." In 2017, the *Baltimore Sun* didn't change that narrative by looking closely at the investigators' work.

* * *

Lisa Snowden was hired at the *Baltimore City Paper* in 2015 as writer and associate editor. She says the *City Paper's* "long-form style" gave her the "luxury to focus on storytelling." "I went full Joker as far as journalism, the limits of it, and the way that it abandons people that are in need, especially Black people," she says. While the alternative weekly brought tone, perspective, and distrust of authority to reporting, it still had mostly white male staff in a city with a nearly 65 percent Black population. Snowden later worked at the *Baltimore Sun*, where she was, again, one of very few Black journalists. (George is Black.)

Snowden considers it a form of "violence" that Baltimore has mostly white journalists, usually hired from out of town. "We're deprived of all that intelligence, all that institutional knowledge about the city, all the things that could have helped us fix things and make life in the city better, because people decided that they didn't deserve to be there," she says.[27] She later became the editor-in-chief of the Black-led *Baltimore Beat*.

After Gray's death, the *City Paper* covered the Baltimore Uprising extensively, with less of a focus on the mystery of Gray's death and more on the revolution brewing in the streets. Snowden was asked to cover the Gray trials. She recalls sitting in a section of the courtroom for reporters. "So it's me and mostly white people. So that felt crazy," she says. "They cover this case, and they go home and never have to think about it. They don't have to think about how that could be my brother or my cousin or my son. I'm thinking about it that way."

In an article on Nero's trial, Snowden raised a subtextual truth the media wasn't otherwise addressing: "And there was the ever present question of race—which was never brought up outright, but there all the same. How could preconceived perceptions—real and imagined—have affected the way police dealt with Gray?" Snowden wrote about how Nero's attorney described the crowds at Gilmor Homes as bigger and more dangerous than they were, which the officers used to excuse treating Gray roughly. "It didn't get to be about human experience and trauma," Snowden remembers about the trials.

Snowden's work on Goodson's trial in the summer of 2016 captured a prevalent mood at the time. The trials "Slog On," the headline states. "At every murder trial, the victim's body is part of the evidence," she writes, "but Gray's bones are picked over again and again." She describes how the medical testimony examined Gray's body "vertebrae by vertebrae," while both sides offered incomplete explanations for his cause of death.

* * *

Rob Brune drove from his home in Columbia, Maryland, to record a protest at the Western District station on April 19, after Gray's death was announced. "They took him out the paddy wagon, they beat him again," one protester screams in his video.[28] For several months, in between construction jobs, Brune kept showing up in Baltimore and capturing important moments during the uprising, broadcasting them around the world through Global Revolution Live, a real-time social media platform. He filmed a video of police brutalizing a protester, Larry Lomax, which went viral, and he captured the very beginning of the first night of rioting on April 25. Whereas mainstream journalists were mostly reacting to stories, Brune was often already on the scene.

Very soon after Gray's death, Brune also knew that there were witnesses to whatever happened to Gray and that reporters were missing the story by focusing on protests and press conferences. "I had post-traumatic stress from having people describe in such graphic detail what happened at Stop 2," he recalls. "You know, it was just mind-blowing that they were just ignoring this immediately. I knew it was corruption." He recalls confronting reporters angrily and being met with dismissiveness. One *Baltimore Sun* crime reporter, he recalls, told him the witnesses probably suffered "cognitive dissonance."[29]

Like Brune, Jasen Henderson, known as "suchaputz" on Twitter, investigated the Gray story without the benefits or trappings of a newsroom. He began digging into the audio and video evidence after Gray died. Henderson lives far outside of Maryland and had no history of journalism or activism, but he grew curious about a cover-up that no one else was reporting. In June 2015, he began tweeting at every journalist covering the case about camera 2107. "1 minute of CCTV #2107 was included in 'Gilmore Homes Surveillance' video.

Cuts off right when chase ends. Why?" he asked one reporter.[30] He guessed, properly, that the video would show something BPD didn't want out.

Henderson became a Baltimore police radio aficionado, often having police-related news before anyone else. On October 22, 2015, he tweeted at a *Baltimore Sun* journalist that there was a suicide call to the Gray family house, which he learned by listening to the police scanner and looking up the address. The next day, it was reported by the media that Gray's mother had attempted suicide.

Some of the dispatch audio played during the trials sounds strange to Henderson. It doesn't remind him of authentic conversations, with more natural back-and-forth with the dispatcher and background noise. The radio calls in the Gray case surely sound clipped and incomplete compared to the other dispatch he saved from April 2015. There are also discrepancies here and there between the audio evidence and CCTV video or CAD reports.

Henderson's attention to the police radio developed his understanding of traditional police practices. He knew cage cars were used to transport prisoners in April 2015 when transport vans weren't available. He saved clips from around that time with officers putting prisoners in cage cars. Cage cars have long been a part of Baltimore policing and are mentioned in David Simon's *Homicide: A Year on the Killing Streets* (1991). If cage cars were an option on April 12, then Goodson had no reason to return to North Avenue to pick up Allen instead of dropping Gray off at Central Booking, aside from helping to cover up what happened.

Independent investigators of all political leanings were looking at the Gray case and making significant contributions missing from mainstream reporting. The *Conservative Treehouse* had a writer named Sundance—a Mosby hater and future Donald Trump supporter—who dug into some of the discrepancies in the case. He located the person that was likely the source of Peter Hermann's mistaken identification of the other prisoner in the van, another prisoner with the last name Allen who was arrested on April 12.[31]

The Freddie Gray story offers a chance to consider the difference between journalism as an act and as a profession. Arguably, the most important journalism in the case was done by Kevin Moore and Brandon Ross with the videos they filmed. Both videos not only broke the story of what happened to Gray but provided essential microinformation. Without their videos, Gray's story would have likely been about a prisoner who swallowed some drugs and/or caused his own injury in a van, whichever story BPD chose to make public, and not about a man killed by police.

CHAPTER 16

REFORM AND REVOLUTION

Two movements converged in the aftermath of Freddie Gray's death in Baltimore. Protests against police abuse were already happening on the streets across the country, with an uprising the year before in Ferguson, Missouri, following the police killing of Michael Brown. The Black Lives Matter (BLM) movement—together with the rise of cell phones and social media—brought mainstream attention to deadly police force. Within big police departments across the country, a second movement was happening in response to BLM. This "police reform" movement sought to address policing outside of its purported aims—to enforce laws and reduce crime—by focusing on mitigating its harms, including racial disparities in enforcement and excessive force. By 2015, BPD was led by a self-described "reform commissioner."

The events surrounding Gray's death offer a case study in not only the limits of the police reform movement of the 2010s but also its costs and harms. In *The New Jim Crow*, Michelle Alexander explains how, while the Barack Obama presidency was "celebrated as evidence of America's triumph over race" and promised criminal justice reform, in fact it "revved up the drug war" through even more funding for "the militarization of policing, SWAT teams, pipeline drug task forces" and other "drug-war horrors" than his Republican predecessor.[1]

The Baltimore Uprising—and the real story of how the Baltimore riots started—similarly shows "reform" leaders promising reconciliation and understanding while using a massive police budget, militarized equipment, and a propaganda campaign to control and suppress the movement to end police violence in Baltimore.

* * *

Baltimore was touting a renaissance in the form of the "Baltimore Miracle" in the early 2010s, after Mayor O'Malley left office. Arrests were cut in half, while the homicide rate hit a historic low. For the first time in forty years, the city's population held steady rather than declining. Under Commissioner Frederick Bealefeld III, BPD's mission was no longer "zero tolerance" but catching "bad guys with guns." Still, BPD continued to be plagued by accounts of corruption and abuse.

When Bealefeld retired in 2012, his young deputy, Anthony Barksdale, took over as acting commissioner. Barksdale came from West Baltimore and was credited by many with leading the reduction of crime. He was the likely choice for commissioner, but he had a blunt manner and wasn't politically smooth. Mayor Rawlings-Blake instead went in another direction, choosing someone from the West Coast, Anthony Batts, who had a PhD and spoke the language of progressive reform. He also had a history of ignominious departures from leadership roles in two cities.

Batts started his career in Long Beach, California, where in 2002 he was named its youngest police chief ever. He was also only its second Black chief. In 2008, three whistleblowers won a $4.1 million lawsuit against Batts and the city in a case that became known as "Lobstergate." They had reported on Port Security Unit officers for diving for lobsters while on duty, falsifying time cards, and more. In the lawsuit, the whistleblowers outlined the retaliation they faced, from vandalized belongings to denied opportunities and IAD cases opened against them. Batts took the stand and insisted that the plaintiffs were average employees, despite written evaluations to the contrary.[2]

A year later, Batts left Long Beach to become chief of the Oakland Police Department. It didn't go well. He was given a three-year contract but stayed for only two years. A local reporter found he was constantly leaving town while he was supposed to be at work. Then, halfway through his three-year contract, the mayor learned that he'd applied for another job in California and forced him out. Batts gave interviews about his departure, blaming everything from the mayor to activists, the budget, and even the quality of bullets. He insisted that Oakland residents came up to him on the street expressing how much they loved him.[3]

Batts headed east, where he whitewashed his reputation, attending the Harvard Kennedy School of Government and the Police Executive Research Forum (PERF). He joined police reform commissions, copublished papers, and built connections with influential leaders like William Bratton and Chuck Ramsey, both PERF board leaders and city-hopping commissioners.

Bratton and Ramsey were two leaders in an unofficial think tank of well-funded police consultants—a group the Marshall Project deemed "America's Rock Star Cops"—who have shaped how US policing operates for decades.[4] Bratton led the New York Police Department under Mayor Rudy Giuliani and popularized "broken windows" policing. At the time, he and others described it as a reformist, community-oriented approach. Within ten years, "broken windows" policing was the "original sin" that needed redeeming, and Bratton and his allies had the solutions.

The cycle of original sin and redemption continued into the 2010s. "Can America's Top Cops Save the Police?" the Marshall Project asked in a 2015 story that featured Bratton, Ramsey, and their

colleagues problem-solving the issues exposed by the BLM movement, as if they weren't the architects of a lot of what went wrong.

Alex Vitale writes in *The End of Policing* about how the Obama
administration funded a "large industry of well-paid 'experts' who
make their living trying to 'reform policing.'" They focus on "procedural reforms" like training and policies, as well as trying to "restore
trust" in policing.[5] Ramsey was the cochair of Obama's 21st Century
Task Force on Policing in 2015. With such allies, Batts was well-
positioned to secure his place among the police reform intelligentsia.
All he needed was a job.

PERF played a big role in getting Batts hired in Baltimore. The
mayor and her top advisor, Ken Thompson of the law firm Venable
LLP, contracted with PERF to find and screen applicants.[6] PERF
put Batts's name forward, but a group of Black pastors and some city
council members opposed the nomination. They wanted Barksdale
and sought to continue the lower-than-usual rate of killings and
shootings that he was credited with helping to achieve. PERF
responded by lobbying the media, filling articles with statements
from allies. "Tony Batts is one of the best there is in American policing today," Bratton told the *Baltimore Sun*.[7]

PERF is a dirty word within some BPD circles. Many cops resent
the role it plays in pushing leaders like Batts, and it has become
shorthand for the consultants in general that profit off of the failures
of BPD. Soon after getting the job in Baltimore, Batts gave Bratton's
firm a six-figure contract to help reshape BPD by writing a strategic
plan.[8] The double-dealing that is PERF's bread and butter—getting
hired by police departments to place its own paid members—
becomes triple-dealing when its new placements give PERF leaders
lucrative contracts.

After Gray's death, BPD was put under a federal consent decree
designed to improve policies, training, and systems. Venable won
the $1.475 million annual contract to monitor its implementation

indefinitely. The lead monitor of the consent decree is Thompson, who headed up the team that brought Batts to Baltimore and earns more than $200,000 per year in the role. Ramsey is the principal deputy monitor, earning more than $82,000.[9] In 2012, they promised to reform BPD by selecting and supporting Batts. By 2017, they began profiting off reforming many of the issues that Batts seemingly made worse in Baltimore.

* * *

Batts started turning off rank-and-file officers in Baltimore almost immediately after he was hired. He described seeing, on the streets of Baltimore, drugs being exchanged inside a red balloon. That was a West Coast phenomenon, not something that happened in Baltimore.[10] He also exaggerated the role of large gangs in the city. Batts never fought the appearance of being an outsider, bringing in other outsiders to support him and pushing out commanders who might not be loyal. "I didn't break it, but I'm here to fix it," he said about BPD in 2014, two years into his administration.[11]

Guided by Bratton's strategic plan, Batts instituted sweeping changes to the department. He offered more of everything—more administrative positions, departments, policies, and even an additional patrol shift, from three eight-hour shifts to four ten-hour shifts—but he gave the rank-and-file less clarity. He didn't offer anything like Bealefeld's succinct "bad guys with guns" mission. According to retired BPD Captain Lisa Robinson, PERF and the new policies were "under the auspices of saying we are creating new policing." But with so much disruption and superficial change, Batts "was also building and developing the ability for corruption to thrive in that kind of environment."[12]

Batts's bête noire in Baltimore was excessive force. It kept coming up, and he struggled to respond meaningfully. To lead Independent

Review Board (IRB) investigations into in-custody deaths, he hired an outside consulting firm. But the IRBs inevitably absolved officers of responsibility, rubber-stamping the police investigations, including in the case of Tyrone West, who was choked to death by police in 2013.

Batts's promises of accountability around police use of force were put to the test in his response to whistleblower Detective Joe Crystal, who reported on his sergeant and another officer for beating up a handcuffed suspect. Crystal testified against them in 2014 and faced comprehensive retaliation. "I would call for backup multiple times and nobody came," he said. Multiple supervisors and colleagues threatened him. Someone put a rat on his car windshield.

Crystal was, by most measures, a good cop. He won an award in the academy and was promoted very quickly out of patrol into a detective squad. "We have to recognize that we're police," he told a reporter. "We have to hold ourselves to that higher standard."[13] After Crystal filed a lawsuit and made his story public, Batts announced he would open an independent investigation, hiring more of his out-of-town allies. Instead, IAD investigated Crystal himself, digging up a minor vehicle policy violation. It was Lobstergate 2.0. Ultimately, Crystal was forced out of the department. After he left, to be "Joe Crystalled" was to face an inferno level of retaliation from crossing the thin blue line.[14]

* * *

While Batts was ostensibly reforming BPD from the top, activists were building grassroots responses to policing on the street. Duane Davis, a.k.a. Shorty, became the godfather of the Baltimore street protest movement in the 2010s. He is best known for his barbeque truck, from which he feeds the homeless and activists, and his toilet bowl art installations, which are decorated with newspaper clippings and serve as political commentary. In 2011, one of those toilet bowls, placed outside of a courthouse, landed Shorty in jail, facing charges of terrorism and accusations of planting a bomb. Davis was acquitted by a jury. There was no bomb, only a decorated toilet bowl. Shorty has a way with words. "Freddie Gray got killed because of reckless eyeballing. He looked the white man in his eyes," he says.[15]

Around 2012, Shorty met Payam Sohrabi while they were both out filming the police. They formed Baltimore Bloc, an anonymous collective, which conducted protests over police violence and other issues and held meetings and classes on political resistance at a local worker-led bookstore. The group created social media memes like "Wanted Wednesday" signs, which would portray problem cops as criminals. Shorty saw his role as Bloc's "Jiminy Cricket." "I'll go out front and push you around and talk crazy to you. I'm gonna make you listen to Tawanda."

Tawanda Jones started "West Wednesday" protests each week shortly after her brother Tyrone West's 2013 death in police custody. Like Kevin Moore, she faced harassment from becoming a public figure of resistance. Her tires were slashed constantly, she says. She remembers a cop driving by miming cutting his throat. Jones describes herself as a mother of four, a "Christian woman," and a preschool teacher. "And I am an advocate and freedom fighter, you know, and that didn't happen until my brother passed away." Baltimore Bloc showed up for West Wednesdays, promoting and broadcasting the demonstrations online.

Ralikh Hayes joined up with Bloc about six months before Gray's death. Before then, he had been perhaps Baltimore's most precocious activist, leading demonstrations from as young as thirteen with the Algebra Project, a tutoring and advocacy program. Hayes calls Bloc a "shadowy collective" that did direct actions but also aimed to be an "alternative press opposing the police narrative." There were other groups protesting in Baltimore at the time too. The People's

Power Assembly was run by Reverend C. D. Witherspoon, who was extremely vocal during most protests.

Hayes describes Bloc as "the bastard stepchild" of Baltimore's resistance. "Everybody else wanted to, you know, talk policy and negotiate," he says. "We're angry. We try and turn up while still keeping people safe."[16] Hayes dealt with slashed tires himself as well as infiltrators at Bloc meetings and Stingray technology intercepting his cell phone communications. Independent journalist Rob Brune recalls being unable to livestream at Baltimore protests because signals were jammed.

Early in 2015, Hayes had a premonition. "I'm telling you. I feel like something's coming. Like I'm real certain that Baltimore is going to happen at some point. I can feel it in my bones."

Brune remembers the same. "I heard people in Baltimore saying: this is a pressure cooker, and it's about to explode over police brutality."

*　*　*

It wasn't experienced organizers who drove the first wave of protests following Gray's death but his own friends and neighbors. "We were kind of just showing up and providing support and coordination," Hayes recalls. It started with a march from Gilmor Homes to the Western District police station on Saturday, April 18, that culminated in a demonstration. Community members stood on the lawn of the police station and yelled in anger. Gray's stepfather, Richard Shipley, told the crowd, "If this happens to him, it could happen to any of you."[17] The footage from these first nights at the police station includes scenes of Black men weeping, a representation of the uprising that wasn't prominent in the mainstream media.

When Gray's death was announced early the next morning, April 19, the protesters returned to the police station with more organizers and some media. Reverend Witherspoon stood on the steps of the police station, asking: "Who needs the Baltimore City police department? You've been nonresponsive. We haven't heard anything from the police."

"It's been a whole week!" one of Gray's friends shouted.

"Seven days ago, we watched the police throw this man into the back of a van and break his neck," Witherspoon yelled. "And now you're telling us we've got a police commissioner who can't come out here and speak to us? That's some bullshit."

The crowd chanted, "We want justice!"[18]

Brune was on the scene filming. His footage captured a tense dynamic between local protesters and a group of out-of-towners led by well-known activist Linda Sarsour, wearing "Justice League NYC" T-shirts. The tension came to a head when an officer pulled up and got out of his police car. It was Porter, whose involvement in Gray's death wasn't public yet. A young man approached, wanting to speak to him. One of the women from New York got in his way and started yelling at everyone there. "Brothers and sisters of this community. We are outraged! We are angry! But there is still a way to organize to fight the forces that be. . . . There must be order in every movement. Or else you just sound like you yelling and screaming! So we should get away from these police cars, because you cannot fight one cop."

"I just wanted to talk to him," the young man said, not yelling or screaming at all. In retrospect, Brune wonders what was really motivating Sarsour's group. He points out how they actively drowned out Witherspoon's speech with songs and chants. "It turned us off politically. Like you gotta go," Hayes recalls of the New Yorkers. "The Baltimore came out in us."

Marches from Gilmor Homes to the Western District station took place daily, growing bigger and more diverse, as the police set up barricades in front of the station. "All night, all day, we gonna fight for

Freddie Gray," people chanted. "No justice, no peace." On April 21, the community held a vigil near the site of Gray's arrest. That night, the police got more aggressive, arresting two journalists who were filming. James A. MacArthur, a radio host and independent journalist, was one of them. "To make a statement, if you will, of all the people to arrest, Baltimore police decide they want to put us, as journalists, in handcuffs," he told Brune.[19]

After five days of protest at the police station, organizers led a mass demonstration of hundreds if not more than a thousand people to City Hall and back on Thursday, April 23, with unions and student groups participating. BPD tried a soft response, tweeting: "Earlier we told you about 2 arrests that we made. There have been no additional arrests. The protesters remain peaceful. #WeHearYou."

Another major demonstration was planned for Saturday, April 25. Malik Z. Shabazz of Black Lawyers for Justice promised thousands of demonstrators. He wanted to "shut down" the city. "Things will change on Saturday, and the struggle will be amplified," he said. "It cannot be business as usual."[20]

* * *

For some, Shabazz himself was responsible for what happened on the afternoon of Saturday, April 25, when some rioting broke out downtown near Camden Yards, home of the Baltimore Orioles. A scene played on the evening news nationwide: Allen Bullock, a friend of Gray's, stood on top of a police car, breaking its windows with a traffic cone. Jones recalls Shabazz steering a few hundred protesters past City Hall toward Camden Yards earlier that afternoon. It made her uneasy. Shabazz, who came from DC, was one of the "outside agitators" the mayor liked to blame.

Brune's camera captured the beginning of the clash between police and protesters outside of Camden Yards. A woman police officer wagged her finger at the protesters, shouting at them and setting some of them off. Eyewitness Kiona Craddock was there, trying to calm down some of the angry crowd. Deputy Commissioner Davis was also there, acting like a calming force on the scene but also setting up barricades and lines of cops to kettle the protesters into one area, which didn't help. "Please go home!" the crowd shouted at the cops and their cars before some young people, including Bullock, jumped on top of them.[21]

As the police chased some of the kids away from Camden Yards, photographer Devin Allen captured a moment that became a *Time* magazine cover: one young man chased by an army of riot cops holding batons. Hayes remembers being next to Allen when he took that picture, trying to get him to keep running. "I'm happy he didn't listen to me, because, you know, that was the image of a lifetime."

Another incident happened as the crowd made its way back onto the commercial street. The protesters passed a strip of bars where mostly white baseball fans were outside drinking before a game. Josh Reynolds, who was working at one of the bars, recalls the protesters chanting, "Black Lives Matter!" and the white patrons of Pickles Bar chanting back, "We don't care!" as well as "Run them over!" to a car behind them.[22] A fight broke out. Protesters threw trash, a trash can, and the barricades. Bar patrons threw bottles and trash back.

Jones remembers hearing a bar patron call Gray the n-word and saying he got what he deserved. "Someone threw a bottle at him, and it was on and popping," she says. "Horses come running past. It seems like a scene out of the Wild Wild West. I couldn't believe my eyes." She wasn't dreaming. The police had deployed some cops on horses that day.

The April 25 protests continued into the night, with demonstrators gathered in front of the Western District station and police in a different mood. "Get off these streets right now or we will be arresting," a loudspeaker message played on a loop.[23] A tight group of riot cops smacked their shields. Two photojournalists were assaulted by police that night. One was also arrested. Hayes says it was common for BPD to play nice during the day and provoke aggression at night.

It was a tense day and night, and then Gray's family requested peace and quiet. On Monday, April 27, Gray's funeral was held at Shiloh Baptist Church in West Baltimore. The funeral was a major production, with reporters from all over the world, packed crowds, and celebrities in attendance. "You would've thought Jesse Jackson died," Sierria Warren says about the crowd. Jesse Jackson was there, with a front-row seat. Some of the audience had to sit in an overflow room and watch on a screen.

Most of the speakers turned Gray into a symbol of something. Congressman Elijah Cummings asked, "Did anybody recognize Freddie when he was alive?" A flashing sign hung behind the pulpit saying, "Black Lives Matter," followed by "& All Lives Matter."[24]

"This isn't the time for sitting on the corner drinking malt liquor or playing lottery," Reverend Jamal Bryant declaimed, "or walking around with our pants hanging down past our behind."

"My peoples wasn't feeling it," Warren says. "Why's there so many people in here concerned about this shit? Ain't nobody really worried about the justice part. Everybody just coming out to be seen."

Jones had a bad impression too, calling Gray's funeral a "dog and pony show" full of "camera chasers and poverty pimps." She wonders, "Where the hell was that when my brother died?"

Organizers had planned on a quiet day after Gray's funeral, respecting his family's wishes. There were no protests scheduled. Still, there was rioting that night. The story of how that happened has less to do with the protest movement and more to do with Commissioner Batts.

* * *

Batts's problems as a leader came to a head in his handling of what happened to Gray. On the day of Gray's death, this reform-minded commissioner said, "All lives matter. All lives matter in this city." At a press conference the next day, he couldn't pull off the appropriate tone and demeanor for the moment. He spoke at length about independent boards, policy, and training. He enumerated a long list of Gray's body parts that might provide a clue as to his cause of death. He whispered and giggled while the CCTV video was playing.

For a while, the *Baltimore Sun* seemed to be on Batts's side, publishing stories about emails he sent to staff that made him seem like a good leader.[25] In the real world, a group of Black ministers asked him to resign, and the protests got bigger and angrier.

Batts took back the narrative and asserted control on April 27. At 11:43 a.m., during Gray's funeral, his media spokesperson issued a statement claiming, "The Baltimore Police Department/Criminal Intelligence Unit has received credible information that members of various gangs, including the Black Guerilla Family, Bloods, and Crips have entered into a partnership to 'take out' law enforcement officials." Then, it stated, "This is a **Credible Threat**" in bold letters.[26] Batts doubled down the next day, calling the threat "valid and verified." The FBI later discredited it.

The Freddie Gray case files show the apparent source of the warning. On April 16, FIT Detective Teel sent an email to the Watch Center with the subject "Threat on Police Gilmor Homes." It relayed a message from a Central District sergeant:

I respectfully wish to report that on 4/16/15 at about 0500hrs an unknown black male called the Central District and . . . advised that there was BGF, Bloods, and Crips in the Gilmore [sic] Homes area and that these gangs were going to kill any police who comes in there and for officers to be careful, it stems from the Gilmore Homes incident this past Sunday.

The caller didn't give his name and hung up immediately after delivering the message, according to the sergeant. The "threat" circulated a bit; a reporter asked about it at an April 20 press conference. Then, two weeks after the anonymous call, on April 27, Batts announced it to the public as if it were urgent and credible.

Vitale writes about the "Miami Model" used by police to gain control over protests and make them seem more violent than they are. In 2003, Miami officials were concerned about demonstrations outside of the Free Trade Area of the Americas negotiations. In addition to establishing a heavy militarized presence, they initiated a propaganda campaign, warning about "violent anarchists." City leaders even enacted temporary ordinances against gatherings of eight or more people without a permit.

The Miami police were criticized and sued for their actions, but that style of protest control has been widely adapted. As Vitale explains, "This style is characterized by the creation of no-protest zones, heavy use of less lethal weaponry, surveillance of protest organizations, negative advance publicity about protest groups, preemptive arrests, preventative detentions, and extensive restrictions on protest timing and locations."[27]

On April 27, BPD put into action an extreme form of the Miami Model—extreme because there weren't any protests scheduled that day to mischaracterize or exacerbate. BPD had to invent them. Mere hours after the "credible threat" announcement, BPD issued an entirely different warning: Teenagers were planning a "purge" that afternoon, in the style of a couple of movies released in 2013 and 2014. It was going to start at Mondawmin Mall in West Baltimore. Mondawmin is a major transit hub next to two high schools and a university.

CNN reported later, "In a sobering example of life imitating art, the chaos sweeping the streets of Baltimore may have been partly inspired by a series of action-horror movies. Baltimore police said rioting at a shopping mall and elsewhere Monday afternoon started amid rumors, spread on social media, of a 'purge' led by large groups of marauding high school students."[28]

There is no evidence to support the claim that "marauding" teenagers descended on the mall that afternoon to "purge." *Mother Jones*, the only mainstream news outlet to catch the real story, published a piece the next day that focused on eyewitness accounts of a transit shutdown: "The police were stopping buses and forcing riders, including many students who were trying to get home, to disembark. Cops shut down the local subway stop. They also blockaded roads ... and essentially corralled young people in the area. That is, they did not allow the after-school crowd to disperse."[29] BPD and school police had been ordered to show up at Mondawmin before 3:00 p.m. in riot gear.

On May 1, 2015, a website called the *Baltimore Eclipse* published a piece called "The Battle of Mondawmin," with images and videos from helicopters, witnesses, and recorded testimony from the ground, including from James MacArthur. It shows, at first, young people standing around in small groups, as teenagers do, wearing backpacks and looking confused by all of the riot police. Some of them hold up their arms, saying, "Hands up, don't shoot." Many are filming the police. Several cops suddenly rush a boy, pinning him against the bus stop wall and dragging him to the ground.[30]

The images and videos are startling and strange. A group of cops in tight formation cross Liberty Avenue toward a small group of young people who escaped onto the porches of homes across from the bus stop. The cops then walk backward, still in formation, as if in a police training video. An armored truck arrives on the scene. Law enforcement personnel arrive in army fatigues carrying munitions. Police set up vans to arrest kids. At most, a handful of kids have thrown debris at the cops by this point.

Meg Gibson, an elementary school teacher, posted her testimony on Facebook: "They were waiting for the kids. . . . I saw the armored police vehicle arrive. Those kids were set up, they were treated like criminals before the first brick was thrown."[31]

At 3:39 p.m., the police tweeted, "A group of juveniles are still in the area of Mondawmin Mall. We are hearing reports of bottles and bricks being thrown at officers."

Helicopter footage shows where the stand-off became especially violent: A group of teenagers retreats down Westbury Avenue, a residential street at the east edge of the mall that hits a dead end. For whatever reason, a group of cops follows them. Some kids throw stones or other objects at the cops, and some police, including a commander in a white shirt, respond by throwing objects back. The kids then approach the police en masse and the police retreat. A smoke bomb lands at the feet of one of the kids. The kids disperse. At some point, a child lies down in the road to block an armored vehicle.

At the end of the standoff, the police are in formation moving the kids away from the mall, driving them south on Reisterstown Road while still pelting smoke bombs in their direction. Less than a mile down the road is the intersection of Pennsylvania and North Avenues, where the riots started that night.

As for the alleged purge threat, it was linked to a flier, with distinctive vertical and horizontal white lines, and a message: "All high schools Monday @3. We going to purge. From Mondawmin to the Ave. Back to downtown. #FDL," which the Urban Dictionary explains means "fucking down low." The background of the flier is one of the media images from two days before, with kids on top of a police car outside of Camden Yards.

At 2:30 p.m. on Monday, just before the Mondawmin lockdown, *Baltimore Sun* reporter Carrie Wells posted the flier to her own account. Many comments asked her for the link to the original post or some evidence of a teenager posting it. "It wasn't like I was the only one who saw it," she responded. "Our reporters were seeing it on social media/getting sent it all weekend." The flier didn't exist *all* weekend; its image was from late Saturday. "I don't really get the obsession over it to be honest with you," Wells later tweeted. "People certainly purged that day."

Fair and Accuracy in Reporting (FAIR) investigated the purge flier and found no instances of it being organically shared by teenagers or other protesters intending to purge.[32] It was mostly shared by journalists, commentators, and concerned parties. The flier circulated during the same weekend BPD members shared false stories about Gray having a preexisting injury and banging his own head into unconsciousness. Baltimore wasn't the first city with a questionable purge threat. In 2014, sheriffs in Albany, New York; Louisville, Kentucky; Orlando, Florida; and other cities were put on alert over alleged purge fliers. One flier from that time had lines cutting across it, similar to the one in Baltimore.

In the weeks, months, and years that followed, police and other city leaders continued to promote the purge narrative at Mondamin. The *Baltimore Sun* reported that high school students planned a "walk out" at 3:00 p.m., though in fact that was when the school day normally ended for most students. The *Sun* has also reported for years on dispatch calls and messages among police leaders insisting that up to a hundred kids were on the scene between 2:30 and 3:00 p.m. committing crimes and abusing cops *before* the transit shutdown. Since the afternoon in question, there have been eyewitness accounts and videos that disprove that story.[33]

* * *

Rioting did happen on the evening of April 27 after the events at Mondawmin. It started at the Penn North metro station and extended into parts of the city. On Mount and Baker Streets, at Stop 2, a corner store was burned down. "They should've burned the police department, not the shit that we used," Sierria Warren says. She recalls the owner of that store looking out for people, giving away food and diapers. "At the same time, the police are getting off a little bit too easy, so they made them do some work," she says.

In July, after Batts was fired, BPD released two long CCTV videos to the media showing how the riots started at Penn North. The videos show a surreal scene with various dramatic set pieces across a broad intersection over two hours that don't look like a riot but do raise questions about city leaders' intentions that night.[34]

When the first video starts, a mass of kids in backpacks is heading down Pennsylvania Avenue from Mondawmin Mall at around 4:30 p.m. They spot a police car on North Avenue, which is, for some reason, empty and parked in the middle of the street. By the time the camera pans over, the kids are searching it and eventually breaking its windows and jumping on it. One kid stands on top of it and raises his arms in the air, as if climbing a mountain and planting a flag.

Over the next two hours, different groups of kids and adults visit that one car, poking through it, smashing it, or just taking pictures. It becomes a tourist attraction. Meanwhile, someone has also destroyed another police car on the other side of Pennsylvania Avenue, parked to the east of a CVS. The intersection is bustling with people, but the vast majority aren't involved in the damage to the police cars.

After twenty minutes or so, a line of about twenty-five cops appears on the north end of Pennsylvania, almost a block back from the CVS store, with riot shields. An armored truck filled with cops also arrives and parks near the second damaged police car. According to juvenile public defender Jenny Lyn Egan, who was on the scene observing with the Baltimore Action Legal Team, similar lines of cops also appeared on either end of North Avenue.[35]

In the videos, the cops stay in position for more than an hour, doing nothing, as the following occurs: Someone lights the second vandalized police car on fire. A police van behind it also catches fire. They burn for more than an hour, while no fire trucks arrive. Also, the CVS is looted, only about 150 feet from the brigade of law enforcement. Eventually, hundreds of people of all ages run into CVS, leaving with bags or carts of goods for over an hour. A group of people also breaks into the check-cashing place across the street from the CVS.

After about an hour, the riot cops are still in the same position but have doubled in number. Then, two things happen. The police make a move, setting off a loud sound cannon (according to Egan and other observers) and approaching North Avenue while banging on their riot shields. By that time, the intersection is mostly cleared of rowdy youth. Around the same time, gray-brown smoke from a fire begins pouring out the broken doors and windows of the CVS. The wall of cops creates a boundary around the CVS.

Based on the video evidence alone, the most reasonable conclusion anyone could draw about how the riots started would sound like a conspiracy theory. Did Batts hope to set off a "purge" on April 27? Police allowed and promoted criminality in their sight for almost two hours on an otherwise ordinary Monday afternoon at a busy intersection. They left a vandalized police car in the middle of the street, which blocked two lanes of traffic. They let two cars burn dangerously. And they allowed hundreds of people to loot a CVS. A CitiWatch camera operator was observing all of this too. This summary doesn't include some of the suspicious behavior Egan and others noted on the ground, including what she describes as a possible plainclothes officer leaving the CVS before the fire broke out.

It is often forgotten, in the local discussions of the riots, that the *Purge* movies are based on the premise that the government sanctions a period of lawlessness, withholding any help by first responders. Whatever their goal, Baltimore city leaders did succeed, on April 27, in keeping the damage contained to mostly West Baltimore. The sports fans downtown weren't affected, as they had been two nights before.

According to an after-action report by the FOP, Batts did issue a "stand-down" order, insisting that officers not respond to protesters even if pelted with rocks. The mayor made a statement on April 26 supporting the policy: "We also gave those that wished to destroy space to do that as well," she said.[36]

Batts at first denied that he gave this order, then apologized to the officers, then told the media that it was for their own protection. It was an approach he advocated in Oakland as well: "We allowed the protesters to start breaking into Foot Locker," he told an Oakland reporter in 2011. "We had to do that because we didn't want to look like this was a police action, where we were responding too soon."[37] "Stand down" is part of the story, but it's also a simplification of what really happened at Mondawmin Mall and Penn North on April 27. It leaves out the police provocation.

* * *

Both President Obama and Mayor Rawlings-Blake called the rioters "thugs" and contrasted them with good and peaceful demonstrators. The Penn North videos offer a different way to look at the so-called thugs. The young people mostly targeted police cars at first. At one point, some of them broke into the trunk of a police car and located a large amount of caution tape. They tried to cordon off the north end of Pennsylvania Avenue, blocking the line of cops from the intersection. That didn't work, so they took a bunch of items that they got from CVS or found on the street—a stone blockade, what looks like a wipes dispenser, a traffic cone—and laid them across the street. Someone lit some of the items on fire. They created a makeshift barrier to the police—a political statement, if you will, though it wasn't an effective barrier. The cops walked right over it later.

As for the "thugs" who looted the CVS, they were people of all ages mostly stealing necessities under the permitting gaze of the police around the corner. In the CCTV videos, people are clearly running out of the store with paper goods, diapers, and food.

The "thugs" narrative was powerful. The next day, a video went viral of a woman who found her teenage son in the streets and smacked him in the head while he tried to get away. Batts lauded her: "I wish I had more parents who took charge of their kids tonight," he said. The son, he said, was wearing "a hood on his head." National news outlets referred to her as a "hero mom" and "mom of the year."[38]

Lisa Snowden, *Baltimore Beat* editor-in-chief, recalls this incident as "loaded": "What it was supposed to show us is that, 'See, this mother is great. She's being a good mother and disciplining her child.' And also, the right thing to do for some Black person that's acting up is to beat him, that beating your kid is going to change them in any way." Snowden contrasts the media's easy condemnation of one kid's small act of resistance to its silence over "all of the violence enacted by decades of Baltimore City government that created these moments where everyone was just kind of fed up."[39]

* * *

Batts called off his stand-down order at some point on April 27. More than 250 people were arrested over the next forty-eight hours, about one-third of them released without charges. The next day, the community engaged in cleanup while city and state leaders went into occupation mode. Governor Hogan declared a state of emergency and called in the National Guard and state police. Thousands of troops in army fatigues showed up in Baltimore. The mayor announced a curfew, restricting anyone from being outside in the city from 10:00 p.m. to 5:00 a.m.

On April 30, Congressman Cummings stood on North and Penn with a bullhorn just before 10:00 p.m. "I want to thank the clergy for being here and lifting us up spiritually. Give them a hand," he shouted, while people clapped. After he was done thanking people, he begged everyone to go home.[40]

In one of Brune's videos, MacArthur tries convincing Cummings to use his influence to end the curfew, citing the trauma for children to have to see assault weapons in their neighborhoods. "It looks like they're here to engage the enemy, except we have nothing but citizens here," he said. The curfew stayed in effect for almost a week, long after there was any rioting. The streets at night were occupied by faceless cops in riot helmets banging on their shields and pepper-spraying citizens. Many stories came out about unlawful, excessively forceful, and/or arbitrarily enforced arrests and police actions during the occupation.

It was during this week that Hogan expedited the autopsy and Mosby announced charges. For the next six years, Mosby would be accused by Hogan, Batts, Rawlings-Blake, and others of rushing charges against the officers, but they all benefited from her choice. She did what they couldn't: she effectively ended the would-be revolution. One day after her announcement of charges, people danced along North Avenue to Bob Marley's music. Within a few days, the Baltimore Uprising was over. "Directly after the uprising," Hayes says, "90 percent of the people that were active disappeared."

CHAPTER 17

PROGRESSIVE PROSECUTOR

When Marilyn Mosby walked down the steps of the Baltimore War Memorial on May 1, 2015, and announced charges against six officers, "It was like watching a movie and that was the end," journalist Lisa Snowden remembers. "I think for most people who had a surface understanding it was like, okay, we're taken care of now." A cheer erupted when Mosby announced "second-degree depraved heart murder" for Goodson. She followed that up by outlining various additional charges Goodson and five other officers, including manslaughter, second-degree assault, misconduct in office, and false imprisonment.

While Mosby's team had clearly staged a moment with a dramatic backdrop, she appeared to be all business, wearing a plain black suit and charmingly pissed-off disposition. A reporter asked, "What do you think needs to be done to make sure what happened to Freddie Gray doesn't happen again?"

Mosby shrugged and said, "Accountability," looking around for the next question.[1] Her presence was an antidote to the wordy promises from other city leaders in the weeks prior.

"I'm exuberant. I'm happy. I'm every positive word you can think of," Kevin Moore was filmed shouting in the streets that afternoon. "I love you, Marilyn Mosby. Please don't ever leave Baltimore."[2] Eleven days later, Mosby appeared on stage at a Prince concert, which, based on many reactions online, took a little away from the luster of the all-business moment.[3]

Mosby wasn't the first prosecutor to criminally charge officers in a death-in-custody case, but it didn't happen often. An ACLU study found that thirty-one people were killed by police in Baltimore between 2010 and 2014, but only one was criminally charged, and he was off duty at the time of the killing.[4] Mosby's predecessor, Gregg Bernstein, declined to prosecute the cops that killed Anthony Anderson in 2012, despite an autopsy determination of homicide from "blunt force injuries." Bernstein claimed Anderson had a liver disease that made him bleed internally.[5]

Mosby's charges in the Gray case helped her build a national image as a "progressive prosecutor," part of a movement of prosecutors, including Philadelphia's Larry Krasner, who seek to reform criminal justice. She sustained this reputation on the national stage for years. "I Was the Prosecutor in the Freddie Gray Case. Here's What Minneapolis Should Know" was the headline of an op-ed she wrote for the *Washington Post* after George Floyd was killed by police in 2020.[6]

Locally, Mosby was a more complicated figure. Her progressive bona fides were called into question by activists, defense attorneys, and other close observers, beginning with her choices in the Gray case. "You had the people behind you, Marilyn Mosby. You had us, you fed us the shit that tasted so good," Moore told the *Guardian* in July 2016, a year after he cheered her on. "This judge knows this shit inside and out, he does it for a living. He ate right through those bullshit charges."[7] Today, Moore calls Mosby's prosecution "a performance" that was "built for them to get the police off the hook for what they did."[8]

Moore remembers Mosby and her staff buying him lunch and making him feel important after Gray's arrest. Not only wasn't he invited to testify, but he wasn't allowed in the courtroom. "They immediately told me to leave or they were gonna lock me up." He showed up for Porter's trial in December 2015 wearing CopWatch gear. "The whole thing was just crazy. And it made me feel like I was going crazy," he recalls. He steadily lost faith as Mosby's office prosecuted Nero, Goodson, and Rice over the next eight months without introducing evidence of excessive force at Stops 1 and 2.

The SAO presented a case over four trials that omitted testimony from Moore and most of the other eyewitnesses. It was also missing Freddie Gray. Prosecutors neglected to introduce him as a complete and sympathetic figure. The case centered the voices and claims of the officers involved in Gray's arrest. It was a homicide case built on the statements of the defendants. SAO's choices are illuminated by the backgrounds and personalities of the prosecutors who led it.

* * *

Mosby's election in 2014 seemed like a made-for-the-movies upset. Mostly unknown on the political landscape, the thirty-five-year-old defeated Bernstein with a fraction of his campaign dollars and endorsements. Mosby and her husband, Nick Mosby, then a state delegate, shored up support from community leaders and ran an energetic campaign.

Originally from Boston and the daughter and granddaughter of police officers, Mosby had worked as an assistant state's attorney at SAO in Baltimore for five years before becoming a private insurance attorney. Most of her campaign rhetoric came from the standard tough-on-crime template. "When you turn on your news and when you open up your newspaper, do you feel safer?" she asked. She criticized the incumbent for letting "repeat violent offenders" back on the street.[9] Bernstein had run four years earlier on a similar platform to defeat an incumbent.

Tawanda Jones joined Mosby's campaign. "When Greg Bernstein decided to laugh at my family in their face and tell us he was not going to do anything about the officers that murdered my brother, I told him not to get comfortable in his seat," she recalls.[10] The endorsement of activists like Jones helped Mosby paint a portrait of Bernstein as part of an old-white-boys' club that protected dirty cops.

This message was reinforced by several news stories just before the election that linked Bernstein to a seemingly corrupt BPD officer, Captain Robert Quick, his friend and former client. WBAL's David Collins reported that Bernstein had protected Quick in 2012 by shutting down an investigation into fraudulent use of overtime.[11] Another layer to that story emerged in a different news outlet. Attorney Janice Bledsoe told *City Paper* that she had led the 2012 overtime investigation into Quick, and Bernstein had forced her to resign after she confronted him about the conflict of interest.[12] As discussed, Bledsoe was in a relationship with WBAL reporter Jayne Miller. WBAL broke the Quick story but didn't mention Bledsoe.[13]

Mosby used the Quick stories to her advantage. She issued a press release with the heading, "Bernstein Protects Dirty Cop Who Stole From Taxpayers." Less than a week later, Mosby defeated Bernstein. Once in office, she named Bledsoe as her Deputy State's Attorney.

Jones also helped Mosby get elected but didn't get anything in return. She had been hoping that the officers who killed her brother would be criminally prosecuted. Yet once Mosby was elected, Jones recalls, "She said she couldn't do anything about my brother's case, because it didn't happen during her tenure. You know that's BS. There's no statute of limitations on murder." Mosby did promise Jones she would look into possible "next steps" if her office gained any new information. So Jones had her brother's body sent for an independent autopsy. That ME concluded he was killed by positional asphyxia, or choking, and not a preexisting heart condition.

According to Jones, Mosby's office took this new information but never answered her calls again.

* * *

Four months into Mosby's new administration, SAO put together a team of homicide and other prosecutors with decades of combined experience to work on the Gray case. By June 2015, it was decided that the case would be tried in court by the two top-ranking officials in the department after Mosby, Chief Deputy Schatzow and Deputy Bledsoe, both appointed only in January. The experienced prosecutors steadily left or were pushed off of the case.[14]

Schatzow and Bledsoe weren't veteran prosecutors themselves, which contributed to the perception, pushed by the defense, that SAO's case was more political than legal. Schatzow had been doing mostly corporate litigation for thirty years. He supported Bernstein during the election, but Mosby made a political move by bringing him on board. Bledsoe had spent most of her career as a criminal defense attorney, apart from a year and a half when she worked under Bernstein running the Police Integrity Unit.

Bledsoe had a specific earlier connection to Gray. In 2013, she represented him on charges of possession with intent to manufacture and distribute narcotics. A video from the court proceedings shows the attorney and client frustrated with each other. She had arranged a plea deal for time served and probation, but he believed he had a good alibi: he was in jail when his mother's house was raided. "Do you want to plea or not?" she asked him curtly. The judge finally gave a speech about old men in prison regretting moments like this, when they had a chance at freedom. Gray took the deal but let the judge know he was unhappy with his counsel. Two years later, Bledsoe was his advocate in court again.[15]

* * *

Mosby promised the world that her office had conducted an "independent investigation" into Gray's death: "My team worked around the clock, twelve- and fourteen-hour days, to canvass and interview dozens of witnesses, view numerous hours of video footage," she said during her May 1 announcement.[16] Yet a pretrial proceeding and notes from her office reveal that SAO's investigation was not as independent or thorough as promised.

In her May 1 statement, Mosby indicated that her office had acted as a law enforcement agency. Consequently, just like the police, SAO was required to turn over its investigation to the defense. During a September 2015 hearing before the first trial, Judge Barry Williams asked, "It has been stated many times that the state's attorney's office did their own thorough independent investigation. And so based on the request . . . what did you turn over?"[17]

Bledsoe replied that she had turned over a witness interview of Kiona Craddock and a video of "three unidentified community members who would not identify themselves." That was the video of Davonte Roary and two other young men walking along the path of the chase. Besides that, she said, she had turned over some canvassing notes that could have fit on one page.

"Okay. And so there were no other interviews that you had, because, if you did, then you would have turned those over?" Judge Williams asked.

"That is absolutely correct," Bledsoe replied.

Kevin Moore, Sierria Warren, and Jacqueline Jackson all recalled speaking to SAO during April. Warren's name appears in SAO's internal notes from April, and she remembers seeing Brandon Ross at SAO's offices. SAO's notes also mention a Stop 2 witness named Darren Green. There were no recorded statements with any of these witnesses included in the discovery evidence turned over by the state to the defense.

SAO ended up turning over an additional seventeen pages of notes from its investigation to the defense, covering April 21 to April 30, which included Schatzow's notes from his settlement discussions with attorney Billy Murphy.[18] SAO's notes show Mosby's office considering a wide range of possible charges while at the same time just beginning to collect and review evidence in the case. The notes alternate between evidence to-do lists—cameras, black box, cell phones, dispatch, and so on—and detailed considerations of possible charges. They contain no independent analysis of the police's version of events, besides a note that Gray was thrown "face down in the van" at Stop 2.

After the trials ended, Mosby and her team were asked by reporters if they had rushed the charges. Mosby responded, "When the ME came back and determined that it was a homicide, that's all that we needed. We had all the officers' admissions, so we had a story and a timeline as to how the incident occurred."[19]

Schatzow offered a similar explanation: "I think that much of the evidence was in the statements of the officers who gave statements, and those statements were all in by April 17th."[20] In their responses, Mosby and Schatzow both confirmed that the initial statements of the defendants formed the basis of their investigation, despite those statements being often contradictory and unclear.

Retired BPD Detective Lewis remembers that prosecutors were uninterested in evidence from the BPD task force that didn't fit their case. "For her not to use it and then to build a case on *we don't know what*, I just felt like this is all a sham, right?" she says. She says she "lost faith in the system" from working on the Gray case and afterward stopped doing investigative work altogether.

Even so, Lewis looked forward to the trials revealing more information than she got from the police investigation. "All you are is just a piece of the puzzle. You don't know how you fit together with everybody else's pieces. And I was looking forward to finding out how my little piece fit. I never got that," she says.[21]

* * *

The case against the Baltimore 6 was prosecuted over four trials, but it also played out in more than three hundred pretrial motions, many of them more informative and juicy than what happened in court. The knife, for instance, wasn't mentioned once in court, but in the motions it was a topic of heated and suspenseful debate.

The defense team was aggressive, seeking to dismiss charges and/ or force Mosby to recuse herself based on prosecutorial misconduct, failure to charge for a crime, conflicts of interest, and more. In one defense motion, Mosby was accused of being a witness in the case.[22] A few weeks before Gray's arrest, an assistant state's attorney (ASA) sent an email on her behalf to the Western District major. It requested that police do something about a drug shop located outside of a mentoring program across North Avenue and a few doors down from where Gray was chased. The major forwarded the email to his lieutenants, including Rice, with a demand for increased enforcement around Mount and North generally, which wasn't the ASA's specific request.

A *Baltimore Sun* article on the email—"Baltimore Prosecutor Asked Police to Target Area Where Freddie Gray Was Arrested"—led to a popular understanding of Gray's arrest as kicked off by Mosby herself.[23] The defense technically lost most of the motions to dismiss or recuse, but they often won them in another sense, through the *Baltimore Sun*'s coverage.

The defense was more successful legally in addressing SAO's discovery violations. Under *Brady v. Maryland* (1963), prosecutors have to turn over any "exculpatory" evidence or information that could benefit the defense. SAO was accused of violating *Brady* rules repeatedly, and the judge usually agreed. "I'm not saying you did anything nefarious. I'm saying you don't understand what 'exculpatory' means," he told Schatzow at one point.[24]

* * *

On December 2, 2015, SAO opened its first case, against Officer William Porter, before a packed courtroom of reporters and observers and a crowd of protesters outside. Porter was charged with manslaughter, or killing without malice aforethought, as well as second-degree assault, misconduct in office, and reckless endangerment, all pertaining to his failure to seat-belt Gray or call for medical attention at Stops 4 and 5. Schatzow and Bledsoe, who co-prosecuted all four trials, planned to use Porter as a witness in subsequent trials to prove Gray was injured by Stop 4.

Schatzow kicked off Porter's trial by supporting the police's insistence that Gray was not harmed at Gilmor Homes. Referring to Gray's ability to "lift his head, lift his neck" and "bear his weight" in Moore's Stop 1 video, he concluded that "those things are evidence of the fact that when Mr. Gray went into the van, there was nothing wrong with his spine." As for Stop 2, Schatzow repeated the police's uncorroborated story:

> *After the door was closed, Mr. Gray was kicking that door from the inside. And not only was he kicking the door from the inside, he was shaking the van. And as you know, that's not something you could do while you're lying on your stomach, you have to be up to bounce to get it to move. So he was able to get to his feet.*

Schatzow was essentially asking the jurors to disregard anything of serious concern on Kevin Moore's and Brandon Ross's cell phone videos, which they watched later that day.

After opening statements, the state called six witnesses in succession who were BPD employees to discuss training, policies, how policies are distributed, and other administrative matters. The state's seventh witness worked for the city and purchased seat belts for the vans. Though Porter was charged with violating specific laws, SAO was focusing on his violations of BPD policy.

The state's first major argument was that Porter should have seat-belted Gray at Stop 4. Yet at the same time, prosecutors were arguing that Gray was fatally injured by that point. In other words, they argued that Porter should have seat-belted a dying man with a broken neck. BPD's long-standing prisoner transport policy, K-14, gave officers discretion around seat-belting, stating, "This procedure should be evaluated on an individual basis so as not to place oneself in danger." The officers who testified said that given the tight space, they rarely, if ever, seat-belted a prisoner in the van.

Three days before Gray's arrest, on April 9, BPD had sent an email to all personnel with an updated policy on prisoner transport, 1114, that mandated seat-belting with no exceptions. The new prisoner transport policy was fifteen pages long and was attached to an email with five other new policies.[25] It wasn't discussed during roll call. Still, prosecutors argued that the officers should have followed it. They claimed Porter could have checked his work email at home; as evidence that he was computer savvy, they mentioned that he used to build computers professionally.

In response, Porter's attorney characterized BPD as essentially dysfunctional, with broken computers and poor policy transmission, and countered that individual officers shouldn't be blamed for systemic problems. As an example of poor training, he shared an anecdote about Porter witnessing a gun instructor shoot a trainee in the head by accident.

SAO's second main argument was that Porter knew Gray was in medical distress at Stops 4 and 5 and didn't call for a medic. As proof, prosecutors played Porter's April 17 statement to FIT detectives. Porter testified in his own defense, describing Gray as more energetic than he did in his initial statement—making eye contact, holding a full conversation, and using his own strength while Porter helped him onto the bench. Schatzow jumped on that last point, accusing Porter of changing his story and lying on the stand: "When you were interviewed by detectives Teel and Anderson, on April 17, you never said that Mr. Gray helped in any way to get from the floor to the bench."

Porter responded that he "thought it was obvious" that he couldn't have lifted Gray all by himself. Schatzow never questioned the bench story, even though it deserved scrutiny. Porter had initially told FIT detectives he sat Gray up on the floor at Stop 4; he only added the bench part forty minutes into his statement. Also, Gray was on the floor and not the bench at Stop 5, according to all of the officers who checked on him.

Porter's April 17 statement to detectives wasn't solid proof of Gray's medical status at Stop 4, so prosecutors focused on Teel's written notes from her phone conversation with him on April 15. She wrote, "Officer Porter advised that he asked Mr. Grey [sic] what he needed at which time he stated that he couldn't breathe." Bledsoe called Teel the "most credible" witness in the trial in her closing statement. Yet Teel's notes were hearsay, and Judge Williams excluded them from future trials. Even the medical examiner had to discuss her autopsy conclusion without reference to Gray having trouble breathing at Stop 4.

Prosecutors put more stock in Teel's thirdhand account of Gray at Stop 4 than they did in Moore's video evidence at Stop 1, which starts with Gray screaming, ". . . breathe!" followed by, "I need attention." According to Schatzow, "Somebody asks a police officer for a medic, you get them a medic," underscoring Porter's omission. Yet SAO didn't charge Miller and Nero with crimes related to medical neglect in apprehending Gray.

Neill Franklin, a former BPD training commander, says Gray should have gotten medical attention from the minute he was screaming for it: "From what we've seen in the video of his arrest, and what appears to be his inability to stand and walk once they were about to put him in the transport van, there's enough to indicate to me that something is possibly wrong here with his physical health."[26] Franklin testified for the state in the subsequent trials of Officers Nero and Goodson. During Goodson's trial, he ended up acknowledging that Gray might have already been injured at Stop 1.

Porter's overall defense was to insist that Gray was not fatally injured at Stop 4, as far as he could tell. But his attorney also made it clear that Gray's safety and medical care were the responsibility of Goodson, not Porter. This defense became an ongoing problem for prosecutors, who had indicted multiple officers for the same neglectful actions.

Prosecutors struggled to build a successful case. They based their understanding of the cause and timing of Gray's death on Dr. Carol Allan's autopsy report, but her findings, which she admitted were inconclusive, didn't survive cross-examination. She acknowledged that she lacked any evidence to support her belief that Gray got up after Stop 2 and was thrown forward before Stop 4.

Prosecutors also spent a lot of time on procedural and other minutiae that sometimes lacked an obvious payoff. Judge Williams generally came off as fair, agreeable, and rigorous with both sides, but he didn't hide his frustration with prosecutors when they seemed to go on aimless explorations. Bledsoe interrogated Officer Gladhill about a time when he drove a pregnant woman to the hospital rather than call for a medic. She repeatedly asked questions about Gladhill's starting location and the distance to other locations. After eight sustained objections in a row, Judge Williams, audibly annoyed, finally said, "It is not relevant. Please ask another question."[27]

* * *

SAO's files contain a list of thirteen civilian witnesses who gave taped statements to BPD detectives. For the first two trials, the prosecutors called only Ross, Gray's close friend who had witnessed most of Stops 1 and 2. He testified at the end of the first day of Porter's trial and gave "the most compelling testimony," according to the *Washington Post*.[28]

Ross held back tears for the first half hour of questioning while he identified Gray in photos and videos. Gray's mother started sobbing as Bledsoe played Moore's video, so the court went to recess. Judge Williams spoke to Ross about being too emotional. Moore's video was played with the sound off during subsequent trials.

The media picked up on Ross's charisma, not just the tears but also his dry and literal delivery. "If I told you this was Officer Porter, would you disagree?" Porter's attorney, Gary Proctor, asked him, pointing to a CCTV still image.

"I can't believe what you say," Ross answered, getting laughs.

"When you wanted to make a complaint, the officer you approached to do so was Officer Porter, right?" Proctor asked Ross.

"No, I told him to get a supervisor," Ross responded.

"The person you trusted with that complaint was Officer Porter, wasn't it?" Proctor asked.

"I wouldn't use the word 'trust,'" Ross answered.[29]

Ross sounded coached when questioned on the stand by Bledsoe. She asked what he heard when running toward Stop 2. "I heard more screaming and noises that sound like a Taser—or possible shackles—coming around the corner," he said. Prosecutors believed that Gray wasn't tased. Ross found a way to support their story, even though he had been confident with FIT detectives on April 13 that the sound he heard was a Taser.

* * *

The defense called on Officer Porter and some of his colleagues—Zachary Novak, Mark Gladhill, and Matthew Wood—to present a counternarrative of what happened during Gray's arrest. This was a coordinated approach over the four trials. Different officers testified for each defendant, but they all told the exact same story, one that had evolved considerably from what many of them initially told FIT detectives.

It was a tale of sudden, shifting extremes. At Stop 2, the officers said, Gray was so combative that he needed shackles. Then, he suddenly became like a "dead fish" or "dead weight" when Rice pulled him into the van, which served to explain how he appeared on Ross's video. Then, after the doors closed, Gray got back up and became combative again.

One by one, the officers repeated a refrain with three notes: banging, shaking, and yelling. "I could tell the wagon was, uh, shaking back and forth," Officer Wood testified in Porter's trial. "I thought I heard that someone was yelling . . . someone was banging around."[30]

"At the second stop, Mr. Gray was banging around inside of the wagon, causing the wagon to shake, and screaming all the time," Miller testified during Nero's trial.[31]

"He then started to bang, yell, scream, violently shake the wagon, side to side," Nero testified in Goodson's trial. When Nero first told his story to FIT detectives, he never mentioned the van shaking at all. By the trials, he testified that he had never seen a van shake so much in his career.[32] Finally, after all of that banging and shaking, the officers described Gray as "lethargic" and tired out at Stops 4 and 5.

Prosecutors didn't challenge any part of this story during Porter's trial, except to interpret Gray's alleged lethargy as a sign that he was injured from a rough ride after the van left Stop 2. Rather, they challenged the officers on microdetails, like Porter's story of how Gray got on the bench at Stop 4. SAO's approach seemed to be to try to undermine the officers' credibility by treating them as if they were lying. Bledsoe asked Officer Aaron Jackson if he recalled seeing Gray put in the wagon at Stop 2. He said he didn't recall it. "You don't recall it, or you don't remember it?" she asked, appearing to pick an argument over two words that mean the same thing.[33]

* * *

Porter's trial concluded after ten days of testimony. Bledsoe gave the state's closing statement, in which she accused Porter of committing "negligent assault." According to Todd Oppenheim, Baltimore felony public defender, there is no such crime in Maryland. The jury instructions only offer three choices for second-degree assault—direct battery, attempted battery, or intent to frighten.[34] "The more appropriate crime would be reckless endangerment," Oppenheim says, which Porter also faced. In his closing statement, Porter's attorney argued that the state provided "literally no evidence" as to how Gray was killed.

Schatzow gave the rebuttal statement to close for the state. As he sometimes did during all of the trials, he brought up a point that seemed out of step with SAO's case. He discussed how evasive Porter was with FIT detectives about what he saw at Stop 2 and asked: "What was he trying to cover up? Was he covering up his own knowledge of what had happened there?" Up until then, SAO hadn't argued that there was anything to cover up at Stop 2. Whatever Schatzow meant, SAO did subtly change its position on Stop 2 in the subsequent trials.

The jurors deliberated for two and a half days before concluding that they could not come to a resolution on any of the charges, so, on December 16, Judge Williams ruled the case a mistrial. Press reports indicated the jurors were leaning toward acquittal on the serious charges and guilt on the two lower offenses: misconduct in office and reckless endangerment.[35] After that outcome, the rest of the officers opted for bench trials, meaning Judge Williams would determine their verdicts.

SAO had intended to try Officer Caesar Goodson and Sergeant Alicia White next, using Porter as a key witness in those trials, despite having just impeached his credibility. But because Porter was still under indictment after the mistrial, Judge Williams ruled that he could testify only if granted limited immunity—that is, none of his testimony could be used against him in a retrial. Williams's decision was challenged by the defense but ultimately affirmed by the Court of Special Appeals. Mosby also sought to use other indicted officers as witnesses. Her requests and the defense's objections caused delays, forcing a change in the order of the trials. Officer Nero ended up facing trial second. This was unfortunate for SAO, because its case against Nero was its weakest.[36]

* * *

On May 12, 2016, Officer Edward Nero faced trial for second-degree assault, misconduct in office, and reckless endangerment based on his actions at Stops 1 and 2, including not seat-belting Gray. Prosecutors argued that Miller and Nero committed assault by handcuffing and moving Gray without reasonable articulable suspicion of a crime. Rice called out the chase but never told Miller or Nero why. "A reasonable officer would seek additional information as soon as possible," Franklin testified.[37]

Schatzow seemed to forget about his legal argument at one point. "Mr. Gray was not assaulted there," he said about Stop 1 during a bench conference, "just as he was not assaulted at Stop 2."[38] SAO had charged officers with literally "assaulting" Gray at both stops.

Nero had an easy defense: he didn't arrest Gray, his attorneys argued. It was Miller who detained, handcuffed, and moved Gray before the officers found a knife. In response, SAO pointed to where

Miller and Nero used "we" in their statements, calling it a "joint arrest." Schatzow interrogated Miller on this point. "Well, let me ask you this. Did Officer Nero remain on his bike at the intersection of Bakbury and Presbury?" he asked. "Or did he—well, that's the question. Did he remain?" Miller explained that Nero left his bike briefly and then went to get Miller's bike. In a long back-and-forth, Schatzow failed to show how Nero participated in Gray's initial detention. In his decision after the six-day trial, Judge Williams rejected the joint arrest argument. He found Nero not guilty on all charges.

Another notable moment occurred while Miller was on the stand. Like his fellow officers, Miller testified that Gray was shaking the van at Stop 2. Schatzow challenged him on that, playing CCTV video from that stop. He asked Miller to let him know when he saw the van shaking, which never happened. Schatzow didn't address the implications of the van not shaking, as though he raised the point only to impugn Miller's credibility. Still, SAO was pivoting on a key part of its Stop 2 story.

* * *

The last two trials, of Officer Caesar Goodson and Lieutenant Brian Rice, took place during the summer of 2016, each running for seven days, repeating most of the arguments from prior trials, and ending with no convictions. Goodson's trial brought more of the behind-the-scenes drama to the fore, including accusations of Detective Dawnyell Taylor working for the defense and Officer Novak coaching Donta Allen at the Western District station after the van ride.

Schatzow introduced the term "rough ride" for the first time during his opening statement to Goodson's trial on June 9 to make the case for second-degree depraved heart murder, which requires both consciousness of and disregard for extreme risk.[39] "He was injured because he got a rough ride," Schatzow argued. "There was no good reason not to seat-belt Mr. Gray, except to bounce him around, because Mr. Gray had caused a scene." Prosecutors played the video of Goodson's wide turn after Stop 2 as evidence of reckless driving.

For the rest of the trial, prosecutors backed away from Schatzow's initial claim that Goodson gave Gray a purposeful rough ride with intent to harm, focusing instead on his negligent behaviors like not seat-belting. They had no proof to offer of Goodson's intent, let alone that he drove roughly. It was too late; the damage to SAO's case was done. Defense attorneys brought up the "rough ride" claim repeatedly during the trial, pointing out the state's lack of evidence to support it. Judge Williams took exception to the rhetoric, interrupting Schatzow during his closing rebuttal statement: "The state said to the world, it was a rough ride," he noted. "Where's your evidence?"[40] He called the phrase "inflammatory" and "not to be taken lightly."[41] He then found Goodson not guilty on all charges.

Lieutenant Rice's trial started on July 7 and ran briskly. Attorneys rehashed the same seat belt policy and medical neglect arguments presented in prior trials in order to make the case for manslaughter and assault, calling many of the same witnesses to testify. Judge Williams sped the testimony along. It was as if the trials in the Freddie Gray case were by now a well-rehearsed production and trial four was a quick run-through. The large crowd of protestors who had stood outside of Porter's trial had dwindled to two people with signs.

Prosecutors characterized Rice as senselessly malevolent in his decisions to stop the transport van at Stop 2, shackle Gray's legs, and leave him on the floor of the van rather than seat-belt him on the bench. "No rational explanation can be given," Bledsoe stated about Rice not seat-belting Gray.[42] She also showed video of him harassing witnesses at Stops 1 and 2.

Despite the harsh portrait, prosecutors withheld a lot of damaging evidence against Rice from their presentation in the courtroom.

During the trials of Officers Porter and Nero, prosecutors had played their FIT statements in full, holding some of their statements up to scrutiny. Goodson's trial was next, but he had never given a taped statement. Prosecutors not only declined to play Rice's statement in court but fought to keep it out. Rice's attorney wanted to bring it up, but prosecutors objected. Judge Williams called a bench conference. "I was curious. You're not doing the statement?" he asked Bledsoe.

"Nope, I stayed completely away from it in my direct examination," she responded. If the state didn't introduce it, the defense couldn't use it.

The judge agreed but said he was "surprised."[43]

The consequence of that deliberate omission was that the public never learned about Rice's insistence in his FIT statement that Gray was banging his head in the van after the doors were closed. Nor did the public learn that Rice was the first to introduce the influential theory that Gray got back up on his feet to shake the van before it left Stop 2. If prosecutors had played Rice's statement, they would have exposed that the autopsy report hinged on a theory first introduced by one of the defendants, who even admitted at the time to detectives that it was "just an assumption."

Schatzow ended Rice's trial by attempting to connect the seatbelt policy issue to criminal liability in his closing statement: "The injury is foreseeable, because you have policy K-14, which specifically talks about avoiding injuries to prisoners, you have the seat belt inspection, you have the seat belts in the van."[44] Rice should have anticipated Gray's injury when he failed to seat-belt him, Schatzow argued.

Schatzow then made a claim that was in direct opposition to how he opened the first trial seven months before:

> *If you were to credit the testimony that, despite the absence of evidence on the CCTV, that the van is shaking violently, why doesn't*

Rice take action then? Why in the world would he let the van drive off, with this crazed prisoner in the back shaking the van wildly? It's just more evidence that the van wasn't shaking, your honor.[45]

In his opening to Porter's trial, Schatzow had presented Gray shaking the van at Stop 2 as a matter of fact; here, he presented it as fiction. Prosecutors had been quietly shifting their position on the van shaking over the previous three trials, but in throwaway moments, not consistently. They still allowed some officers to testify that the van was shaking without challenging them.

The media, for its part, never picked up on SAO changing its story from the beginning to the end of the trials. Yet, without Gray shaking the transport van at the end of Stop 2, the state had no reason to exclude from consideration that he could have been fatally injured before the van left Gilmor Homes.

* * *

Brandon Ross continued to testify for the state after Porter's trial, but he appeared during the last three trials in handcuffs, with a sullen, distraught, and withdrawn disposition. SAO was holding him in prison pretrial in an assault case dating from March 2016.

Ross's testimony swung back and forth between what he initially told detectives about Stop 2—that the officers "threw him in the van headfirst, on his belly, on his stomach"[46]—and the state's story—that he saw Gray "kneeling" out of the van while his legs were shackled and then "placed" into the van by officers. Because the attorneys weren't debating how the officers got Gray back into the van at Stop 2, they let such moments slide.

Ross's own assault case was repeatedly delayed while he appeared as a witness in the Gray trials. He had been charged with stabbing someone, but prosecutors didn't have a weapon, video evidence, or firsthand witnesses. Then, three weeks after Mosby dropped the charges against the remaining officers in the Gray case, her office dropped Ross's charges too.[47]

Prosecutors may have realized that the optics—their only civilian witness was in handcuffs and clearly reluctant to testify—weren't great. So they summoned Gray's friend Jamel Baker, the single father, to testify in the last two trials as another eyewitness. In doing that, prosecutors selected the one Stop 2 witness who was never entirely sure if he saw Gray thrown, put, slid, lifted, or flipped into the van, because he was looking down from two flights up and busy getting his window screen out of its frame.

In court, Baker was mostly asked about Gray's sneakers. He told the court he recognized Gray hanging out of the van from his new turquoise New Balance shoes. It provided a memorable moment for the media, but Baker didn't like it. "They were too focused on the shoes," he says. He recalls the theatrics of Bledsoe pulling out Gray's shoes: "Well, how did you know it was him?" he recalls her asking. "Da-da, da-da! Then they pulled the shoes out the bag. It just seemed pointless." After he testified, Baker decided the trials were "a waste of time" and SAO "wasn't looking to win."[48] It's a sentiment shared by many of the witnesses. Alethea Booze calls the trials a "front" to "stop the rioting."[49]

Oppenheim thinks they have a point: "The cops are essentially the investigative wing of prosecutors' offices, and the state's attorneys have to rely on officers for most cases," he explains. "Thus, it would stand to reason that the state is going to be mindful of maintaining a good working relationship with the police department while putting on the most high-profile cop prosecution in decades, but still appeasing public sentiment."[50]

Schatzow and Bledsoe were asked during a press conference after the trials whether they had interviewed eyewitnesses. Bledsoe said,

"You have to understand that the community is very reluctant to give names and addresses, but our investigators were out there every day."[51]

Booze disagrees. "Everyone that saw what happened wanted to appear in court, but they didn't call any of us," she says.[52]

A reporter asked Schatzow about Booze in particular. "The name doesn't ring a bell with me," he replied. Booze's statement was in SAO's discovery evidence. Schatzow suggested witnesses should have called the office. "We've been around for fourteen months. We answer the phone."[53]

* * *

On July 27, 2016, Mosby, who had been publicly quiet about the case since her May 1, 2015, press conference, announced that she was dropping the charges that remained against Miller, White, and Porter, citing the "dismal likelihood of conviction."[54] The timing of the announcement suggested another reason. Prosecutors were scheduled to attend a hearing that morning concerning a "clean team" of new prosecutors who were supposed to be taking over for the remaining trials to ensure that the testimony Porter and Miller gave in prior trials wouldn't be used against them. The hearing would address claims by Miller's attorney that SAO wasn't following the rules around keeping the clean team untainted by the current prosecutors. Rather than proceed with the hearing, Mosby dropped the charges. Schatzow insisted in a press conference the next day that Mosby's decision had nothing to do with the clean team. Both clean team prosecutors quit SAO within the following week.[55]

With the end of the Gray case and the judge's gag order lifted, Mosby gave interviews to the *New York Times*, *Vogue*, and others. She spun her losses as valiant victories in that they had led to reforms. She also appeared conciliatory toward BPD. She and the new commissioner, Kevin Davis, who had overseen the Freddie Gray task force, made public statements of mutual support.

Mosby closed the Gray case, but her office continued pursuing another case that involved police brutality, one that didn't gain national attention at the time. On June 7, 2015, Baltimore police, responding to a robbery call from a cab driver, chased Keith Davis Jr. into a garage and shot at him more than thirty times. Miraculously, he survived. Police said Davis was in possession of a gun, which they reportedly located on top of a refrigerator he hid behind. As it turned out, all of the shell casings on the scene belonged to the officers. The Force Investigation Team handled the case but focused more on investigating Davis for the alleged robbery than on investigating the police who shot him.[56]

In February 2016, Davis was acquitted on all charges, including "handgun on person," except for one. Six months into the case, SAO had added a charge called "firearm possession with a felony." Davis was a convicted felon who was therefore not allowed to be within grabbing distance of a gun. Days after he was acquitted for the robbery-related charges, SAO charged Davis with murder, linking the gun on the refrigerator, which his attorneys believed was planted by police, to a murder committed a mile away on the same day of his violent arrest. Davis had no connection to the murder victim.

BPD's choices were predictable in the Davis case. It was Mosby that provided the surprise. She didn't charge the officers. Instead, she would not stop prosecuting Davis for murder despite two hung juries and two overturned convictions, one resulting from a discredited jailhouse informant. Mosby seemed to take one path publicly in the Gray case and the opposite path in the Davis case.

Davis's wife, Kelly, became a vocal advocate against Mosby, mobilizing Baltimore Bloc members and others. In 2022, a judge cited Mosby with a "presumption of vindictiveness" based on statements made and actions taken by her and Bledsoe against the Davis family and their supporters.[57] The broad coalition of people who sought change during the Baltimore Uprising splintered around Mosby's leadership. She lost the support of many activists who supported Tawanda Jones and Kelly Davis, both mothers of four. Others, including the local NAACP, remained passionately aligned to her. She won reelection in 2018.

In January 2022, Mosby was indicted by the federal government for financial crimes, including mortgage fraud. She gave one of her trademark passionate speeches while declaring her innocence. "You see, ever since I walked down the steps of the War Memorial on May 1, 2015, and announced charges against six police officers in the killing of Freddie Gray, I have had a target on my back, and I get it," she said. "I've used my power and my discretion to do things that a lot of people in this country just don't like."[58] At the time of her speech, Mosby was prosecuting Davis, a police brutality victim, for the same murder for the fifth time.

CONCLUSION

THE FEDS

Money poured into West Baltimore after Freddie Gray's death. A program called "One Baltimore" was one of many initiatives that promised to transform the neighborhood by raising millions in funding. Within two years, the program folded.[1] Its failure was emblematic of what happened across Baltimore within government, activism, and community service, where heroes seemed to rise out of the ashes of the uprising only to fail to deliver on promises or be exposed for seeking personal gain.

The federal government also swooped into Baltimore in 2015, promising another set of eyes on BPD and the Gray case. The feds positioned themselves as the adults in the room and took a watchdog role over BPD in the years that followed, through the criminal and civil divisions of the Department of Justice (DOJ).

On April 16, four days after Gray's arrest, representatives from the DOJ Community Oriented Policing Services (COPS) program, which had already been advising BPD, held a "town hall" in West Baltimore, where scores of angry city residents, including Tawanda Jones, lined up to share story after story of abuse and corruption from the police and government. The COPS representatives seemed, at times, overwhelmed by the outpouring.[2]

Then, on April 21, Attorney General Loretta Lynch announced that the DOJ Civil Rights Division would open an investigation into Gray's death. Case files show the local Federal Bureau of Investigation office had been receiving evidence from BPD—and surveilling the protests heavily—but Lynch was speaking about a civil rights investigation, which would address Fourth and Fourteenth Amendment rights against false arrest and unreasonable force.[3]

The announcement contributed to the idea that the feds were coming to save Baltimore. On April 30, then–State Senator Catherine Pugh, who later became mayor, was confronted on the streets by journalist Rob Brune. He told her that witnesses weren't being interviewed in the Gray case. "We're waiting for the federal investigation," she said. "I promise you. I'll give the information to the feds tonight."[4]

On May 8, Attorney General Lynch announced that the DOJ would also conduct a full "pattern or practice" investigation into BPD. Mayor Rawlings-Blake offered hope: "If, with the nation watching, three black women at three different levels can't get justice and healing for this community, you tell me where we're going to get it in our country."[5] Presumably, she was referring to herself, Lynch, and Mosby.

"Three black women? What's that mean?" Officer Nero asked his colleagues in a text conversation.

"Guess it's the mom, girlfriend and grand mom," Officer Miller responded.[6]

Two months prior to Lynch's announcement, the DOJ had announced findings in a double investigation into the Ferguson Police Department and Michael Brown's shooting. Its report found that the department had a pattern and practice of civil rights violations but that Officer Darren Wilson was not at fault in shooting Brown. It was the system, not the individual officer, the feds determined. The DOJ ordered the Ferguson Police Department to enter into a consent decree agreement, which would place the department under federal oversight.[7]

The outcome was similar in Baltimore. The DOJ published the results of its broader investigation into BPD on August 10, 2016, exposing that BPD officers routinely violated the rights of civilians, used excessive force, and discriminated against Black citizens, women, and the disabled.[8] Baltimore was placed under a consent decree. A year later, the DOJ determined that police officers were not at fault in Gray's death.

The consent decree team in Baltimore responded to the problems outlined in the DOJ report with an investment in training, policies, and the types of "procedural reforms" outlined by Alex Vitale in the *End of Policing*. A new commissioner, Michael Harrison, was brought to Baltimore in 2019 by PERF and marketed as a "consent decree commissioner," just as the same group had marketed Batts as a "reform commissioner" years before. Harrison later became PERF's board president while still running BPD. Policing in Baltimore has been guided by the same network of consultants for decades.

Ray Kelly, executive director of the Citizens Policing Project, was hired to work on the consent decree as its lead community liaison but left that role after feeling disappointed by what he saw. "None of the parties of the consent decree were representing the people," he says. He saw a lot of the money go to trainings but also "helicopters, police cars, computers, body cameras, laptops, you name it." Meanwhile, those in charge lacked the "political will" to enforce serious changes because they couldn't let go of thinking they needed to get "crime under control" before addressing human rights, he says.[9]

According to former federal prosecutor Paul Butler in his book *Chokehold: Policing Black Men*, "When the federal government takes over a police department, it does not necessarily improve the situation it seeks to address. About half the time, police violence actually increases after an intervention by the U.S. Department of Justice."[10] Consent decrees give police departments more money to oversee their own internal accountability, with guidance from police-friendly consultants.

Just as the consent decree was getting established in Baltimore, in February 2017, federal prosecutors indicted eight police officers who were part of the Gun Trace Task Force (GTTF). Formed in 2016 and trumpeted in the press as an elite, successful crime-fighting unit, the squad was found on wiretaps to be stealing from residents, dealing drugs, and planting evidence. Squad members had garnered more complaints than any other BPD officers but were still given enormous freedom and unlimited overtime.[11] GTTF officers testified in court that higher-ups had enabled their criminality by burying evidence and coaching them through statements. They described a level of corruption that policies, training, and body cameras couldn't repair. Numerous other indictments followed.

In the last few years, the GTTF scandal and its fallout have dominated media stories about Baltimore police corruption. The GTTF story has been told in books, podcasts, an HBO series by David Simon, and a comprehensive report by an outside consulting group.[12] The death of Freddie Gray has served as the opening chapter to most of these accounts, with Mosby's charges and the riots framed as a dramatic inciting incident. After the riots, the story goes, crime soared, and the police response paved the way for corrupt police officers to have unchecked power. The details of the Gray case are immaterial in this narrative.

Yet the media never exposed the full story of what happened to Gray and how it was covered up by multiple city leaders, including many of the same leaders who have been accused of looking the other way when GTTF officers faced misconduct allegations. The media never revealed that numerous witnesses had consistent accounts of seeing Freddie Gray tased, beaten, and thrown headfirst into the transport van during Stops 1 and 2; that these witnesses began sharing stories with investigators immediately after Gray's arrest; that Lieutenant Rice and Officer Novak pushed a story to investigators and medics that Gray banged his own head, and they appear to have used Donta Allen to promote that narrative; that Rice was also the original source for the unsupported theory that Gray got up at the end of Stop 2 in order to shake the van, which influenced the autopsy and prosecution; that the bike officers were looking for a reason to arrest Gray after they had him in custody, and BPD continued considering options after he was hospitalized; that the Crime Scene Unit was delayed an hour before coming to the police station, during which time Officer Goodson drove the van away from the scene; that investigators and city leaders sought to limit blame to Goodson from very early on; that BPD manipulated footage from publicly released CCTV videos; that the medical examiner was seemingly never given civilian eyewitness statements, which could have influenced her cause of death finding; that prosecutors were talking about a rough ride theory before reviewing most of the evidence; and more.

If these facts were known, the real story of Gray's death might occupy a different narrative function in the GTTF story. If Baltimore had honestly reckoned with the corruption behind how Gray's death was handled in 2015, what followed could have been mitigated.

The city's recovery from the GTTF scandal was the latest in Baltimore's cycle of original sin and redemption. From zero tolerance policing to Gray's death to GTTF, ongoing issues in BPD have been historically suppressed until they finally explode and become national news stories. City leaders respond with speeches expressing shock and dismay followed by hearings and policy changes, like the body cameras and mandatory seat-belting BPD introduced after Gray's death. The narrative of original sin and redemption has allowed BPD to write a story in which it reforms itself constantly, with the help of its criminal justice partners. Yet BPD's sins are not the rare events the department claims. There have been consistent local news reports for decades of unlawful arrests and police brutality, corruption, and criminality.

Baltimore Beat's Lisa Snowden characterizes what happened with the Gray case as an example of this cycle: "Baltimore police have a long history of hurting and killing Black people. Freddie Gray is one that burst through the bubble and made national attention," she says. "Leaders responded to that acting like that's the only one that has ever happened. They said, 'We will acknowledge that happened because we have to, but we haven't had any more of the uprisings that happened after his death. We have it under control now.'" To Snowden, the only thing that changed after Gray's death was a rhetorical shift. "They figured out how to use this kind of soft and cuddly language for violence that is still happening," she explains.

* * *

The DOJ promised an independent investigation into Gray's death, but there were no signs of it for more than a year. Sources working on both sides of the criminal case shared that they were never contacted about it or asked for any evidence during 2015 and 2016. Yet BPD used the promise that a federal investigation was under way to deny media outlets access to police files after Mosby dropped the remaining charges in July 2016.

Finally, on September 12, 2017, one day after BPD announced that the internal affairs investigation was done and disciplinary hearings were scheduled, the DOJ announced that it had also closed its investigation into Gray's death.[13] The timing suggests there was coordination between BPD and a federal investigation that was supposed to be independent. The DOJ has rejected repeated Freedom of

Information Act requests for its files in the Gray case, citing "attorney work product."

While the DOJ report on Michael Brown's shooting in Ferguson was eighty-six pages long. Gray's death received only a press release. In it, the DOJ assured the public that it had comprehensive access to evidence, including CCTV video and civilian witness statements. It then outlined a "factual summary" of the case, repeating the official six-stop story.

Without exception, the DOJ's narrative of Gray's arrest gives credence to the statements of the officers who were the very suspects under investigation. It accepts Porter's claim that Gray was "talking, able to maintain a seated position, and supported his own neck" at Stop 4, despite no independent verification. That Porter might have had an incentive to lie isn't considered. Here again, the Gray case illustrates that the criminal justice system is built around and biased toward the word of cops. As such, it doesn't easily adjust to the possibility of police as criminal suspects. Even the GTTF prosecutions relied more on BPD cops pointing fingers at each other than the testimonies of the countless civilian victims of the officers' crimes.

The DOJ's press release in the Gray case makes a surprising claim about Stop 2, one that wasn't made by any officials or even the officers' defense attorneys: "Once the wagon doors were shut, Rice, Miller, Nero, Porter and multiple civilian witnesses heard Gray yell and bang against the wagon from the inside, causing it to visibly shake." There are no recorded statements of "multiple civilian witnesses" describing Gray causing the van to shake at Stop 2. Numerous witnesses have insisted the van was never shaking. Brandon Ross testified, "I can't really see the van shaking, but I heard a noise."[14] CCTV evidence shows the van not shaking.

It is possible that Gray kicked the van's door at Stop 2 in a plea for help, causing it to briefly move. Ross did tell FIT detectives he heard Gray kicking the door at one point, and Michelle Gross said she heard it on Ross's video. Rice's van shaking story could have had its origins in a tiny kernel of truth.

That wouldn't change the bigger truth, which is that "multiple civilian witnesses" saw Gray appear suddenly quiet and lifeless at Stop 2, as he appeared on Ross's cell phone video. It is also true that multiple civilian witnesses told investigators that several officers used the kind of "headfirst" force that corresponds to the mechanism of Gray's fatal injury, as identified by the medical examiner and expert medical witnesses in court, but their tapes were buried. It is furthermore true that multiple civilian witnesses shared this information on April 12 before they knew that it was their friend in custody and/or that he was in a coma, giving them no apparent reason to lie.

The final word about the Gray case from the feds—the last great hope for accountability in Baltimore—was to silence the real voices of "multiple civilian witnesses," rewrite the testimony they provided, and rubber-stamp the narrative written by Lieutenant Rice and his Baltimore police colleagues.

ACKNOWLEDGMENTS

THIS PROJECT WOULD NOT HAVE been possible without its catalyst, Amelia McDonell-Parry, who kicked off this investigation with me for the *Undisclosed* podcast. I am grateful for her input and permission to continue our investigation on my own, as well as that of the *Undisclosed* team. Jasen Henderson has been extremely generous with his time, insights, and analysis as well.

This book is informed by years-long conversations about Baltimore and policing with attorneys, activists, police officers, journalists, and residents. In particular, I thank Rob Brune, Angela Burnecko, Joe Crystal, Carrie Everett, Megan Kenny, Keesha Ha Patterson, James MacArthur, Anna Mantegna, Brandon Soderberg, Lisa Snowden, D. Watkins, and many regular sources who require anonymity. I offer additional respect and appreciation to the informative, angry, funny, uncompromising, and highly specific community known as "Baltimore Twitter."

Thanks to my editor, Cal Barksdale, whose close attentiveness, rigor, and profound insight have greatly improved the manuscript. Thanks also to Leslie Conliffe for being an unrivaled manager and to Murray Weiss for his belief in this project and efforts to make it happen.

I am grateful for the love, support, and wisdom of my father, Austin Barron, and my late mother, Marilyn Barron, who both taught me not to trust institutions or their propaganda.

Finally, and above all, I offer respect and appreciation to all of the Gilmor Homes community witnesses named in this book for their testimonies over the years. This book is for them.

CHRONOLOGY

April 12, 2015 (Sunday)

BPD's official arrest timeline:

8:38 a.m.: Freddie Carlos Gray Jr. is chased by three officers on bikes and arrested in the Sandtown-Winchester neighborhood of West Baltimore.

8:40 a.m.: Gray is detained on Presbury Street at Gilmor Homes. (Stop 1)

8:47 a.m.: The van stops again at Mount and Baker Streets, still in Gilmor Homes. Gray is removed, his legs are shackled, and he is returned to the van. (Stop 2)

8:57 a.m.: The van stops at Fremont Avenue and Mosher Street, and the driver checks in the back. (Stop 3)

9:00 a.m.: The van stops at Druid Hill Avenue and Dolphin Street in the Central District, where Officer William Porter checks on Gray. (Stop 4. Unconfirmed.)

9:11 a.m.: The van stops at West North Avenue near Pennsylvania Avenue, where Sergeant Alicia White and several officers check on Gray. The bike cops put Donta Allen into the other side of the van from Gray. (Stop 5)

9:18 a.m.: The van arrives at the Western District, where Gray receives medical attention. (Stop 6)

By 10:00 a.m.: Medics transport Freddie Gray to University of Maryland Shock Trauma Center.

10:45 a.m.: BPD's Force Investigation Team opens use-of-force investigation into Gray's injury in police custody.

April 13: BPD gives a press conference, sharing that Gray was chased by officers on bikes and found in a coma at the police station.

April 16: BPD acknowledges Stop 2 in a press release but claims Gray was "conscious and speaking" at this stop.

April 18: First protest march from Gilmor Homes to the Western District police station.

April 19 (Sunday): Freddie Gray dies in the early morning. Surgical autopsy examination is performed. Second march from Gilmor Homes to the Western District. Protests continues daily. BPD task force established to take over criminal investigation of Gray's death in police custody. BPD releases charging documents showing Gray was charged with switchblade possession.

April 20: News conference by city leaders, including Mayor Stephanie Rawlings-Blake, BPD Commissioner Anthony Batts, and Deputy Commissioner Jerry Rodriguez. BPD explains van's journey to Central Booking and Stops 4 and 5. The mayor introduces the idea that Gray's death "happened in the van."

April 21: US Attorney General Loretta Lynch announces that the Department of Justice (DOJ) Civil Rights Division will open an investigation into Gray's death.

April 23: A major demonstration converges on City Hall.

April 25: Rioting breaks out in downtown Baltimore near Camden Yards before an Orioles baseball game.

April 26–May 1: Media outlets report on leaks from anonymous sources claiming Gray died from a variety of causes, including hitting his own head, a preexisting injury, hitting a bolt in the van, and swallowing drugs.

April 27: Freddie Gray's funeral. BPD issues warnings about attacks on police and teen "purge," shutting down transit and blocking streets in West Baltimore. Rioting is permitted and expands into other parts of the city. Nighttime curfew imposed by Mayor Rawlings-Blake, and National Guard ordered by Governor Larry Hogan to patrol Baltimore.

April 30: Autopsy report determines Gray's death to be a homicide. BPD announces discovery of Stop 3 and end of the task force.

May 1 (Friday): State's Attorney Marilyn Mosby announces charges against six BPD officers.

May 8: Attorney General Lynch announces that DOJ will also conduct a full "pattern or practice" investigation into BPD.

Trials and Outside Investigations:

November 30–December 16: Trial of Officer William Porter, ending in a mistrial, as jurors fail to reach a verdict on any of the charges.

May 12–19, 2016: Trial of Officer Edward Nero, ending in acquittal on all counts.

June 9–20: Trial of Officer Caesar Goodson, ending in acquittal on all counts.

July 7–14: Trial of Lieutenant Brian Rice, ending in acquittal on all counts.

July 27: Marilyn Mosby announces she is dropping the remaining charges against the officers in the death of Freddie Gray. Montgomery County, Maryland, is contracted to lead the internal affairs investigation with help from Howard County.

August 10: DOJ publishes the results of its "pattern or practice" investigation into BPD.

September 12, 2017: DOJ announces that it has closed its civil rights investigation into Gray's death, determining none of the officers to be at fault.

October 10: Officers Miller and Nero accept a five-day suspension for their role in the Gray case and avoid disciplinary hearings.

October 27–November 14: BPD holds disciplinary hearings for Officers Porter, Goodson, and Rice based on the investigation conducted by outside counties, finding none of them guilty of any internal charges. Commissioner Kevin Davis drops all internal charges against Alicia White.

NOTES

This book is sourced by interviews with more than sixty people, some interviewed for *Undisclosed* podcast in 2017 and most interviewed over the last three years. This book is also sourced by news reports and thousands of primary case documents, photographs, and audio and video files gathered from sources and Public Information Act requests.

Introduction: True Crime

1 Computer-aided dispatch (CAD) report #F151020146.

2 Robert Brune, "#FreddieGray Rally at the Baltimore Police Station 4.19.15," YouTube video, April 19, 2015, https://www.youtube.com/watch?v=Us44ZTuFMi4.

3 "Deaths in Custody 2003–2020," Office of the Chief Medical Examiner, Maryland. (For reasons that are unclear, this data sheet doesn't include Trayvon Scott, who reportedly died from an untreated asthma attack while in police custody in February 2015.)

4 Kevin Rector, *Baltimore Sun*, April 25, 2015.

5 Benjamin Hancock, "Geraldo Confronted about Fox News Coverage of Baltimore," YouTube video, April 29, 2015. https://www.youtube.com/watch?v=UTcJwYVHi6w.

6 Marilyn Mosby, press conference, May 1, 2015.

7 Sheryl Gay Stolberg and Jess Bidgood, *New York Times*, December 14, 2015.

8 Hillary Nelson, Vulture, July 2018.

Chapter 1: The Timeline

1 The information in the official timeline was shared during Baltimore Police Department (BPD) press conferences on April 12, 20, 24, and 30, 2015, and Marilyn Mosby's press conference on May 1. Some information emerged during the trials, as noted.
2 BPD press conference, April 12, 2015.
3 Freddie Gray autopsy report, April 30, 2015.
4 Mosby press conference, May 1, 2015.
5 Mosby press conference, July 27, 2016.

Chapter 2: Foot Chase

1 Editorial, "Why Freddie Gray Ran," *Baltimore Sun*, April 25, 2015.
2 BPD press conference, April 13, 2015.
3 BPD press conference, April 20, 2015.
4 Stacia L. Brown, *New Republic*, April 30, 2015.
5 "Goodson Pre-Stop 1" video in discovery evidence.
6 Brandon Ross testimony, *State v. William Porter*, December 3, 2015.
7 Shawn Washington statement to BPD detectives, April 27, 2015.
8 The route of the chase is informed by the following evidence: "Goodson Stop 1" video in discovery evidence; accounts of the chase from officers and witnesses; video timelines created by SAO and internal affairs investigators; *Baltimore Sun*'s The Dark Room, "Freddie Gray's Girlfriend Recalls His Last Day"; and a video of a walking tour of the chase with Davonte Roary and two unnamed witnesses, taken by SAO (hereafter "Davonte Roary walking tour"), undated.
9 Jernita Stackhouse interview with author, June 29, 2019.
10 Davonte Roary walking tour, undated.
11 Jayne Miller, "Police Release Timeline in Arrest of Freddie Gray," WBAL, April 16, 2015.
12 Seth Stoughton email to author, July 25, 2022.
13 Brandon Ross testimony, *State v. Edward Nero*, May 13, 2016.
14 BPD press conference, April 20, 2015.

15 Sean Hannity, "Baltimore on Lockdown," Fox News, May 1, 2015.

16 University of Maryland Medical System hospital records for Freddie Gray, April 12–19, 2015.

17 Christopher J. Keary et al., "Toxicological Testing for Opiates: Understanding False-Positive and False-Negative Test Results," *The Primary Care Companion for CNS Disorders*, 14, 4 (2012).

18 Wolf Blitzer, *The Situation Room*, CNN, April 20, 2015.

19 Note: Maryland Judiciary Case Search online database no longer shows dropped or expunged cases.

20 Jenny Lyn Egan interview with author, May 10, 2022.

21 Catherine Rentz, "Freddie Gray Remembered as Jokester Who Struggled to Leave Drug Trade," *Baltimore Sun*, November 22, 2015.

22 Michelle Alexander, *The New Jim Crow: Mass Incarceration in the Age of Colorblindness*, 10th anniversary edition (New York: The New Press, 2020), 8.

23 Ibid, 77, 118.

24 Governor's Office of Crime Control & Prevention, "Maryland's Comprehensive State Crime Control and Prevention Plan, 2010–2014."

25 Alex Vitale. *The End of Policing*, 2nd edition, (London: Verso, 2021), 162–163.

26 *The Rush Limbaugh Show*, Premiere Radio Network, April 30, 2015.

27 Larry Hogan. *Still Standing: Surviving Cancer, Riots, a Global Pandemic, and the Toxic Politics That Divide America* (Dallas: BenBella Books, 2020), 107.

28 David M. Perry, PhD, and Lawrence Carter-Long, "The Ruderman White Paper on Media Coverage of Law Enforcement Use of Force and Disability," March 2016, 1.

29 Erin J. McCauley, "The Cumulative Probability of Arrest by Age Twenty-Eight Years in the United States by Disability Status, Race/Ethnicity, and Gender," *American Journal of Public Health* 107, no. 12 (December 1, 2017): 1977–1981.

30 David Montgomery and Michael Wines, "Dispute over Sandra Bland's Mental State Follows Death in a Texas Jail," *New York Times*, July 22, 2015.

31 Carol Ott interview with author, April 14, 2022.

32 Michael Tomasky, *Daily Beast,* May 5, 2015.

33 Miller self-reported his weight on a "personal information" sheet before he was interviewed on April 12, 2015.

34 Wes Moore, @iamwesmoore, Instagram video, July 15, 2020, https://www.instagram.com/tv/CCrkHAWpgZb/?igshid=e1fm851qlus4&hl=en.

35 ABC, April 13, 2021.

36 Terrance McCoy, "How Companies Make Millions off Lead-Poisoned Poor Blacks," *Washington Post,* April 25, 2015.

37 Kimberley Richards, "CNN Under Fire for Calling Freddie Gray 'Son of an Illiterate Heroin Addict,'" *HuffPost,* December 1, 2015.

38 Terrance McCoy, "Freddie Gray's Life a Study on the Effects of Lead Paint on Poor Blacks," *Washington Post,* April 29, 2015.

39 D. Watkins interview with author, March 2, 2017.

40 Jamel Baker interview with author, June 30, 2019.

41 Sierria Warren interview with author, June 22, 2020.

42 Stefanie Mavronis, "Voices of the Freddie Gray Protest: Part 1," YouTube video, April 27, 2015, https://www.youtube.com/watch?v=K8GZ7Pxh9Js.

43 Alethea Booze interview with author, June 29, 2019.

44 Stackhouse, June 29, 2019.

45 Peter Moskos, *Cop in the Hood: My Year Policing Baltimore's Eastern District* (Princeton: Princeton University Press, 2008).

46 Peter Moskos and Leon Taylor, "Nero Should Have Never Been Charged," *Baltimore Sun,* May 25, 2016.

47 Jaselle Coates interview with author, June 29, 2019.

Chapter 3: The Lieutenant

1 William Porter testimony, *State v. William Porter,* December 9, 2015.

2 Open Baltimore, "BPD Arrests" data sheet.

3 Dispatch audio played in *State v. Edward Nero,* May 13, 2016.

4   It was probably Miller, but it might have been Nero who placed the radio calls after the officers detained Gray, "We got one," and "1700 Presbury, Gilmor Homes." Miller and Nero have similar voices on the radio. The caller wasn't listed on any documents, and the calls don't show up on Computer-Aided Dispatch reports.

5   "Bicycle Patrol Units," *Baltimore City Police History*, September 11, 2013, https://baltimorepolicemuseum.com/en/bpd-units/bicycle-unit.html.

6   Davonte Roary walking tour, undated.

7   Lisa Robinson interview with author, May 23, 2022.

8   Retired BPD commander, speaking to the author on the condition of anonymity, February 3, 2017.

9   Carrie Everett interview with author, September 29, 2021.

10 Brian Rice statement to detectives, April 12, 2015.

11 "Goodson Stop 1" video in discovery evidence.

12 BPD, "2106," YouTube video, April 24, 2015, https://www.youtube.com/watch?v=dBq_i9Jyf_Y&t=727s.

13 Everett, September 29, 2021.

14 Michelle Alexander, *The New Jim Crow: Mass Incarceration in the Age of Colorblindness*, 10th anniversary edition (New York: The New Press, 2020), 7–8.

15 Ray Kelly interview with author, May 18, 2022.

16 ACLU of Maryland, "ACLU, NAACP File Class Action Lawsuit over Illegal Arrests in Baltimore City," news release, June 15, 2006.

17 The officers' arrest histories were obtained from Open Justice Baltimore, a civilian-led criminal justice data enterprise.

18 For a discussion on how Baltimore homicide and arrest numbers correspond, see Brandon Soderberg, "Reckoning with the Legacy of Baltimore's 'Zero Tolerance' Crime Policy This Election Season," *Real News*, March 18, 2022.

19 "Info on Prisoner Transport Vehicle," BPD investigative binder 6.

20 BPD press release, April 16, 2015; BPD press conference, April 24, 2015.

21 Measurements detailed in email from a Thomas Wisner, crime lab technician, to Detective Dawnyell Taylor, June 1, 2015.

22 Oliver Laughland, "Baltimore Officer Made Taser Threat to Witness Who Filmed Freddie Gray Stop," *Guardian*, May 20, 2015.

23 "Goodson Stop 2," video in discovery evidence.

24 Jon Swaine and Oliver Laughland, "Baltimore Officer Suspended in Freddie Gray Case Accused of Domestic Violence," *Guardian,* April 21, 2015. "Baltimore Police Officer Who Chased Freddie Gray Had a Pattern of Violence—Court Filings," *Guardian*, April 23, 2015.

25 "Baltimore Police Officer in Freddie Gray Arrest Once Hospitalized over Mental Health," Associated Press, April 30, 2015. "Records Show Worry over Baltimore Cop's Mental Health," Associated Press, May 1, 2015.

26 Westminster Police Department report, June 22, 2012.

27 Swaine and Laughland, "Freddie Gray Officer Threatened to Kill Himself and Ex-Partner's Husband, Court Document Alleges," *Guardian*, May 5, 2015.

28 IAD records indicate a suspension, though of unclear length. Maryland Judiciary Case Search records show Rice wasn't named on any arrests for months during 2013 and parts of 2014. Normally, he was named on several arrests per month. That could indicate an administrative suspension ("desk duty"). Open Baltimore salary records show him receiving a gross pay that was lower than his salary during that fiscal year, indicating at least one unpaid suspension. Normally, gross salary is significantly higher with overtime pay.

29 Swaine and Laughland, "Officer in Freddie Gray Case Demanded Man's Arrest as Part of Personal Dispute," *Guardian*, May 8, 2015.

30 Pamela Foote interview with author, February 4, 2022.

31 "Chasing Justice: Addressing Police Violence and Corruption in Maryland," ACLU of Maryland, August 2021.

32 State of Maryland Motor Vehicle Accident Report, August 8, 2014; court files, *Kathy Smith and James Dashields v. Brian Rice, Mayor, City Council, et al.*, September 2015.

33 Seth Stoughton, email to author, September 30, 2021.

34 Alison Knezevich, "Lieutenant Brian Rice Charged in Freddie Gray Death Had Weapons Seized in 2012," *Baltimore Sun*, May 2, 2015.

35 Fraternal Order of Police press conferences, April 22, 2015 and May 1, 2015.

36 Former commander, direct message to author on condition of anonymity, September 28, 2021.

37 Everett, March 27, 2022.

Chapter 4: Freddie's Crew

1 Where not indicated, the sources for this section included statements to detectives; interviews with the author; CCTV, security, and cell phone videos; trial testimony, and media stories, most of which are cited later in this chapter.

2 Brandon Ross first 911 call.

3 Jamel Baker interview with author, June 30, 2019.

4 Kevin Moore statement to detectives, April 12, 2015.

5 Baker statement to detectives, April 12, 2015.

6 Daquontay Walker statement to detectives, April 13, 2015. (He was not a witness, but he turned over a copy of Ross's Stop 2 video.)

7 "Facebook," BPD investigative binder 8.

8 Ross statement to detectives, April 13, 2015.

9 "Cell Phone Video Captures Police Incident Now Under Investigation," CBS Baltimore, April 13, 2015.

10 "Goodson Stop 2" video in discovery evidence (from CitiWatch camera 2102, not included in the public release).

11 Ross's second 911 call.

12 Ross testimony, *State v. Edward Nero*, May 13, 2016.

13 BPD press conference, April 20, 2015.

14 Seth Stoughton, email to author, July 25, 2022.

15 *Anderson Cooper 360*, CNN, April 20, 2015.

16 Cheryl Conner, "Neighborhood Remains Peaceful, but Protest His Death," WMAR, April 20, 2015.

17 Duane Day statement to detectives, April 21, 2015.

18 Davonte Roary walking tour, undated.

19 Moore interview with author, April 11, 2022.

20 Catherine Rentz, "Videographer: Freddie Gray Was 'Folded like Origami,'" *Baltimore Sun*, April 23, 2015.

21 BPD press conference, April 24, 2015.

22 Rentz, "Freddie Gray Arrest Witness Accuses Police of Intimidation," *Baltimore Sun*, April 25.

23 Maryland Judiciary Case Search records and courthouse files for Davonte Roary.

24 Moore interview with author, April 11, 2022.

25 Baker interviews with author, June 30, 2019, and March 26, 2022.

Chapter 5: Neighbors

1 Alethea Booze interview with author, June 29, 2019, and interview for *Undisclosed* podcast, January 16, 2017

2 Harold Perry interview with author, June 29, 2019.

3 Jaselle Coates interview with author, June 29, 2019.

4 Jernita Stackhouse interview with author, June 29, 2019.

5 *CNN Special Report: Who Killed Freddie Gray?* CNN, January 19, 2016.

6 Shawn Washington statement to detectives, April 27, 2015.

7 Yolanda White statement to detectives, April 24, 2015.

8 Perry, June 29, 2019.

9 BPD, "2101," YouTube video, April 24, 2015, https://www.youtube.com/watch?v=QbYJuvtohw8&t=674s.

10 US Census Bureau, American Community Survey (ACS), 2011–2015 estimates.

11 William Porter testimony, *State v. William Porter*, December 9, 2015.

12 Ray Kelly interview with author, May 18, 2022.

13 ACS, 2011–2015.

14 "The State of Gilmor Homes Since the Baltimore Uprising," *Mark Steiner Show*, October 12, 2015.

15 Carol Ott interview with author, April 14, 2022,

16 Christian Schaffer, "Lawsuit: Maintenance Crew Demanded Sex for Work," WMAR, September 29, 2015.

17 Lawrence T. Brown, *The Black Butterfly: The Harmful Politics of Race and Space in America* (Baltimore: Johns Hopkins University Press), 2021.

18 Jeremy Ashkenas et al., "A Portrait of the Sandtown Neighborhood in Baltimore," *New York Times*, May 3, 2015.

19 Kevin Moore interview with author, April 11, 2022.

20 Mayor's Office, "Fiscal 2015: Summary of the Adopted Budget."

21 Tobias Sellers interview for *Undisclosed* podcast, December 2016.

22 Sierria Warren statement to detectives, April 12, 2015.

23 Warren interview with author, June 22, 2020.

24 Kiona Craddock statement to SAO investigator, April 14, 2015.

25 Jacqueline Jackson interview for *Undisclosed* podcast, March 13 and 27, 2017.

26 Thomas Wisner email, June 1, 2015.

27 "Freddie Gray Death Protests Intensify in Baltimore," *New Day*, CNN, April 23, 2015.

28 State of Maryland Office of the Chief Medical Examiner, "Post Mortem Examination Report: Freddie Carlos Gray, Jr.," April 30, 2015.

29 "Goodson Stop 1" video in discovery evidence.

30 Robert Brune, "Freddie Gray Arrest Eyewitness Michelle Gross 04.28.15," YouTube video, May 20, 2015, https://www.youtube.com/watch?v=3qiQMzyqKYM.

Chapter 6: Lieutenant Rice's Crew

1 Garrett Miller testimony, *State v. Edward Nero*, May 16, 2016.

2 Maryland Judiciary Case Search database and courthouse files.

3 "Investigation of the Baltimore Police Department," US DOJ, August 6, 2016.

4 Lisa Robinson interview with author, May 23, 2022.

5 Miller text, April 21, 2015.

6 Miller text, April 27, 2015.

7 Edward Nero statement to detectives, April 12, 2015.

8 Garrett Miller statement to detectives, April 12, 2015.

9 "Goodson Stop 2" video in discovery evidence.

10 CSU photograph of leg shackles against ruler in BPD case files.

11 "Wagon Shaking Demonstration" video in discovery evidence.

12 BPD press conference, April 20, 2015.

13 Joe Rivano Barros, "Lawyers Wrangle over Taser Evidence in Nieto Trial," *Mission Local*, March 7, 2016.

14 The officers' schedule for April provides information on when Goodson was working.

15 Zachary Novak texts, April 28, 2015.

16 Miller IAD disciplinary file.

17 Zachary Novak statement to detectives, April 12, 2015.

18 BPD, "2113," YouTube video, April 24, 2015, https://www.youtube.com/watch?v=hNKjyNm0Ou4&t=10s.

19 Angelique Herbert statement to detectives, April 23, 2015.

20 "1034 N. Mount St. Audio 04-12-2015," dispatch audio recording from the Baltimore City Fire Department.

21 Matthew Wood statement to detectives, April 26, 2015.

22 Mark Gladhill statement to detectives, April 26, 2015.

Chapter 7: Pocketknife

1 Marilyn Mosby press conference, May 1, 2015.

2 Baltimore City Charter & Code, 59-22, "Switch-blade Knives."

3 Peter Moskos, "A Primer on the Freddie Gray Trials," Cop in the Hood, May 14, 2016.

4 "First Look at Video Evidence of Knife Found on Freddie Gray," WMAR, October 31, 2016.

5 Michael Janofsky, "Baltimore Opening High-Tech Central Booking Center," *New York Times,* November 23, 1995.

6 BPD, "Proposed eLearning Modules: Stops, Searches, and Arrests/Fair and Impartial Policing" (training manual), 69; BPD policy 1117: Adult Booking Procedures, January 14, 2015.

7 Dispatch audio played in *State v. Caesar Goodson,* June 14, 2016.

8 Wayne Brooks, BPD Legal Affairs, letter dated April 19, 2019.

9 Brian Rice statement to internal affairs investigators, December 27, 2016.

10 Wayne Brooks, BPD Legal Affairs, email to author, June 20, 2017.

11 Knife Chain of Custody Report.

12 BPD policy 1401: Control of Property and Evidence.

13 Zachary Novak grand jury testimony, May 19, 2015.

14 Novak statement to internal affairs investigators, November 4, 2016.

15 Carrie Everett interview with author, March 27, 2022.

16 To explain why the CAD reports don't show Miller's CC request in the morning, *Undisclosed* podcast considered the possibility that the trial audio was edited to make Miller's nighttime call seem like it happened during the morning, with one line of the conversation (the dispatcher announcing the CC and CAD numbers) edited from another conversation. The dispatcher responded to Miller in that conversation with Novak's unit number, adding another layer to the confusion and/or mistakes. That said, there is other evidence to suggest Miller did call the dispatcher during Stop 2, including the call seeming to be playing in the background after Brandon Ross's first 911 call, as the dispatcher seeks assistance (which *Undisclosed* hadn't yet obtained). Still, nothing is conclusive, and the CAD reports are far clearer on the fact that Miller made a CC request at night in relation to the Gray case.

17 CAD reports #151020698 (Miller) and #151020695 (Nero).

18 Mosby press conference, May 1, 2015.

19 BPD press conference, April 13, 2015.

20 It's not possible to independently verify when the charging documents were filed, so Rodriguez could have been telling the truth that charges weren't filed yet and the forms were backdated. There are tracking numbers, but they run along a different sequence for warrants and summons that is not entirely in order. One reason to question the documents is that the original is missing. It was supposed to be in the court files, but they only contain copies. The police binders and discovery files also only contain copies. Another reason is that the court commissioner's unit number matches someone named Ricky Parker, but his signature doesn't look like that name. It looks a lot more like how Officer Garrett Miller signed his name on the same document. In emails during August 2022, the courthouse representative insisted that documents were valid and submitted that night but refused to provide any evidence to support this.

21 Knife Chain of Custody Report.

22 Xan Martin interview with author, March 5, 2017.

23 Hearing Before the Committee on Interstate and Foreign Commerce, United States Senate. April 17, 1958

24 United States Code 1241, Title 15, Chapter 29, section 5, "Manufacture, Transportation, or Shipment of Switchblade Knives."

25 Edward Nero statement to internal affairs investigators, February 6, 2017.

26 Sarah Elkins interview with author, February 23, 2017.

27 "Motion in Limine to Preclude Reference to or Argument About the Legality of the Knife Recovered from Mr. Gray in the Course of his Detention and Arrest," February 1, 2016.

28 Michael Schatzow and Janice Bledsoe press conference, July 28, 2016.

29 Ibid.

30 There was another knife in evidence in the Gray case. It belonged to Officer Goodson. It was reportedly found clipped to his pants pocket when detectives raided his house on April 28. Strangely, it was noted

in paperwork and filed into evidence, but there were no pictures of it included in the public release. A few pictures are missing from that set, as compared to the photo log. It's possible prosecutors were referring to that knife in their statement about one of the officers in the case having the same "type of knife" as the one recovered from Gray, but their statement was unclear.

Chapter 8: Baltimore in Black and Blue

1   Sheryl Gay Stolberg and Richard A. Oppel, Jr., "Suspects in Freddie Gray Case: A Portrait of Baltimore Police in Miniature," *New York Times*, May 9, 2015.

2   Caesar Goodson statements to detectives, April 12 and 22, 2015. (He declines to speak on the record.)

3   Goodson statement to internal affairs investigators, February 15, 2017.

4   Matthew Wood statement to internal affairs investigators, November 1, 2016.

5   Zachary Novak and Mark Gladhill statements to internal affairs investigators, both November 4, 2016.

6   BPD, "1115," Youtube video, April 24, 2015. https://www.youtube.com/watch?v=aEgDnNKuyRQ&t=1s.

7   Michael Schatzow opening statement, *State v. Caesar Goodson*, June 9, 2016.

8   Jay Hwang interview, March 9, 2017.

9   *Washington Post*, September 3, 2015.

10 William Porter testimony, *State v. William Porter*, December 9, 2015.

11 Jamel Baker interview with author, June 30, 2019.

12 Porter texts, April 30, 2015.

13 Porter statement to FIT detectives, April 17, 2015.

14 Angelique Herbert testimony, *State v William Porter*, December 7, 2015.

15 BPD "728," YouTube video, April 24, 2015, https://www.youtube.com/watch?v=d6Ksrd3PSC0&t=1086.

16 "Goodson Stop 5 Part 4," video in discovery evidence.

17 Sheryl Gay Stolberg and Richard A. Oppel, Jr., "Suspects in Freddie Gray Case: A Portrait of Baltimore Police in Miniature," *New York Times*, May 9, 2015.

18 Gladhill statement to internal affairs investigators, November 4, 2015.

19 Carrie Everett interview with author, March 22, 2022.

20 Vanguard Justice Society press conference, May 10, 2015.

21 Lisa Robinson interview with author, May 23, 2022.

22 Marcia Chatelain, "Baltimore Police and the Reign of Commissioner Batts," *Undisclosed* podcast, 2017; "African American Police," Baltimore Police Historical Society, September 11, 2013, https://baltimorepolicemuseum.com/en/bpd-history/afr-amer-police.html.

23 *Vanguard Justice Society vs. Hughes et al.*, 1979. White's height was self-reported on a "Personal Information" sheet before she was interviewed.

24 "Defendants Opposition to State's Motion for Joinder and Motion to Sever Co-Defendants," July 14, 2015.

25 Alicia White statement to FIT detectives, April 12, 2015.

26 White statement, April 17, 2015.

27 White and Novak text conversation, April 18 and 21, 2015.

28 "Sgt. Alicia White, Officer Charged in Freddie Gray Case, Tells Her Story," WMAR, November 18, 2016.

Chapter 9: Rough Ride

1 BPD press conference, April 24, 2015.

2 Lakishna Lewis interview with author, August 22, 2015.

3 Porter statement to detectives, April 17, 2015; supplemental report written by Anderson, undated.

4 "Sources: 2 Officers in Gray Case Had Trouble Before," WBAL, April 22, 2015.

5 Justin George, "Looking for Answers, Part 1: Police Begin Investigation into Freddie Gray's Death," *Baltimore Sun*, October 9, 2015.

6 Justin George, "Looking for Answers, Part 3: Riots Complicate Police Probe into Freddie Gray's Death," *Baltimore Sun*, October 9, 2015.

7 BPD press conference, April 30, 2015.

8 CNN Newsroom with Carol Costello, April 30, 2015; "Inside Scoop on Freddie Gray's Arrest and Injuries," *Anderson Cooper Tonight*, April 30, 2015.

9 Ben Ashford, "EXCLUSIVE: Cop Charged with Murder of Freddie Gray Told Family He Begged Arresting Officers to Restrain Dead Man," *Daily Mail*, May 1, 2015.

10 "Timeline: Freddie Gray's Arrest and Death," *Baltimore Sun*, http://data.baltimoresun.com/news/freddie-gray/index.html.

11 Caesar Goodson statement to internal affairs investigators, February 15, 2017.

12 John Bilheimer testimony, *State v. William Porter*, December 3, 2015.

13 BPD policy G-01.

14 BPD YouTube videos "2019," "2015," "2018," April 24, 2015. Also "1211 Druid Hill Ave." video in discovery evidence. The security camera at 1211 Druid Hill Avenue, from a camera attached to a Head Start program located in Union Baptist Church, showed a van headed toward Stop 4 and a police car following. The *Baltimore Sun* reported that the action in the video was a few minutes earlier than the timeline provided by BPD (Kevin Rector, "The 45 Minute Mystery of Freddie Gray's Death," April 25, 2015). Case files show that the time on the security camera in general was about six minutes ahead of real time (or ahead of the time on a detective's cell phone), which was why BPD requested earlier footage. The same issue happened with the security camera footage of Stop 3, which explains why that video was played in court with the time stamp scrubbed. In other words, the case files do offer support that the BPD timelines did reflect the times those two videos were taken.

15 CAD reports (P151020695, P151020714) locate Novak at Stop 2 and then Stop 5, even though he didn't go to Stop 5. They don't show

him downtown getting gas after Stop 2 and then at the police station, which was his actual journey.

16 Robert Brune, "#FreddieGray Rally at the Baltimore Police Station 4.19.15," YouTube video, April 19, 2015, https://www.youtube.com/watch?v=Us44ZTuFMi4.

17 "SAO Notes on Freddie Gray" in discovery evidence.

18 Joshua Insley email to author, July 18, 2022.

19 Jon Swaine, "Death of Baltimore Man Freddie Gray in Custody Sparks Call for Independent Inquiry," *Guardian*, April 19, 2015.

20 "MFM Seeks Justice and Truth behind the Death of Freddie Gray," Murphy Falcon Murphy news release, April 19, 2015.

21 "Baltimore Investigates Death of Man in Custody," *New Day*, CNN, April 20, 2015.

22 Yvonne Wegner, "Freddie Gray's Twin Sister: 'Please Stop the Violence,'" *Baltimore Sun*, April 26, 2015.

23 David E. Ralph, Deputy City Solicitor, memo to Board of Estimates, September 4, 2015.

24 *New Day*, CNN, April 20, 2015.

25 Murphy press conference, June 26, 2016.

26 Alethea Booze interview with author, June 29, 2019.

27 Tobias Sellers interview for *Undisclosed* podcast, December 2016.

28 Sierria Warren interview with author, June 22, 2020.

29 Kevin Moore interview with author, April 11, 2022.

Chapter 10: Confidential Informant

1 Kevin Moore interview with author, April 11, 2022.

2 BPD, "728," YouTube video, https://www.youtube.com/watch?v=d6Ksrd3PSC0&t=1086.

3 Garrett Miller statement to FIT detectives, April 12, 2015.

4 BPD, "Proposed eLearning Modules: Stops, Searches, and Arrests/Fair and Impartial Policing" (training manual), 66.

5 Zachary Novak statement to FIT detectives, April 12, 2015.

6 "The Other Man in the Van with Freddie Gray Breaks His Silence," WJZ, April 30, 2015.

7 "Second Man in Police Transport Van Speaks Out," WBAL, April 30, 2015.

8 "2nd Van Passenger: Freddie Gray 'Did Not Hurt Himself,'" *Don Lemon Tonight*, CNN, May 2, 2015.

9 William Porter and Miller text conversation, April 30, 2015.

10 Donta Allen statement to detectives, April 12, 2015.

11 Jeff Noble, email to author, December 20, 2016.

12 Allen testimony, *State v. Caesar Goodson*, June 16, 2016.

13 Ibid.

14 Pretrial hearing, *State v. Caesar Goodson*, June 9, 2016.

15 BPD policy J-12.

16 Novak testimony, *State v. William Porter*, December 9, 2015.

17 Novak statement to internal affairs investigators, November 4, 2016.

18 "SAO Notes on Freddie Gray" in discovery evidence.

19 Affidavit of Matthew Fraling, III, June 5, 2016.

20 Maryland Judiciary Case Search database and courthouse files from York, Pennsylvania, and Baltimore City.

21 U.S. Code Title 18, 921.

22 Doug Donovon, "Panel OKs $6 Million for Police Victim," *Baltimore Sun*, December 2, 2004.

23 Stefanie Mavronis, "Voices of the Freddie Gray Protest: Part 2," YouTube video, April 28, 2015, https://www.youtube.com/watch?v=nJd7pUm2Kzc&t=53s.

Chapter 11: Injured Arm

1 BPD press conference, April 20, 2015.

2 Kevin Rector, "Fire Department Releases Medical Response Timeline in Gray Case," *Baltimore Sun*, April 23, 2015.

3 Dispatch audio played in *State v. Caesar Goodson*, June 14, 2016.

4 Zachary Novak statement to detectives, April 12, 2015.

5 Caesar Goodson statement to internal affairs investigators, February 15, 2017.

6 William Porter statement to detectives, April 17, 2015.

7 Garrett Miller statement to internal affairs investigators, February 6, 2017.

8 Fire department dispatch calls provided by Baltimore City Fire Department.

9 CAD report #F151020146, but it doesn't show a clear arrival time at Shock Trauma. It does show the medic enroute at 9:55. The time was provided officially by the Fire Department spokesperson to the *Baltimore Sun*.

10 Dispatch audio from the Baltimore Fire Department scanner archive, April 12, 2015, downloaded from broadcastify.com.

11 CAD reports #P151020714 and #F151020146.

12 Ibid.

13 Jayne Miller, "I-Team Examines Call For Medical Help in Gray Case," WBAL, April 24, 2015.

14 Porter text, May 4, 2015.

15 Thurman White statement to detectives, April 24, 2015.

16 Lakishna Lewis interview with author, August 22, 2015.

17 Angelique Herbert statement to detectives, April 23, 2015.

18 James Irons statement to detectives, April 28, 2015.

Chapter 12: The Autopsy

1 David Simon, "Mr. O'Malley's Bad Math," *The Audacity of Despair*, May 18, 2015.

2 Simon (@aodespair) tweet, June 11, 2020, https://twitter.com/AoDespair/status/127111775784153907.

3 State of Maryland, Office of the Chief Medical Examiner, Post Mortem Examination: Tyrone West, December 5, 2013.

4 "New Autopsy Says Tyrone West Died of Asphyxiation during Police Struggle," WMAR, December 14, 2016.

5   Tyree Woodson Force Investigation Team file. First reported: Baynard Woods, "What Happened to Tyree Woodson?" *Baltimore City Paper*, May 24, 2017.

6   Memo from FIT Detective Charles Anderson, March 9, 2014.

7   Scott A. Luzi, Judy Melinek, and William R. Oliver "Medical Examiners' Independence Is Vital for the Health of the American Legal System," *Academic Forensic Pathology* 3, no. 1 (March 2013): 84–92.

8   State of Maryland, Office of the Chief Medical Examiner, Post Mortem Examination: Freddie Gray, April 19, 2015.

9   UMMS, hospital records for Freddie Gray, April 12–19, 2015.

10 *Baltimore Sun*'s The Dark Room, "Freddie Gray's Girlfriend Recalls His Last Day," https://vimeo.com/146275343.

11 Morris Marc Soriano testimony in *State v. William Porter*, December 7, 2015.

12 Adam Lipson, *Undisclosed* podcast, May 22, 2017.

13 Leigh Hlavaty, *Undisclosed* podcast, May 22, 2017.

14 Colin Campbell, "Man Injured in Gilmor Homes Arrest Has Spine Surgery, Remains in Coma," *Baltimore Sun*, April 15, 2015.

15 "Baltimore Investigates Death of Man in Custody," *New Day*, CNN, April 20, 2015.

16 Carol Allan testimony, *State v. William Porter*, December 4, 7, 2015.

17 Todd Oppenheim interview with author, July 28, 2022.

18 "SAO Notes on Freddie Gray" in discovery evidence.

19 National Association of Medical Examiners, *A Guide for Manner of Death Classification*, February 2002.

20 "Meeting at OCME" notes, BPD investigative binder 8.

21 Kevin Moore interview with author, April 11, 2022.

22 Sierria Warren interview with author, June 22, 2020.

23 "Meeting at OCME" notes.

24 Jason Szep et al., "Special Report: How Taser Inserts Itself into Investigations Involving Its Weapons," Reuters, August 24, 2017.

25 Brianna da Silva Bhatia, "Excited Delirium and Deaths in Police Custody: The Deadly Impact of a Baseless Diagnosis," *Physicians for Human Rights*, March 2, 2022.

26 Ellen M. F. Strommer et al., "The Role of Restraint in Fatal Excited Delirium: A Research Synthesis and Pooled Analysis," *Forensic Science, Medicine, and Pathology* 16, (2020): 680–692.

27 State of Maryland, Office of the Chief Medical Examiner, Post Mortem Examination: Anton Black, January 23, 2019.

28 E.g., Law Enforcement Action Forum newsletter, January 2011, includes "adrenaline dump" in its outline of how excited delirium works https://www.mml.org/insurance/risk_resources/publications/leaf_newsletter/2011_01.pdf.

Chapter 13: Missing Footage

1 BPD press conference, April 20, https://www.youtube.com/watch?v=KeVqlJn8Z9c (footage has the hot mic moment).

2 BPD, YouTube video, April 22, 2015, https://www.youtube.com/watch?v=e-rOT9G_SuQ&t=918s.

3 Sierria Warren interview with author, June 22, 2020.

4 Harold Perry interview with author, June 29, 2019.

5 "Under Close Watch," *American City and County*, August 2007.

6 Mayor's Office, "Fiscal 2015: Summary of the Proposed Budget."

7 BPD press conference, April 24, 2015.

8 Catherine Rentz, "Gaps Found in Surveillance Footage of Freddie Gray's Arrest, Transport," *Baltimore Sun*, May 14, 2016.

9 Ibid.

10 "Control Center Quick Reference Guide," DVTel, February 2014.

11 This angle on the April 20, 2015, press conference captures the Stop 2 video being played: https://www.youtube.com/watch?v=s1XGPJtS_6g.

12 BPD YouTube video, "2108 (1)," May 20, 2015, https://www.youtube.com/watch?v=HWUYAnVprKo&t=8s (first of nine).

13 Robert Brune, "#FreddieGray Rally at the Baltimore Police Station 4.19.15," YouTube Video, April 19, 2015, https://www.youtube.com/watch?v=Us44ZTuFMi4.

14 Todd Oppenheim interview with author, July 28, 2022.

15 BPD YouTube videos "2101," "2106," and "2104," April 24, 2015.

16 Matt Howerton, "Report: APD Could Have Altered Copies of Lapel Footage Given to Public," KDAT, March 25, 2017.

17 Evan Sernoffsky, "Edited Body Camera Footage Raises Questions about Police Accountability," KTVU, September 22, 2020.

Chapter 14: Force Investigation

1   Mosby press conference, July 27, 2016.

2   BPD press conferences, April 13 and April 20, 2015.

3   Michael R. Bromwich et al., "Anatomy of the Gun Trace Task Force Scandal: Its Origins, Causes, and Consequences," January 2022.

4   Lakishna Lewis interview with author, August 22, 2022.

5   Syreeta Teel testimony, *State v. William Porter*, December 4, 2015.

6   Seth Stoughton, email to author, July 22, 2022.

7   Text from Zachary Novak to Garrett Miller, April 13, 2015.

8   Novak text, April 15, 2015.

9   Jennifer Anderson testimony, *State v. William Porter,* December 3, 2015.

10 Sandra Guerra Thompson interview with author, February 21, 2017.

11 FOP press conference, April 22, 2015.

12 Brian Rice statement to internal affairs investigators, December 27, 2016.

13 Novak statement to internal affairs investigators, November 4, 2016.

14 Jamel Baker interview with author, June 30, 2019.

15 "Initial Offense Report," BPD investigative binder 1.

16 Novak grand jury testimony, May 19.

17 Novak statement to internal affairs investigators, November 4, 2016.

18 Baynard Woods, "What Happened to Tyree Woodson?" *Baltimore City Paper*, May 24, 2017. Force Investigation Team case file: Tyree Woodson.

19 Michael Boyd testimony, *State v. Edward Nero*, May 13, 2016.

20 Lewis interview with author, August 22, 2022.

21 BPD press conference, April 20, 2015.

22 Las Vegas Metropolitan Police Department force investigation flow chart: https://www.lvmpd.com/en-us/InternalOversightConstitutionalPolicing/Documents/Use%20of%20Force%20Review%20Process%20Flowchart%20V9.pdf.

23 BPD policy 710.

24 BPD homicide detective, interview with author on condition of anonymity, July 2019.

25 Wayne Brooks, BPD Legal Affairs, email to author, April 24, 2017.

26 Justin George, "Looking for Answers, Part 1: Police Begin Investigation into Freddie Gray's Death," *Baltimore Sun*, October 9, 2015.

27 BPD Policy 710.

28 Tawanda Jones interview with author, May 10, 2022.

29 Tyrone West Force Investigation Team file.

30 Task force activities and progress are mostly documented in BPD investigative binders 1–9.

31 Justin George, "Looking for Answers, Part 2: Pressure Builds as Police Investigate Freddie Gray's Arrest," *Baltimore Sun*, October 9, 2015.

32 BPD investigative binder 8.

33 Letter from attorney Craig S. Brodsky to the author and publisher, February 9, 2023.

34 "Wagon Shaking Demonstration" video in discovery evidence.

35 "Lead Detective Knife Video" in discovery evidence.

36 BPD policy 1007. A motion filed by the defense in July 2015 cited *Gattus v. State* as precedent for this rule.

37 "Baltimore Police Union Faces Backlash for Freddie Gray Tweets," *The Hill*, June 25, 2016.

Chapter 15: The Media

1 Kevin Rector, *Baltimore Sun*, April 25, 2015.

2 David A. Graham, *Atlantic*, April 22, 2015.

3 "Joint Motion to Dismiss and in the Alternate for Recusal of Baltimore City State's Attorney's Office," May 10, 2015.

4 Jayne Miller, "Questions Arise after Man Injured in Police Custody," WBAL, April 15, 2015.

5 Miller, "Witness Says Prisoner Thrown into Police Vehicle," WBAL, April 17, 2015.

6 MSNBC, April 23, 2015.

7 MSNBC, April 29, 2015.

8 MSNBC, April 30, 2015.

9 "Donta Allen Wanted in Pennsylvania on Forgery," WBAL, September 4, 2015.

10 Miller interview with author, June 16, 2022.

11 Sierria Warren interview with author, June 22, 2020.

12 Lee Fang, "Baltimore Radio Host Airs Outlandish Theories about Freddie Gray," *Intercept*, April 29, 2015.

13 Mark Puente and Doug Donovan, "The Truth about Freddie Gray's 'Pre-Existing Injury from a Car Accident,'" *Baltimore Sun*, April 29, 2015.

14 Michael E. Miller, *Washington Post*, April 30, 2015.

15 Carlos Miller, "Baltimore Cop Claimed on Facebook Freddie Gray Broke His Own Neck in Police Van before Deleting FB Page after Social Media Backlash," *PINAC*, April 26, 2015.

16 Brad Bell, "Law Enforcement Sources Say Freddie Gray Suffered Head Injury in Police Transport Van," *WJLA*, April 30, 2015.

17 Jon Swaine and Oliver Laughland, *Guardian*, May 1, 2015.

18 Justin Fenton, "Gray Suffered Head Injury in Prisoner Van, Sources Familiar with Investigation Say," *Baltimore Sun*, April 30, 2015.

19 Lynh Bui, Arelis Hernández, and Matt Zapotosky, "Findings Indicate Gray Got Head Injuries in Van," *Washington Post*, May 1, 2015.

20 Carol Allan testimony, *State v. Brian Rice*, July 7, 2016.

21 Daniel Bates, "Where's the Bolt That 'Killed Freddie Gray'?" *Daily Mail,* April 30, 2015.

22 Sean Hannity, "Baltimore on Lockdown," Fox News, May 1, 2015.

23 Memo from Sergeant John Herzog to Major Dennis Smith, May 1, 2015; interview notes dated December 9, 2015.

24 Justin Fenton, "Freddie Gray Alleged Back Injury Detailed in Unsealed Report," *Baltimore Sun,* December 31, 2015.

25 BPD press conference, April 30, 2015.

26 "Freddie Gray Investigation: Full Case File," *Baltimore Sun,* December 20, 2017.

27 Lisa Snowden interview with author, May 6, 2022.

28 Robert Brune, "#FreddieGray Rally at the Baltimore Police Station 4.19.15," YouTube video, April 19, 2015, https://www.youtube.com/watch?v=Us44ZTuFMi4.

29 Rob Brune interview with author, March 22, 2022.

30 Jasen Henderson tweet, June 2, 2015, https://twitter.com/suchaputz/status/605928495542235137?s=20&t=XwSMD98YNpg-ZGiW9U-un7Q.

31 Sundance, "The Freddie Gray Transport Van—Reconciling Disparate Witnesses," *Conservative Treehouse,* May 8, 2015.

Chapter 16: Reform and Revolution

1 Alexander, *The New Jim Crow: Mass Incarceration in the Age of Colorblindness,* 10th anniversary edition (New York: The New Press, 2020), 315.

2 "Chief Batts Takes the Stand in 'Lobstergate' Trial," *Long Beach Telegram,* February 1, 2008.

3 Tasion Kwamilele, "Anthony Batts, the Exit Interview," *Oakland North,* November 7, 2011.

4 Simone Weichselbaum, *The Marshall Project,* October 16, 2015.

5 Vitale. *The End of Policing,* 2nd edition (London: Verso, 2021), 246. The "procedural reform" trend in policing precedes President Obama but

gained extensive federal support under his DOJ, including through the expansion of consent decrees. An earlier example of what Vitale describes is the "Blue Ribbon Commission" report on the LAPD Rampart scandal commissioned by Bratton in 2006. The scandal implicated seventy cops in corruption, yet the report suggested hiring more cops and spending money on outreach efforts to restore community trust in police.

6   City of Baltimore, "Mayor Rawlings-Blake Names Advisory Panel for Police Commissioner Search," media release, June 10, 2012.

7   Justin Fenton, "Batts, New Baltimore Police Chief Pick, Says He's Committed," *Baltimore Sun*, August 28, 2015.

8   Mark Ruetter, "Meet Baltimore's $560-an-Hour Cop Consultant," *Baltimore Brew*, April 24, 2013.

9   "Approved second-year monitoring budget," Baltimore consent decree monitoring team.

10 Justin Fenton, "New Baltimore Police Commissioner Batts Seeks Fresh Start," *Baltimore Sun*, September 22, 2022.

11 BPD press conference, October 3, 2014.

12 Lisa Robinson interview with author, May 23, 2022.

13 "Former Baltimore Police Detective Joe Crystal on Breaking Code of Silence," WBAL, July 20, 2015.

14 "Former Baltimore Cop Speaks on Intimidation," *The Reid Report*, January 5, 2015. Albert Samaha, "This Cop Broke Baltimore's Blue Wall of Silence," *Buzzfeed*, May 15, 2015.

15 Duane Davis interview with author, May 17, 2022.

16 Ralikh Hayes interview with author, June 9, 2022.

17 "Man Critically Injured by Baltimore Police Has Died in Hospital," *RT*, April 19, 2015.

18 Robert Brune, "#FreddieGray Rally at the Baltimore Police Station 4.19.15," YouTube video, April 19, 2015, https://www.youtube.com/watch?v=Us44ZTuFMi4.

19 Robert Brune, "#FreddieGray Baltimore Rally Tuesday 4.21.15 Two Journalists Detained," YouTube video, April 21, 2015, https://www.youtube.com/watch?v=gyLA53nUpeQ&t=113s.

20 Scott Neuman, "After Baltimore March, Clashes between Protestors, Police," NPR, April 25, 2015.

21 "How Did the #FreddieGray Rioting Begin in Baltimore? 04.25.15," YouTube video, April 27, 2015.

22 Josh Reynolds, interview with author, July 29, 2022.

23 Robert Brune, "Agitator In Chief @BaltoSpectator James 11:25pm Saturday 4.25.15 #FreddieGray," YouTube video, April 26, 2015.

24 AJ+, "Live—Freddie Gray Funeral in Baltimore," YouTube video, April 27, 2015, https://www.youtube.com/watch?v=nplG_XNgZrU.

25 Justin Fenton, "Baltimore Police Internal Memo Says Batts Met with Officers in Freddie Gray Probe," *Baltimore Sun*, April 21, 2015.

26 BPD, "Credible Threat to Law Enforcement," media release, April 27, 2015.

27 Vitale, 215.

28 Brandon Griggs, "Baltimore Riots and 'The Purge,'" CNN, April 29, 2015.

29 Jenna McLaughlin and Sam Brodey, "Eyewitnesses: The Baltimore Riots Didn't Start the Way You Think," *Mother Jones*, April 28, 2015.

30 "The Battle of Mondawmin," *Baltimore Eclipse*, May 1, 2015, https://baltimoreeclipse.wordpress.com/2015/05/01/the-battle-of-mondawmin/.

31 Reprinted by Tom Scocca, *Gawker*, April 28.

32 Adam Johnson, "Media's Baltimore 'Teen Purge' Narrative Falls Apart," Fairness and Accuracy in Reporting, April 29, 2015.

33 Kevin Rector, "What Happened at Mondawmin? Newly Obtained Documents Shed Light on Start of Baltimore Riots," *Baltimore Sun*, April 20, 2019.

34 *Baltimore Sun*, "Video Shows Evolution of Riot in Penn-North" parts 1 and 2, YouTube video, July 20, 2015, https://www.youtube.com/watch?v=oIqM3Yug_4I; https://www.youtube.com/watch?v=xz1bIl4On7k.

35 Jenny Lyn Egan, direct message to author, July 28, 2022.

36 Fraternal Order of Police lodge #3, "After Action Review," July 8, 2015.

37 Tasion Kwamilele, "Anthony Batts: The Exit Interview," *Oakland North*, November 7, 2011.

38 Nisha Chittal, "Baltimore 'Mom of the Year' Speaks Out," MSNBC, April 29, 2015.

39 Snowden, May 6, 2022.

40 Robert Brune, "#BaltimoreUprising Curfew—Congressman Elijah Cummings Misleads Crowd about Legality of the Curfew," YouTube video, March 26, 2022.

Chapter 17: Progressive Prosecutor

1   Marilyn Mosby press conference, May 1, 2015.

2   Colleen Curry, "We Spoke to Kevin Moore, the Man Who Filmed Freddie Gray's Arrest," *Vice*, May 1, 2015.

3   Eliot C. McGlaughlin, "Marilyn Mosby Under Fire after Appearance at Prince Gig," CNN, May 14, 2015.

4   ACLU of Maryland, "Briefing Paper on Deaths in Police Encounters in Maryland, 2010–2014," March 2015.

5   Gregg Bernstein, "State's Attorney Gregg L. Bernstein's Prepared Remarks," media release, January 24, 2013.

6   Mosby, *Washington Post*, May 30, 2020.

7   Baynard Woods, "'I Hear the Screams Every Night': Freddie Gray's Death Haunts Man Who Shot Video," *Guardian*, July 20, 2016.

8   Kevin Moore interview with author, April 11, 2022.

9   "Violent Crime Focus of Baltimore City State's Attorney Primary Race," CBS Baltimore, June 4, 2014.

10 Tawanda Jones interview with author, April 4, 2022.

11 David Collins, "Emails May Shed Light on Police Captain's Suspension," WBAL, June 5, 2014; "I-Team Probes Bernstein's Involvement in Police Overtime Case," June 20, 2014.

12 Edward Erickson Jr., "State's Attorney Accused of Conflict of Interest," *Baltimore City Paper*, June 20, 2014.

13 Robert Quick was also one of the officers involved in the shooting death of Larry Hubbard, Jr. who was referenced by Schatzow in SAO's notes. That was the case that involved twenty-three witnesses who "tanked" the cover-up.

14 Homicide prosecutor Lisa Goldberg and Police Integrity Unit prosecutor Albert Peisinger were both originally on the case, per various case documents. On May 1, 2018, Peisinger posted to his Facebook page about his experience: "As the weeks passed, I made clear that my opinion was not in alignment with that of the State's Attorney's team. From that point on, I was no longer involved in discussions concerning the case."

15 Hearing, *State v. Freddie Gray*, Baltimore City Circuit Court, May 20, 2013.

16 Mosby press conference, May 1, 2015.

17 Hearing, *State v. Caesar Goodson et al.*, Baltimore City Circuit Court, September 10, 2015.

18 "SAO notes on Freddie Gray" in discovery evidence.

19 "Baltimore City State's Attorney Marilyn Mosby Explains Decision," WBAL, July 27, 2016.

20 Michael Schatzow and Janice Bledsoe, press conference, July 28, 2016.

21 Lewis interview with author, August 22, 2022.

22 "Supplement to defendant's joint motion for recusal of Baltimore City State's Attorney," June 9, 2015.

23 Kevin Rector, *Baltimore Sun*, June 9, 2015. The article dropped just as a motion from the defense exposing the email dropped.

24 Hearing, *State v. Caesar Goodson*, June 9, 2016.

25 Peter Moskos argues in a December 8, 2015, article on his website (and emails to author on September 22, 2022) that the policy was likely backdated, based in part on his BPD sources who do not remember receiving it. The policy is extremely on the nose of the Freddie Gray case, seeming to predict it. It discusses seat-belting and medical care and

demands that van drivers not make stops. SAO did call to the stand the head of BPD IT to verify its transmission, and a hard copy of it exists inside of a document that includes nearly 1,500 emails sent to Officer Miller. (The author of the seat belt email incidentally was Robert Quick, the one Bledsoe investigated for overtime fraud and one of the officers involved in Larry Hubbard, Jr.'s death.)

26 Neill Franklin interview with author, January 30, 2017.

27 Mark Gladhill testimony, *State v. William Porter*, December 10, 2015.

28 Lynn Bui, Justin Jouvenal, and Rachel Weiner, "Freddie Gray's mother sobs in court after seeing footage of son's arrest," *Washington Post*, December 3, 2015.

29 Brandon Ross testimony, *State v. William Porter*, December 3, 2015.

30 Matthew Wood testimony, *State vs. William Porter*, December 10, 2015.

31 Garrett Miller testimony, *State v. Edward Nero*, May 16, 2016.

32 Edward Nero testimony, *State v. Caesar Goodson*, June 17, 2016.

33 Aaron Jackson testimony, *State v. Edward Nero*, May 17, 2016.

34 Maryland Pattern Jury Instructions—Criminal, 4:01.

35 Justin Fenton, "Freddie Gray Case: Juror from Trial Breaks Silence," *Baltimore Sun*, July 29, 2016.

36 "Petition for a Writ of Certiorari and Motion for Expedited Review," Attorney General of Maryland, February 10, 2016.

37 Franklin testimony, *State v. Edward Nero*, May 13, 2016.

38 Bench conference during Nero testimony, *State v. Caesar Goodson*, June 17, 2016.

39 Maryland Pattern Jury Instructions 4:17.1, Second Degree Murder.

40 Schatzow rebuttal statement, *State v. Caesar Goodson*, June 20, 2016.

41 Verdict by Judge Williams, *State v. Caesar Goodson*, June 23, 2016.

42 Bledsoe closing statement, *State v. Brian Rice*, July 14, 2016.

43 Bench conference during Michael Boyd testimony, *State v. Brian Rice*, July 8, 2016.

44 Schatzow rebuttal statement, *State v. William Porter*, December 14, 2015.

45 Schatzow rebuttal, *State v. Brian Rice*, July 14, 2015.

46 Ross testimony, *State v. Edward Nero*, May 13, 2016.

47 Circuit court file for Ross's assault case.

48 Jamel Baker interview with author, March 26, 2022.

49 Alethea Booze interview with author, June 29, 2019.

50 Todd Oppenheim, email to author, November 7, 2022.

51 Schatzow and Bledsoe press conference, July 28, 2016.

52 Alethea Booze interview with author, April 2020.

53 Schatzow and Bledsoe press conference, July 28, 2016.

54 Mosby press conference, July 27, 2016.

55 "Prosecutor's Departure Latest Ripple in Freddie Gray Case's Fallout," CBS Baltimore, August 2, 2016.

56 Ron Cassie, "The Many Trials of Keith Davis, Jr.," *Baltimore Magazine*, November 2021. Amelia McDonell-Parry, "*Undisclosed* Podcast: The State v. Keith Davis Jr.," 2019.

57 Madeleine O'Neill, "Judge Won't Toss Davis Murder Case but Finds 'Presumption of Vindictiveness' in Other Charges," *Daily Record*, June 30, 2022.

58 Mosby press conference, January 14, 2022.

Conclusion: The Feds

1 Erin Cox, "Years Before Trump's Attacks, Gray's Death Sparked a Huge Effort to Heal Baltimore. It Wasn't Enough," *Washington Post*, August 1, 2019.

2 Robert Brune Media, "DOJ COPS Office Town Hall in Baltimore," YouTube video, https://www.youtube.com/watch?v=Pv83UYzXrz8.

3 DOJ, "Federal Officials Decline Prosecution in the Death of Freddie Gray," press release, September 12, 2017.

4 Robert Brune Media, "Rep Elijah Cummings Steps into the #BaltimoreUprising Crowd," May 1, 2015, https://www.youtube.com/watch?v=12m7ss-6bcc&t=60s.

5 Amanda Sakuma, "Black Women Front and Center of Power in Baltimore's Aftermath," MSNBC, May 5, 2015.

6   Garrett Miller and Edward Nero text messages, May 5, 2015.

7   DOJ, "Department of Justice Report Regarding the Criminal Investigation into the Shooting Death of Michael Brown by Ferguson, Missouri Police Officer Darren Wilson" and "Investigation of the Ferguson Police Department," both March 4, 2015.

8   DOJ, "Investigation of the Baltimore Police Department," August 10, 2016.

9   Ray Kelly interview with author, May 18, 2022.

10 Paul Butler, *Chokehold: Policing Black Men* (New York: The New Press, 2017), 171.

11 "Chasing Justice: Addressing Police Violence and Corruption in Maryland," ACLU of Maryland, August 2021.

12 Michael R. Bromwich et al., "Anatomy of the Gun Trace Task Force Scandal: Its Origins, Causes, and Consequences," January 2022.

13 DOJ, "Federal Officials Decline Prosecution in the Death of Freddie Gray," press release, September 12, 2017.

14 Brandon Ross testimony, *State v. William Porter*, December 3, 2015.